DISCOVERING THE MIND OF A WOMAN

KEN NAIR
with LESLIE H. STOBBE

OLIVER
NELSON

THOMAS NELSON PUBLISHERS
Nashville • Atlanta • London • Vancouver

Published in Nashville, Tennessee, by Thomas Nelson, Inc., Publishers, and distributed in Canada by Word Communications, Ltd., Richmond, British Columbia.

Unless otherwise indicated, the Bible version used in this publication is THE NEW KING JAMES VERSION. Copyright © 1979, 1980, 1982, Thomas Nelson, Inc., Publishers.

Scripture quotations noted NASB are from the New American Standard Bible, © 1960, 1962, 1963, 1968, 1971, 1972, 1973, 1975, 1977 by The Lockman Foundation. Used by permission.

Scripture quotations noted KJV are from The King James Version of the Holy Bible.

Scripture quotations noted AMPLIFIED are from The Amplified Bible: Old Testament, copyright © 1962, 1964 by Zondervan Publishing House (used by permission) and from The Amplified New Testament, copyright © 1958 by the Lockman Foundation (used by permission).

Scripture quotations marked NIV are taken from the HOLY BIBLE, NEW INTERNATIONAL VERSION®. Copyright © 1973, 1978, 1984 by International Bible Society. Used by permission of Zondervan Publishing House. All rights reserved.

Library of Congress Cataloging-in-Publication Data

Nair, Ken, 1936–
    Discovering the mind of a woman / Ken Nair, with Leslie H. Stobbe.
        p.   cm.
    ISBN 0-7852-7811-7 (pbk.)
    1. Marriage—Religious aspects—Christianity. 2. Interpersonal relations—Religious aspects—Christianity. 3. Wives—Psychology.
I. Stobbe, Leslie H.   II. Title.
BT706.N35   1995
248.8'425—dc20   95-21445
                                                                                          CIP

Printed in the United States of America.

23 PHX 06 05 04

CONTENTS

FOREWORD

I am glad for this book. After fifty-five years of Christian marriage, I find thoughts here that will help me be more thoughtful of my wife's needs. It has helped me understand why and how she thinks differently than I do about so many things.

A husband, as this book points out, is to live with and love his wife with understanding. So the Bible teaches. And here is important help in achieving that understanding. This change in a husband and the consequent response by a wife can result in life-changing home life, and together radiate to many others, for the glory of Christ.

Kenneth N. Taylor
Translator of *The Living Bible*

1

A DISCOVERY THAT CHANGED MY MARRIAGE

If you are a man over forty-five, you might identify with me (and a lot under forty-five may as well!). I was the kind of husband who believed that I loved my wife, but I also believed that her role was to make life beneficial for me.

Even though we were both working, when I came home weary with office stress and ready for refreshment, my wife was supposed to be there for me. She was always supposed to provide encouragement, an opportunity to relax, and a hassle-free home environment.

When I look back, I'm embarrassed because I thought I was an excellent example of a good husband. I was not guilty of gross immorality, of severe physical or mental abuse. In spite of my selfishness, my wife loved me and genuinely supported me. In fact, some people thought we had a model marriage that could be used to illustrate what a Christian marriage was like.

I didn't ask the Lord what He thought of our marriage. It never dawned on me to ask Nancy how she felt about it. And because she had such a gentle disposition, she never raised a big stink. So I assumed the Lord must be pleased with my efforts as well.

What I didn't realize was that our marriage was a parody of what God really wanted for us. It was based on misconceptions passed down from generation to generation in the Christian church—liberally influenced by concepts gained through the secular media.

The Lord in His mercy saw fit to shake me up, to destroy my Christian complacency. He wanted me to learn three major biblical concepts absolutely vital to a truly successful marriage—concepts that were not even on the fringe of my understanding about marriage, but whose implementation totally changed my marriage over time.

A CASE OF COLLUSION

When God set out to intervene in how I was behaving toward Nancy, He built a brick wall, and I ran headlong into it. The brick wall resulted from collusion between God, my wife, and my boss. Here's how it happened.

The leaders of a nationally known Christian organization saw that my dedication to their ministry was unlimited (in retrospect, that alone should have been a hint of a problem). So they invited me to join their staff in December 1970. I considered it a most enviable opportunity, for I knew many men had dreamed of working for this organization—and *I* was the one who had been *invited*.

My wife will be the first to admit that she was also excited about this special privilege. After all, she, too, was committed to my commitment to Christian service. So we packed our household furnishings into a moving van and left for our destination in a suburb of Chicago. Since we flew, we arrived several weeks sooner than our furniture did.

We had been in our barren house for three weeks when the leaders of the organization announced a multiday staff retreat several hundred miles away. I was delighted to have a chance for more intensive interaction with other staff members and leaders.

Nancy was not the least bit excited about my news, so she tried to influence my decision to go with some news of her own. The movers had called and informed her that our furniture was about to arrive. And its arrival just happened to be scheduled for the very day we as staff were to leave for the retreat. Not only was she unaccustomed to having her husband away for several days; she was not at all enthused about having to oversee the unloading of a truck full of household furniture and goods. Nor was she thrilled about trying to get the house organized with two young children underfoot and no husband to help.

It was the middle of winter in Chicago, with snow and slush everywhere. And while I was gone, more snow could arrive—and I would not be there to remove it from our walk and driveway.

You guessed it—she became very discouraged and upset over the combination of events. In fact, I got an earful from my very distressed wife. She felt so strongly that I ought to stay home from the retreat to play the roles of husband and father while supervising the movers when they arrived—and helping with the unpacking—that she refused to be swayed to my thinking.

I WAS EMBARRASSED

I was mortified. I thought, *How can my wife embarrass me like this? She's going to ruin my reputation as a husband who has everything and everyone in the family in line. She's going to make me look bad in the eyes of my new boss. And she's going to ruin my chances of being with the staff on this special outing if she continues to insist that I stay home and help her with move-in days. Worse yet, she may ruin my chances of being part of this great ministry. What shall I do?*

I tried to explain to her that I had no choice in the matter. After all, it was standard policy and practice at this organization to take getaway retreats.

You see, I was convinced that my business success was more important than anything else in the world—and without her interference I could be successful. Why couldn't she just stay in her place and be a submissive wife?

It didn't occur to me that God might be interrupting my pursuit of my ambition through her and this unique combination of circumstances. So I thought she should take this matter up with my boss, thinking he would straighten her out and we'd go about getting on with the retreat. As far as I was concerned, that idea was a stroke of genius. He would explain to her how unreasonable she was. She wouldn't dare dispute his evaluation about her restrictive attitudes!

What I didn't realize was that God had made her resistant, that God was using that attitude in my wife to bring me to some unusual insights.

She called my boss, and he shamed her by saying, "Your husband is a prisoner of your expectations." But even that didn't change her attitude. To my astonishment, she stood her ground and he backed off.

Although the conversation between them was in the morning, I didn't immediately hear from my boss. All day I waited for a report on the conversation. As I was getting ready to walk home, my boss told me that I would not be going on the retreat. Outwardly, I accepted his decision, but inwardly, I was boiling about my wife's interference in my ministry life.

Walking home, I became even more angry. I was thinking, *How could she do this to me? She's ruined me. Now I'll never be able to work in a meaningful way in this ministry.* I was about thirty yards from home when the Holy Spirit broke through my anger and hit me broadside with some very startling thoughts.

BREAKTHROUGH THOUGHTS

First, He reminded me that the bitterness and resentment within me came from my having to stay home with my family instead of being with others who were practically strangers to me. Then, He reminded me that these thoughts were exactly opposite to how I should have been reacting as a Christian husband and father. In fact, they were also diametrically opposite to the purpose of the ministry I had joined—to build Christian families.

Searching my spirit, I recognized that I didn't *really* want to put my family first, and I wasn't genuinely seeking to meet my wife's needs. I realized I didn't even know how to do that! I didn't know how to genuinely love my wife or anyone else, for that matter.

Then came the really disturbing thoughts. How could I be the spiritual leader in our home if I was not sensitive to my wife's spirit? I began to wonder, *What really is a spiritual leader?*

That moment was the first step in the funeral of Ken Nair's egotistic self-centeredness. It was also the first step in a long journey that has given me a lot of joy.

At that point I asked God to change my focus from angry, reactionary "poor me" attitudes to ones that pleased Him. I specifically pleaded with God for three things:

1. That God would help me learn how to meet the needs of my wife, to understand her mind, her way of thinking, her innermost feelings.
2. That God would show me how to love my wife so that she would be able to experience more than just hearing me say, "I love you." As God's representative, I wanted to have her experience God's loving her through me, to bless her heart through me. That would include learning how to love her from her frame of reference.
3. That I would learn how to be the spiritual leader of my home. That my spirit might become so sensitive that I would become aware of the Holy Spirit leading my spirit.

I had no idea what these three requests would require of me in the future. If I had known then what God would take me through to fulfill my requests, I might have backed off.

So did I instantly become a spiritual leader in my home, sensitive to my wife's spirit? Far from it. My ignorance was such that I went about my tasks that weekend of seeing the furniture put in the right places, unpacking boxes, and so on, without letting my wife know the desires the Holy Spirit had awakened in me. I was so insensitive about communication that I never thought to share my experience with her.

How did Nancy react? She says she was glad I was there to help, that she was at peace that she didn't have to do it all by herself. She was thrilled that she didn't have to face the new community and its environment by herself.

"Ken's attitude that weekend was great. There was no evidence of anger that he had to do it," Nancy says. But it took many months before she realized the major change in attitude that God had worked as a result of that experience.

RADICAL CHRISTLIKENESS NEEDED

You see, I, too, realized only later the radical nature of the three principles of marriage I had stumbled onto as a result of that experience. They have become the foundation stones of my ministry to men ever since then.

In time I began confronting men with what the Holy Spirit had taught me, that *Christlikeness is God's first priority for every man.* That we as men become Christlike in our responses, in our sensitivity to our wives' spirits. In loving them as Christ loved the church and gave Himself for it, we become the spiritual leaders that they will respond to with love and loyalty.

I'm sure you have heard many preachers and Sunday school teachers say that we as Christians ought to be Christlike. But I didn't find anyone in my experience as a Christian who was teaching or demonstrating how to rigorously apply Christlikeness to the husband's role in the marriage relationship or to the father's relationship with his children. Instead, the traditional teaching focused on the need for the wife to be submissive to her husband, no matter what. That teaching had been easy for me to quickly absorb and wholeheartedly accept!

What I didn't recognize, and I still find most men don't recognize, is the full significance of Ephesians 5:25–27:

> Husbands, love your wives, *just as Christ also loved the church and gave Himself for her,* that He might sanctify and cleanse her with the washing of water by the word, that He might present her to Himself a glorious church, not having spot or wrinkle or any such thing, but that she should be holy and without blemish (italics mine).

We basically stop reading and internalizing what God is teaching us after the first part, "Husbands, love your wives." As a result we don't get the full implication of what it means to love our wives as Christ loved the church. If we did, we would begin to discover the minds and spirits of our wives, and that discovery would transform the marriage relationship—just as that recognition totally changed how I have responded to my wife ever since then.

THIS COULD BE DANGEROUS!

Yet before I share with you what I have learned during the nearly twenty-five years since that experience, I need to sound an alert. One of my experiences may help you understand why.

I once watched as a friend did something at a packed-out convention that helped me immensely. Months before the weeklong convention began, it was sold out. Despite that, several hundred showed up, hoping to register on the first day. They were told that if they waited around, there might be a few seats because of cancellations.

Imagine the anticipation as hundreds of people waited nearly three hours to see if there would be any vacancies. Many people expressed their reasons for needing to get in. Finally, the convention began, and my friend said, "We have enough room to let these people in."

"Great," I said. "Let me go tell them."

I wanted to go over to them, get their attention, and tell them, "I've got good news for you. You can all get in." But my friend said, "I'll take care of it." He got their attention by saying, "We have good news and bad news. First the good news. It seems as though there is enough room for you to get in tonight."

The crowd rippled with anticipation. Then he added, "Now the bad news. You probably will have to stand all evening (three hours), which means you will be in the back of the auditorium where it will be difficult to see and to hear. Then, too, if the people who had already registered before you show up tomorrow night, you won't be able to get in for the rest of the week. With this in mind, do you still want to attend?"

Of course, everyone did—but they had been prepared and couldn't later complain that they had been uncomfortable or couldn't see or hear well.

This book requires a similar "good news, bad news" introduction. The good news is that *if you apply* what is in this book, you will reap the following benefits:

- You will gain genuine peace in the home.
- You will develop unbelievable communication skills.
- You will have a much richer love life with your wife.
- You will have more spiritually/emotionally balanced children.
- You will have better relationships at your workplace.
- Your children will learn how to have better and more successful marriage relationships. You will help them avoid many of the pitfalls you experienced.
- God will be able to bless you in many more ways because of your obedience to dying to self.

NO SHORTCUTS

The bad news is that there will be times when you will experience extreme pressure and stress as the flesh struggles to stay in control. You will get so angry as you read this book that you will want to throw it off a cliff, or jump up and down on it and destroy it. There is no shortcut to Christlikeness—and being Christlike is so radically different from what we have called Christianity today that it happens only through a new focus and radical obedience to Jesus Christ. In Hebrews 2:10, we read, "For it was fitting for Him, for whom are all things and by whom are all things, in bringing many sons to glory, to make the captain of their salvation perfect through sufferings." There is no other pathway to Christlikeness.

Thousands of men have attended the Discovery Seminars I present. And almost without exception their wives would admit the need for more Christlike leadership in the home. Most of the men would admit that they were hearing information they have never heard before. They would admit that they didn't know how to practice the biblical principles being taught in this book or the seminars. But less than 5 percent have asked for help in becoming more Christlike.

I remember one seminar led by a friend that was attended by twelve hundred people. At the end, he asked how many people felt excited about what they heard. Applause and cheers broke out. He followed that by asking me to stand, announcing that I was the one who had taught him the principles they were so excited about. He invited anyone who wanted to be trained as I had trained him to get in contact with me. He publicly asked if I would wait and meet them. I agreed. Only one man inquired about the training. And he was there only because his wife dragged him there.

People who have sought discipling range from having typical marriages to high-conflict marriages. Some were already separated and divorced—they were up against the proverbial brick wall. Even though he knew things were bad, one man had to get shot and almost killed by his Christian wife before he got serious about effecting change. Yet of those more than five hundred who have let themselves be discipled on how to be a Christlike husband, all have regained their wives' love and loyalty. I've enjoyed being part of some wonderful remarriage ceremonies!

In this book you will learn how to discover the mind of a woman—the woman who is your wife. The price to pay is that of dying to self and becoming truly Christlike. If you are ready to follow Christ in obedience to His Word, turn the page to chapter 2 to start the ride of your life.

2

MEN WHO MADE THE COMMITMENT

As though Christlikeness in itself isn't worth the effort, no matter what the cost, most men I begin counseling or discipling want dramatic evidence that the results will be in keeping with their efforts. The business world has taught us that results count. The more quickly you can achieve change, the better the approach must be.

Yet for all men I disciple, change comes slowly—and that's true for me as well. After all, we are creatures of habit, of ingrained un-Christlike attitudes learned through years of repeating the same natural-to-man thoughts and actions.

Add the skepticism of wives into the mix and you have double pressure for quick changes. Usually when I start working with a man, helping him understand himself and what God desires of him, he will begin to implement some of what he is learning. Yet it's not unusual for a wife to say to herself (or her husband), "It'll never last. He'll revert to his old self. He's just on another crusade. He's been on so many crusades, so is this the three-month crusade or the six-month crusade? So he's made a few changes. I'm still not impressed. For fifteen years he's been a turkey, and I can still hear the gobbler in him."

As in most marriages, this wife is responding to her husband's past character. He can say to her, "That's not right. You should trust me!" And her response will likely be, "I'm sorry. I still don't trust you. You've blown it too many times."

Why this skepticism when the husband is trying so hard to effect change? It's because the following scenario has happened too often.

WHY WIVES REMAIN SKEPTICAL

Let's say that after three months of one-on-one interaction with me, the husband begins to change. His wife sees the changes, but she senses they are coming out of his head, not his heart. So she says something like, "You haven't changed." And he says, "Don't tell me I haven't changed! I never used to do laundry before! I never used to clean up the bathroom before! I never helped you in the kitchen!"

But her response remains, "I'm not impressed." So he reacts, "This is what I get for all my efforts?" She likely responds, "See, your attitude is proof that it only got into your head, not your heart." And he reacts, "Hang it on your ear. If that's what I get after three months of trying to be Christlike, I'm not going to try anymore."

There is her proof that she was right—his motive was to impress her or get her off his back, not that he wanted to change his whole life. It's only in his head, not in his heart.

I help the husband who is in a discipling relationship to see that the wife's skepticism is healthy and God-given. How else would he discover his wrong motivation if not through his wife's negative reaction?

The man whose spirit responds in a Christlike manner to this healthy skepticism from his wife, who hangs in there for the long term, will, I guarantee you, convince his wife. Later in the book I'll complete the "Timeline of Change," the pattern I see repeated again and again as men get serious about becoming Christlike.

"Hold it," you may be saying. "You don't know my wife. I have moved heaven and earth to keep our love alive, and it didn't work. Why should your approach work? It's put up or shut up time."

Ready for a little show-and-tell?

FORMER FOOTBALL QUARTERBACK

About eight years ago I appeared on the same television program with Travis Turner, the former quarterback of the Nebraska Cornhuskers, shortly after he got married. Off camera, he revealed a strong desire to have a successful marriage.

"I think I need your book," he said. So I gave him a copy of *Discovering the Mind of a Woman,* which I had self-published earlier. Later I wrote him, asking if he could accept the most demanding challenge of his life, to become more like Christ.

He agreed to let me disciple him. Soon it became apparent that he was very hostile about and in his marriage, and often physically violent despite his Christian testimony. A few months into the discipling relationship with Travis, I was at my daughter's house when his wife drove up looking terrified. She said, "He's in a rage."

I went over to his house. I found the front door wide open, so I walked in. I could see the dust had not settled. He had just demolished a bookcase with his fist. I spoke gently as I walked up to him. He spun around and, glowering at me, said, "What are you doing here?"

I said, "Your wife was just over, and I came because I was concerned about you. Is there any way I can help you?"

He responded, "I just want to be left alone."

I told him, "I want you to know that I will be there when you need help. Are you sure you will be okay?"

"Yes, I'll be okay," he snapped.

That was the first of many occasions where his flesh took over. Things got worse as a result. Carol even took the children and left him for a long period. God used that time to break Travis.

Dying to self to become Christlike is very hard. A person's true self gets exposed and confronted during the discipleship process. Travis proved his commitment to God, staying in the battle. He didn't turn and run. He didn't quit. Today he is reaping the benefits. He says his relationship with Carol is better than he ever imagined it could be.

FORMER MAYOR

The second example reveals the power of God to heal the hurts in a marriage that has experienced deadly relationship conflicts.

As opportunities presented themselves, Gary Smalley would ask me to accompany him on speaking engagements. On one of those occasions when we went to a neighboring city in Arizona, Gary and I planned to go out for dinner after the meeting. We asked the pastor about local restaurants, and he invited us to join him and a few other men who were already waiting for him at a restaurant.

When we sat down at our table, there was a big guy on my left. As he talked about his life, I asked myself, *Why does this guy's story sound so familiar?* Then Gary introduced me to him, mentioning that he was the former mayor of an adjoining city.

Suddenly, my mind clicked. I remembered a story I had heard from several people about a former mayor who had been shot by his wife, putting him in the hospital. Part of the tragedy was the negative publicity the case generated in the local news media since he and his wife were prominent evangelical Christians who had helped start two big churches.

Just at that point I heard Gary saying to my neighbor at the table, "Would you like to get your wife back again?"

He said, "I'd do anything."

Gary assured him I could help him regain his wife, opening the door for me to talk with him. Of course when he had said that he'd do "anything," my ears perked up. I asked him if he meant that. He affirmed, "I will do anything."

I thought to myself, *We'll soon find out,* and I told him what it would take to get his wife back, that it would mean dying to self.

"When we meet, we will not talk about how to get your wife back. We'll talk about how you can be more Christlike. Can you commit to that?"

He confidently said, "I'll do it."

At six feet five inches, this man towered over me. During one conversation in a parking lot, I finally stepped onto a concrete tire stop so I could look him in the eye. Combine this with his position as president of his own company and tenure as mayor of a large, growing city, and you can imagine the power and control he was used to exercising. He was accustomed to making the rules. On many occasions he and I stood nose-to-nose and toe-to-toe while he went into a tirade about how he thought things should be.

By contrast, his wife was five feet and possibly four inches tall, weighing maybe a hundred pounds. Yet again and again she demonstrated how God can use a wife to reveal a man's need for Christlikeness.

Once while he and his wife were still in the divorce process, he and I sat in his office discussing his situation. I was on the couch directly in front of him, and he was behind his desk. We were at most eight feet apart. As he shared some of the demands his wife was making, he was very reactionary. I began pointing out his bad attitudes. Suddenly, he slammed both clenched fists on his desk and bolted to his feet, screaming out in rage at me.

Since I was seated, he must have towered four feet over me. Yet because I've been around so many men who reacted with intense hostility to dying to self, I didn't jump when he exploded. Instead, I asked him very calmly, "Is this your Christlike response?" Almost as if the contrast shook him back into reasonableness, he thought for a moment and answered with a subdued tone, "No, it isn't."

Because on occasion his wife lived with that kind of menacing conduct, she responded positively when he let the

Spirit of God convict and change him. She stopped the divorce process after six months. A year later I was invited to a private remarriage ceremony—and they are still happily married eight years later.

DIVORCED AND REMARRIED

But you may say, "My wife is already married again. There's nothing I can do—or want to do."

Really? Why not consider gaining the joy of a new relationship with Jesus Christ, regardless of what it might do for your relationship with your former wife? That's what Craig faced.

Craig had been going to counseling for months after his wife, Linda, divorced him. By the time a mutual friend sent him to me, Linda was already engaged to another man.

After he had met with me a couple of times, Craig said to me, "Do you realize that the counsel you are giving me is in almost all cases the opposite of what I have been receiving? I wish I had heard this stuff before."

Craig began responding well to the discipling, putting into practice what he was learning about becoming a Christlike person. When he and his ex-wife got together because of their son, he no longer argued with her. Instead of telling her how wrong she was, he confessed how wrong he had been. Instead of telling her how to change, he shared how he needed to change. He told her that he wanted God to help him become the man he always should have been but had not been for her. He concluded by admitting how much she had suffered because he wasn't the person God wanted him to be.

After about three months of this interaction, Linda said, "Why didn't you do this before? This is what I always wanted."

He said, "I'm just learning. I didn't know this stuff before."

I've discovered that most wives don't really want a divorce. They just want to stop the hurting, and they reason that a divorce will accomplish that. So when Craig began to really change, he positively affected Linda.

She admitted, "I'm so bewildered. I don't know what to do. I'm supposed to marry the guy I'm engaged to in three months."

So Craig asked me, "What shall I tell her?"

"Don't tell her anything," I said. "You keep working on *you*. You keep focusing on becoming Christlike."

Because Linda was confused, she married the guy she was engaged to. He doted on her, gave her many things, and showed interest in her goals. And he took her traveling, visiting places she had always wanted to go, including a trip to Egypt a month after the wedding.

Five days after they got back from their honeymoon in Egypt, Linda said, "I made a mistake. I should not have married again."

So she had the marriage annulled and came back to Craig. They are still living happily together after more than seven years.

I've seen this time and again. If we can get a man to commit to becoming Christlike, his wife will do a total about-face in her attitude—over time.

IMPOSSIBLE TO LIVE WITH

Many times the wife makes the first move; she is the first to admit the marriage is a sham and something needs to be done. But I never find the solution in counseling the woman alone. I recommend that husband and wife come for counseling together if that is possible. That seems impossible in many situations. Take the case of Rick and Louise.

Louise told her friend Craig that she was going to divorce Rick. Craig suggested, "Tell Rick to go see Ken Nair." She laughed uncontrollably at the idea.

Rick was a biker type. They were both drunk when they were married fourteen years earlier. They were not still into drugs, although they had been. So upon Craig's suggestion, Louise responded, "There is no way Rick would go to a Christian counselor."

But Louise did call and we talked. She related that "Rick doesn't understand me now. I can't talk to him. We've been married for fourteen years, but it's over. I simply cannot handle the mental and emotional abuse I go through every day of my life with him."

I asked her how he abused her. She said, "Rick constantly gives me looks that say, 'You're stupid.' He talks to me like I'm a child. He gives up on me and goes silent for months if I don't see things his way. Rick devotes himself to his job and has no time left for me or our son. We have no physical relationship. I get the feeling he is always mad at me. He simply will not listen when I try to talk to him."

She was convinced that Rick would not dream of coming in for counseling. But just in case he did, and concerned that he would react negatively to my approach, she asked, "Since he's not a Christian, do you have to talk to him about the God stuff?"

I told her, "I'm just going to be me. I'm not on a crusade over him. I'm just going to talk to him about life. We all live in life and need to understand it."

That was okay with her.

So the day she left him, Louise left a note on the kitchen table saying, among other things, "If you want to know why I'm leaving, go see a man named Ken Nair."

So Rick made an appointment. When he came in, he handed me her note as his explanation for showing up. I explained that I would not push the "God stuff" and would tell him why his wife left him.

Using his wife as the model, I explained the innermost nature of a woman to him. I shared with him specific ways a husband can affect his wife. Using other illustrations, we examined how the innermost natures of men and women are different, that women specifically had spiritual needs to which we as men must be sensitive. We talked about being a provider and that providing material needs for a wife is not enough.

Rick immediately identified with the examples I was using. Puzzled that they fit his wife so well, he asked, "How long have you been counseling with Louise?"

I assured him, "I've never met Louise in person. I only talked with her for a few minutes on the phone."

Rick was astounded, and God used that exchange to open the door to his heart. From that moment on, he was so attentive that he was like a sponge, constantly wanting to know more.

My plan was eventually to present Jesus to Rick. I started by asking him if he would like to understand why men have relationship problems. He responded most positively, so I explained, "If you go into an appliance store or an electronics store to buy something, the manufacturer provides instructions on how to properly use it. That's true even for a simple item like a shaver.

"Now God is as wise as any human manufacturer, and He has provided us with instructions on how to live in a family. Yet almost nobody thoroughly reads and implements what is in that manufacturer's instruction manual.

"If you bought a car but didn't read and follow the instructions, no warranty would be upheld on it. The manufacturer wouldn't even talk to you. You would probably say something like, 'I guess I should have read the instructions.'

"Yet people don't believe they must follow the instructions of God's manual, and then things go wrong. Not having followed God's instructions, they find their lives in jeopardy— and even though they didn't read the instructions and things are going wrong because of that, they get mad at God."

I said to him, "You've come to me because you need help. Would you like to know what kind of help this manual provides?"

His positive reply led me to explain what salvation is and why we need it. I asked him, "Have you ever done this yourself?" He said he hadn't. So I asked him, "Do you think this is something you should be concerned about?"

"Definitely," he answered.

I asked, "Would you like to do it?"

He responded, "I sure would."

I said, "Now this is not something I can do for you. You need to feel the urgency yourself. You need to talk to God about this in a manner that expresses your own concerns and your own heart's attitudes. So go home and reflect on what we've talked about and then come back and tell me what you've done."

Rick called me the next day and said, "I did it."

Wanting him to learn how to share his experience, I asked, "You did what?"

"What you told me."

"What did I tell you?"

"To accept Jesus Christ as my personal Lord and Savior. I did it," he responded immediately.

I was elated and said, "I know somebody else who would like to hear that." So I put my wife on the phone and introduced him. He told her, "I did what your husband told me to do." And he told her exactly what he had done. I had him go through this scenario because I wanted him to have the joy of witnessing, of sharing what he had experienced.

Craig, the person who had referred Rick's wife, told me a few days later, "I have never seen such a dramatic conversion in anybody!"

Rick began to live the new life in his relationship with his wife. She came to me and said, "What have you done to Rick? I told you that I didn't want to have anything to do with him anymore. And here I am falling in love with him again."

Rick and his wife were baptized on the same night they repeated their wedding vows. Tears filled my eyes as I participated in it. It was a truly beautiful occasion.

Please remember that the only time I talked to his wife was when she explained why she couldn't live with her husband anymore. Rick told me later that what made him willing to seriously consider everything I said was that I could describe their situation so accurately without having known them. God's work in Rick's life won over his estranged wife.

A CHRISTIAN TALK SHOW HOST

It seems like the men most unwilling to take the hard steps of dying to self and letting the Holy Spirit change them into Christlike men are professional Christians. They have so much at stake in maintaining the facade that nothing is wrong in their marriages.

Eldon and his wife, Martha, were the pastor host and hostess of a TBN talk show in Phoenix in the early 1980s. They were conducting an interview with Gary Smalley while I was sitting in the studio watching the interview on a monitor. As the program progressed, I noticed trouble and despair in Martha's countenance.

After the program, I approached Eldon, and letting him know that I seldom took the initiative as I was about to do, I gently asked, "If I were to perceive that you were struggling with some problems in your marriage, would you be open to talk about it?"

Half curious, half surprised, he guardedly asked, "What do you mean?"

I replied, "Observing Martha, I believe there might be some needs in your marriage, and I'd be open to help you." I began telling him some of the actual problems I sensed existed in his marriage.

"How do you know that?" he repeatedly asked me.

"I just know," I said.

Being embarrassed about his need for counseling, yet at the same time desperate enough to get it, he was willing to come to my house on Wednesday nights. After conducting Bible study, choir practice, and so on at his church, he would bring Martha with him as they drove across town and spent several hours at our house while I focused on his need for Christlikeness.

Having the wife present in these sessions is vital. Often after I've interpreted to a man what his wife is thinking deep in her innermost being, he will ask, "How did you know that?" I'll explain that I've had to learn that from the experiences within my own marriage. I'll then turn to his wife and ask, "Is that what you've been thinking?" She will usually respond, "That's exactly what I'm thinking."

I go through this exercise to prove to a man that it is possible to know what his wife is thinking. Reminding him that I have never met his wife before, I point out, "If I can do it, it's proof that I can teach you to know what is going on in the mind of your wife."

For about six months, Eldon made no apparent progress. He would fight with his wife on the way to our house, fight with her on the way back home, and fight with her during the week. He was reacting negatively to the concept that he was the solution to their problems.

Martha got to the point that she felt it was hopeless, so she bought a ticket and flew back to Oklahoma. Despite her intentions to remain separated, the Lord convicted her, and she came back home.

"GET WHERE SHE IS"

One Sunday night I received a call from Eldon. He was desperate, reporting, "Ken, my wife is on the floor in the sanctuary sobbing her heart out. It looks and sounds like she's having a nervous breakdown. Some of the women in the church are gathered around her trying to comfort her. What do I do?"

For once, it sounded like he was finally ready to do what we'd been talking about. I let him know he would have to follow my counsel very closely.

"Okay," he said, "but what do I do?"

"Step by step, here is what you do."

I first counseled him to leave the phone off the hook so he could report back after going down to the sanctuary.

"I want you to walk in there, and if the women are still there, let them know they're excused. They'll be glad to know that. If your wife is still on the floor, you get down there with her. If she is standing up, you stand with her. If she is sitting, you sit with her. You get where she is.

"You say to her, 'You've had to be the strong one in this family. You've had to be the one who carried the spiritual burden of our marriage. No more. I'm going to be the strong one, and you will be able to lean on me. I want to be there for you.'"

When he came back to the phone, he said, "It worked. Within five minutes, she was lying on my chest saying that for once she had hope in our marriage."

He told me later, "When I said to you, 'It worked,' I could hear you smiling on the other end of the phone."

From that point on, Eldon became responsive. His determination to become Christlike became stronger than the pride of his flesh. He agreed to meet with me in a group of couples. Even so he was so stubborn that one night when a woman asked him to put his arm around his wife to comfort her, he refused.

I asked him, "As a Christian, would you have ever believed you were that stubborn about obedience to Christlikeness?" He answered, "No." I responded, "It's a matter of understanding and surrender. If we want to be Christlike, we must discover how stubborn the flesh can be. We must understand that it doesn't want to yield control before we will recognize the need to make it surrender."

Continuing with discipleship, Eldon and Martha fell more and more in love. Once he heard me say, "My wife and I have such a good relationship that in the light of all the grief in marriages, it almost doesn't seem fair." Eldon now tells me, "I never could relate to that before, but now I can."

Eldon eventually came on staff full-time with Life Partners, a discipleship ministry I founded in 1979 with the goal of eliminating the need for divorce in the Christian community.

Let me repeat, of more than five hundred men who have submitted to the discipline to become truly Christlike in their behavior toward their wives, all have experienced a renewal of their marriages, even if they had already been divorced for several years. Expressing love to your wife like Christ expresses His love to the church is a winner every time!

The experiences of the men in this chapter indicate that one of the biggest hindrances to men discovering the minds of their wives is their own stubbornness. By nature, we don't want to be the kind of husband God wants us to be. So in the next chapter we'll examine what it means to really say, "I want God's will for my life."

3

FOUR MALE PREJUDICES

In this fast-paced, highly competitive business world, companies are constantly examining themselves to determine how they can be more productive. As men, we compare our products with those of other companies to determine how our business can be improved to stay on the cutting edge technologically. We try to eliminate all barriers to achieving our goal.

When we leave the office for home, however, it's as if that spirit of constant self-examination is taken off like a coat and hung on a hook on the back side of the office door. Not seeing the family as a job in which God has expectations of us, we think that all that we need to do is go home and relax in its comforts. We do not see meeting the family as something we need to gear up for so we can give family members serious attention.

You see, a man's instincts tell him that his home is his castle, where he can live in comfort without anyone having any more expectations of him—especially not his wife. And only when there is a genuine crisis at home does he make any real effort to eliminate barriers that might hinder a smoothly running home—and most men think a smoothly running home is the same as a smoothly running relationship.

Yet based on what I've discovered in talking with thousands of men and their wives, this need for self-examination is greater at home than it is in the corporate office. In the light of Scripture calling a man to Christlikeness, I'm convinced the need for genuine self-examination is even greater for us as husbands and fathers today than is the need for self-examination within companies.

WE ARE EXPECTED TO EXAMINE OURSELVES

The Bible is clear that just as we get evaluated regularly at our jobs, we are also being examined for our behavior at home by God Himself:

I, the LORD, search the heart,
I test the mind,
Even to give every man according to his ways,
According to the fruit of his doings (Jer. 17:10).

That's why the apostle Paul wrote, "Examine yourselves as to whether you are in the faith. Test yourselves" (2 Cor. 13:5).

I propose that we need to examine ourselves with regard to four commonly held male prejudices to see if we are reflecting any of these attitudes in our relationships with women, specifically our wives. All four prejudices, negative attitudes about women, act like barriers between us and our wives, preventing us from developing healthy, loving relationships with them. I have found that even when wives have been convinced that they should believe and accept these attitudes as normal, the effect on them is disastrous. Their spirits' needs will not be cared for as God intended. As a result, they will uncontrollably build up resentments that may explode unexpectedly in the faces of unsuspecting husbands.

However, let me warn you that such self-examination will bring discoveries that are as disturbing to you as are the findings of companies that discover they must reinvent themselves. Just as corporate examinations often result in layoffs of large numbers of people, even so when you examine your attitudes in the light of becoming more Christlike, you will be confronted with laying aside many attitudes you have harbored for years, possibly decades. As you read this book, there will be times when you will mutter, "Who does this guy think he is?"

So before you read any further, you may discover the need to pray with the psalmist,

> Search *me*, O God, and know *my* heart;
> Try *me*, and know *my* anxieties;
> And see if *there is any* wicked way in *me*,
> And lead *me* in the way everlasting (Ps. 139:23–24,
>   italics mine).

If you are serious about becoming the person Christ wants you to be, you'll want to memorize those verses. I certainly have needed them whenever I found my ego rising up in self-defense against the truths I have discovered—and will be sharing with you—about my relationship with my wife.

You see, the God who loves us and wants His best for us is bringing reproof into our lives, especially the reproofs we get at home from our wives. He wants us purged of our un-Christlike ways, especially in our relationships with our wives. He wants us to gain the wisdom the writer of the book of Proverbs wrote about:

> The ear that hears the rebukes of life
> Will abide among the wise.
> He who disdains instruction despises his own soul,
> But he who heeds rebuke gets understanding (15:31–32).

We will need this wisdom to accept reproof and instruction if we are to deal effectively with these four commonly held male prejudices that I discovered in my life and will highlight. These prejudices are so acceptable to our male thinking that they are deeply ingrained in our whole culture. And with leadership being held in the hands of men, these prejudices are also pervasive in our Christian churches—so much so that most men initially disagree strongly with my analysis.

I know how threatening it can be when my traditional Christian ways and thought patterns are being challenged. I'm sure that's true of others as well, especially since most of us have lived with our negative thought patterns for years. They have become habitual, so they are also comfortable. They are like good old friends.

I challenged the five men in the previous chapter to "live with your wives in an understanding way . . . and grant her honor as a fellow heir of the grace of life, so that your prayers may not be hindered" (1 Peter 3:7 NASB). That meant coming to terms with their forms of these prejudices, dying to them, and living in the newness of the Christ life, with its new attitudes toward women, especially in the marriage relationship. Their new attitudes won them favor with God and their wives and renewed the relationship so effectively that all five are now in remarkably harmonious marriages. Even more significant, each is enjoying a richer relationship with his Lord.

What are these male prejudices, and what must our attitude be toward them?

1. WOMEN ARE IMPOSSIBLE TO UNDERSTAND!

As difficult as it is to get any two men to agree on any one subject, there is, however, one "truth" that you can get almost all men to agree on—the mysterious nature of women. It is probably the most common source of jokes and laughter among men. You will find out just how united men are on this subject if you ask any group of men, "Do you understand the way a woman thinks?"

"Nobody understands the way a woman thinks, not even women," will be the almost unanimous response, usually accompanied by an air of superiority, laughter, or smirks.

Hey, I grew up with that attitude. I distinctly remember hearing as a boy about the impossibility of figuring out a woman. As I grew up, I became even more aware that many men had accepted as fact that the surest thing about a woman's mind is its fickleness.

I carried that attitude into my marriage—and it nearly destroyed it. That attitude so badly scarred my relationship with my wife, it took years to heal. That's why I began examining my prejudices, to see if they really held water. I discovered I had brought into my marriage attitudes that were neither biblical nor true, although they were culturally acceptable even in the Christian environment in which I lived.

Why is the "mysterious woman" attitude so prevalent? It obviously has strong historical roots, for it is deeply embedded in human society. Very few men have tried to live with their wives in an understanding way. I believe this male prejudice is so widely accepted that few men have ever challenged themselves to try to make even a token attempt to understand their wives. It has become a self-fulfilling prophecy since not making a genuine effort means they will not gain any understanding. Their wives remain nothing more than merely physical beings. Consequently, men can be heard glibly saying, "Women are impossible to understand."

This is not only an American phenomenon. Once as I was talking with a Christian from Africa, he told me that his wife had left him.

"I've been desperately praying that she not leave, but I feel like my prayers are just bouncing off the ceiling," he said. "Despite all my prayers, she has gone back to Africa."

So I inquired, "Do you *understand* your wife?"

He had a really puzzled look on his face as he questioned, "What's that got to do with it?"

I responded, "Scripture says that if you want your prayers to be answered, you need to live with your wife in an understanding way. Do you understand your wife?"

"I don't understand. What is it you're trying to say?" he asked again.

"I just heard you say that you feel like your prayers are bouncing off the ceiling. And I'm suggesting not only that they *seem* to be doing it, but that in essence they are. And the reason they are returning to you unanswered is that God is trying to tell you something. I think He's saying, 'Your prayers are very inappropriate. You're not looking at the situation between you and your wife from My perspective. Instead of asking Me to help you understand how to care for your wife as My Son Christ would, you are saying to Me, "God, straighten out my wife. Make her get her act together and do what's right."' And I'm convinced that God is trying to tell you, 'You are supposed to be the one who is My representative of Christ in your wife's life, and I cannot cause her to get her act together until you, as her spiritual leader, get your act together.' I think you ought to be praying, 'God, indeed, I do not understand my wife as Christ does, and I know it is Your command to me that I be like Christ. I'm seeing the need to have You open my eyes so I may discover why my wife has left me.' Now God can answer that prayer!"

The Apostle Peter Recognized This Prejudice

Even two thousand years ago the apostle Peter recognized the need to encourage new believers by cautioning them to avoid the pitfall of settling for less than God's best. Knowing that men practice this male prejudice as a natural response to life, Peter set out to counteract it by writing, "Live with your wives in an understanding way" (1 Peter 3:7 NASB).

The apostle Peter clearly did not consider living with our wives in an understanding way an impossible task. He considered it absolutely essential to a vital relationship with God. Typically, the problem that most of us men face is that we really don't want to put forth the effort because we consider it so impossible; it is just an exercise in futility, a waste of time to even try, we feel.

I'll be the first to admit that there is a basic difference in the way men and women think, and we'll get into that in depth later. All I want to emphasize now is that we as men use this "mysterious woman" concept as an excuse for not making the effort. We don't understand our wives because the flesh is such a dominant influence in our lives that it even overrides God's Word and lets us dismiss out of hand His command to understand our wives.

With the flesh in control there is no sense of urgency within us to make the effort to become learners about our mysterious wives—even though we take great pains to examine what is going on in the marketplace, why the car engine is not working properly, why we are not improving our golf games. Even if the solutions to our problems in these particular pursuits were extremely demanding, we would consider it reasonable to give ourselves fully to discovering and implementing them because they are easily recognized as legitimate pursuits—but understanding the women we chose as our wives? Why bother? No matter how hard we try, things don't get any better. Everybody knows that women are totally beyond figuring out and "fixing."

So while the item we are marketing becomes state of the art, the car engine problems are solved and the automobile begins to run smoothly, our golf games improve incrementally, *our relationships with our wives deteriorate*. Which, from our limited and admittedly unskilled perspective, only proves that they really are incomprehensible, that there is no way we are going to understand the deep-seated complexities and innermost heart of women.

By now you know that I'm convinced we *can* learn to understand our wives. Once I set out to do that, I made some amazing discoveries and learned how to care for my wife in ways that turned our marriage around. I'll share some of what it takes for you to learn to understand your wife as well in upcoming chapters.

A second male prejudice is that

2. WOMEN ARE THE REAL PROBLEM!

I present seminars in which I emphasize that the single most significant problem in the Christian community is that we men have failed to exhibit the Christlike leadership that God requires of us. If we did, we would be able to cure relationship problems. We demonstrate this lack of Christlike leadership by our unwillingness to take the steps to understand women, which prevents us from bringing lasting solutions to relationship problems.

During our seminars, men often ask, "When are you going to get to the women?" This question reveals who most men believe really is the problem in marriage relationships. It also brings to the surface the struggle most men experience when they are charged with the biblical responsibility of demonstrating Christlike leadership—capable of initiating lasting solutions to marriage problems. Most men do not believe they are at the root of the "real" problem. So they think it would be helpful if I told them how to deal with "those women" because the strange behavior of their wives is the problem.

It's not unusual to hear a husband say things like, "My wife doesn't respect me. She's not submissive like the Bible says she ought to be. I have feelings and I have needs and she is not paying attention to me."

Interestingly enough, I don't know of anyone who has been around seminars for women and has heard women say, "When are you going to get to the men?"

At the heart of this difference is what might be described as a "vending machine marriage" mentality. We men feel that we keep giving and giving, but something must be wrong with the machine because we're not getting back out of it the results we think we should be getting.

Here's a common example of this confused thinking. When a wife complains, "You don't care about me," a husband may fire back, "Hey, I'm putting a roof over your head, clothes on your back, your car runs. What more do you want? You sure have a lot to learn about gratefulness!"

Typically, a husband reasons, "What nerve! After all I've done, she says I don't care." Because he doesn't understand that she is talking about her heart being cared for, he concludes, "Why am I trying so hard? I'm not getting any appreciation in return!"

Continuing with the comparison, when a man doesn't get satisfaction from his vending machine (principally sex but also receiving the joys of eating and sleeping and maybe a little understanding for his own needs), the first thing he does is react to the "stupid machine" by kicking it and hitting it. In a marriage that abuse is always emotional, and all too often it's also physical. So he starts banging on the machine because he believes that treatment is warranted; maybe then he will get his quarter back. In marriage he believes his retaliation is warranted, too, for maybe then he'll get satisfaction from his investment. In neither case does this treatment get him the results he desires.

To carry the analogy a little further, maybe, even unknowingly, the husband puts in counterfeit money. And the machine spits it back out, so he begins kicking the machine instead of evaluating whether or not he is using what is genuinely acceptable. It may need a different coin of the realm—just like his wife may need a totally different kind of input.

This natural-to-men attitude of self-preservation that avoids self-examination by instinctively pointing the finger of accusation away from self, saying, "My wife is the problem," surfaces in some extraordinary ways. And of course, it's always easier to see it in someone else's life. Consider the following example.

Frank (not his real name) was frequently and deeply involved in gross immorality and physical abuse of his wife and children. Yet at home on many occasions, he insisted, no, demanded, that Sue, his wife, be very careful not to violate any Christian standards.

What was Sue doing that caused Frank to feel that he must center his attention on her sinfulness? What glaring fault of hers so successfully distracted him from his wrongdoing? What caused him to become so concerned about how she was violating her obligation to obedience to the Scriptures?

She demonstrated great anger at his infidelity. She lost emotional control and screamed at him about his lack of faithfulness to their marriage. Along with feeling rejected and betrayed, she deeply feared that his conduct was subjecting her and the children to the infections of sexually transmitted diseases.

Ironically, even though Frank initiated the hostile atmosphere, he said he could not "in good conscience" allow Sue to carry on unchecked in her irresponsible behavior. He con-

sidered it "his duty as a Christian" to point out his wife's failure—her inability to control her temper.

An extreme example of prejudiced reasoning?
Unfortunately not, for as I disciple men, I'm finding his attitude an all-too-common one. What really astonishes me is that
almost without exception, the Christian community sides with
people like Frank and against the wives.

In this case, as Frank's wife became more and more public
in her anger toward him, their pastor (who knew I was counseling them) called me in to question why I was not repri-
manding her. It was no secret anymore, since his wife was
becoming more demonstrative. Everyone was questioning
Frank (including their pastor), asking, "What's wrong?" So
Frank would put on his I'm-trying-to-stand-up-under-this-
burden-God-has-given-me-to-bear look and ask everyone for
prayer. He subtly convinced people, by agreeing with their
observations of Sue's uncontrollable, raging temper, that she
was the problem.

Yes, sir, they all thought. *She is his cross to bear.*

And everyone grieved for him, concluding, *What a godly
man!*

I finally alerted the pastor to Frank's immoral behavior
and his domestic violence, letting him know that the only reason he wasn't hearing her side was that Frank's wife was
afraid of the beatings she would get if she told the truth.

I'm still amazed when I hear Christians say, "It's terrible
that Frank would do those things. *But* still, it's not right for
her to get angry like that!"

Only after I presented absolutely incontrovertible evidence of the nature of Frank's behavior was the pastor willing
to consider that Frank might be the real problem.

You and I certainly know that anger is not God's goal. But
let's step back for a moment and take a reasonable look at the
situation in Frank and Sue's home. Surely, it is incongruous for
any Christians to be upset about Sue's anger while minimizing
Frank's sin—which brought on the angry, screaming attacks.
Wouldn't you say that something was wrong, that it would be a
gross miscarriage of justice? Yet that's not how many men think.

This double standard is illustrated by another situation. Larry, a close friend, went to Greg's house for a visit. When he discovered that Greg was gone for the evening, Larry forced himself on Greg's wife. When Greg came home and discovered his wife had been violated, he became violently enraged, vowing to wreak vengeance on Larry.

Was Greg justified in getting violently angry with Larry? Most men would agree that he was indeed justified in becoming enraged at his friend's rape of his wife. That being the case, why was Sue's anger not acceptable? Is it because negative attitudes toward women automatically assume women are the greater problem and must be corrected—by men?

In both cases, there was anger at immorality and violated rights. But no one is likely to automatically think, *Wow, for a woman to act like that toward her Christian husband, there must be something wrong with his capacity to provide her with Christlike leadership.* No, no! Sue was automatically condemned for *her* anger. On the other hand, Greg became the champion of justice when his anger exploded at his friend. In my experience that is because husbands have a tendency to hold wives absolutely responsible while they give themselves the freedom to be irresponsible and unaccountable.

This tendency is not new. Remember the story of Jesus and the woman the Pharisees and scribes dragged in front of Him (John 8:3–11)?

Who Had the Problem?

In your mind, picture Jesus standing with a small group talking over some things as a commotion develops down the road. It's a little too far away to tell what is going on, but it looks like a mob scene with some religious leaders in front of the crowd. A closer look indicates they're dragging someone with them.

The crowd is growing. As the mob gets closer to Jesus, you're able to see that they've been harshly handling a woman they're forcing to come with them. The religious leaders are indignant about something.

You'll remember that these religious leaders have already made a whole series of moves to try to discredit Jesus. So He is definitely on His guard. When they reach Jesus, the person who seems to be in charge says, "This woman was caught in the very act of adultery. Now Moses said that she should be stoned, but what do You say?"

Everyone waits with bated breath, wondering what Jesus will say. The Master responds, "Let the person without sin throw the first stone." This response has a sobering effect on their righteous indignation. One by one, from the oldest to the youngest, they slip away.

Let's freeze the action right there. She was caught in the very act. Seems to me that adultery is a two-person sin, so where is the man they caught in the act as well? Why have they not dragged him down to be stoned?

From where I sit, that story illustrates more than Jesus' wisdom in dealing with the woman. It also illustrates men's consistent shrugging off of their sins by thinking, *The woman's the real problem.*

I have found that women tend to have much more sensitive spirits than men do. You might say they are more tender-hearted, emotionally sensitive. Thus when a wrong has been done in a relationship, a woman's conscience will usually bother her more quickly and much more intensely than a man's would. She is more likely to accept personal responsibility than a man is—and that's one of the reasons I've decided to focus mostly on ministering to men because the Bible clearly makes men responsible not only for their actions but also for the condition of their marriages.

Did I touch a raw nerve with that statement? If I did, you're perfectly normal because most men absolutely bristle when I suggest that God does not allow men to use "my wife's the *real* problem" as an excuse, no matter what problems present themselves in the marriage.

For so long we've blamed those we've labeled the weaker sex as the real problem, we men don't give serious consideration to the notion that we may actually be the key to marriage problems. Yet if we're serious about becoming Christlike, we're going to have to root out the attitude, "She's the real problem," and tackle our negative attitudes and behavior—even those attitudes we say wouldn't be a problem if it weren't for the women causing us to react. We'll get into that in much more depth later in this book, so save your ammunition for that exchange.

The third male prejudice that basically justifies our need to look elsewhere for problem-solving deficiencies in marriage is

3. WOMEN ARE INFERIOR TO MEN

"Hold it," you're saying. "That prejudice died with the birth of the feminist movement—certainly since the successes women have had in the business world today."

I wish it were true that it had died. The attitude that men are superior to women, in fact, that women are basically stupid, is still alive and well—even in Christian circles. I have to admit, to my shame, that I instinctively carried that notion into my marriage, even after I thought I had accepted Nancy as the person God had given me to help me become Christlike.

Nancy would complain to me, "You make me feel stupid." Maybe your wife has never accused you of that. But like most men whose wives have, I would get defensive, explaining, "That's your problem. Don't try to blame that on me." I honestly didn't believe it was true. Having grown up in an orphanage, I knew what it was like to be made to feel inferior, and I thought I was very conscientious about not devaluing others. I really believed I valued her as a person.

But God wanted me to believe Nancy's expression about how I was making her feel. So He used a visit she and I made to a lawyer. I listened very closely throughout the whole process. I especially concentrated on the technicalities so I could recall them with Nancy. Walking back to the car, I asked Nancy, "Do you remember when the lawyer talked about such and such?" She replied, "Yes." And with a desire to help, I inquired, "Do you know what he was talking about?" She answered, "Yes." Doubting, I questioned, "What was he talking about?" She proceeded to clearly explain the topic to me. I remember thinking, *Okay, she knows that one.*

But there was much more to understand. So I proceeded. I asked her about another topic. She again recalled that part of the conversation. So I again inquired, "Do you know what he was talking about?" She responded, "Yes." So I asked, "What was it?" Again, she clearly and simply explained the issue.

God is clever. All of a sudden the thought hit me: *You know what, Nair, you really think your wife is stupid.* So I confessed to her how I had discovered that she was right. I really was guilty of thinking she was stupid, and that's why I approached her so often with a doubting attitude. Yet every time she had accused me, saying, "You make me feel stupid," I disagreed because I honestly didn't know that I thought of her that way.

PREJUDICE REINFORCED BY BIBLICAL INTERPRETATION

The idea that women are inferior, or less than men, is too often substantiated in Christian circles by the current misuse of a particular word found in Genesis 2:18. That word is *help meet.* In the King James Version, God is quoted as saying, "I will make him a help meet." Unfortunately, the word *help meet* has been wrongly reclassified, reinterpreted, and rephrased. We are taught today that the word is *helpmate.* And generations of Bible teachers have continued with that misinformation, teaching that women are helpmates.

For us as men, we readily classify women as helpmates. It allows us, even biblically, to have an on-site mate whose job is to grab the other end of the two-by-four for us.

When I ask men what they think would be a reasonable working definition for the title *help meet* (even though I used the word *help meet,* their frame of reference is *helpmate),* here's what I usually hear: "Someone whose job it is to rear the children, do the housekeeping, the laundry, and the dishes."

Trying to explain how that thinking is a distortion of God's reason for inventing a helper, I follow my question with this line of reasoning: "To get a better idea of the purposes God had in mind when He invented women, let's go back to the beginning of time. Let's imagine God has just finished creating woman and has named her 'helper.' Were there any children?"

The guy says, "No."

"Were there any houses?"

Again, "No."

"Were there any clothes to launder?"

"No."

"Any dishes to do?"

"No."

"That being the case, isn't it reasonable to conclude that we should eliminate those activities as the purpose behind the title *helper* or *help meet*?"

A good question at this point would be, "Then what *did* God mean?"

My reading of the passage tells me that at that very moment, while God was relating with Adam, He said, "It is not good that man should be alone." But wait a minute! Of all the possibilities in which I might feel alone, the time while God was relating with me certainly would *not* be one!

But God, being able to see into the future, knew that after the Fall, He and Adam would be separated. Adam would then indeed be alone, separated from God. In anticipation of that event, God invented a helper, one who could serve to accomplish God's purpose of reestablishing spiritual sensitivity.

Because our separation from God was so extensive, we weren't left with a clue about what godliness is. Even as Christians, we still need help. Were it not for salvation through Jesus Christ and the entrance of the Holy Spirit, now indwelling the Christian's spirit, we would not have any motivation in our spirit to care about God's ways. And being new-baby Christians—still living within the frame of our human beings, and still being spiritually ignorant—we continue to operate on the basis of our human instincts. And therein lies the need for help. God provided a man with a tangible, visible means of discerning whether or not he is on track about becoming more and more like Christ and sensitive in his spirit to the Spirit of God.

Basically, God is saying, "After the Fall, I know you won't have a clue about what godliness is, so I'm providing you with a helper. This helper will provide you with a means of measuring whether or not you are becoming more and more like what I want you to be, spiritually alive and functional. Christ is your example and the way. Then as you become more Christlike, you will also be furnishing your wife with the leadership that provides an example worth following. Together you can reestablish the spirit-to-spirit relationship with God that was lost."

Instead of seeing women in that positive light, many Christian men consider women as not much more than some sort of God-given sidekick, like in the old radio programs Tonto was to the Lone Ranger. Dare I go so far as to add that some men believe God gave women such a wide range of potential so that they could be more useful for men? Their qualities help them to more effectively serve the purpose of making us look good in our social circles, as business executives, as elders in the church. If they perform *as we think God made them to perform,* there is probably no end to how useful they could be. But God forbid that we should consider them equals—partners with God, whose God-given purpose is to help us discover the difference between the standard male attitudes in our hearts and Christlike attitudes.

Let me illustrate. One man I was discipling lived in the Midwest. His character and relationships started changing dramatically, so much so that his life drew attention. That enabled him to begin sharing these concepts with other men—and their lives also started showing signs of improvement. That also drew attention.

The man I was discipling attended a large church. When the pastor became aware of what this man was teaching, he reacted with a verbal attack on this man. So my friend asked me if I would stop by when I was in the Midwest. Maybe I could help him by meeting with him and his pastor to clear things up. I agreed to do it.

The pastor met us at the door. After a perfunctory greeting, he led us through the big church into his office. When he opened the door, was I surprised! The room was full of staff people, fourteen of them (men and women). It was obvious something was going on that included much more than what we thought we had made arrangements for: a get-acquainted-to-clear-up-any-misunderstandings meeting with the pastor.

After making introductions and engaging in some minor chitchat, the pastor said, "Now I want to let you know that I know what you preach. I've read your book, and I know you teach that men should give their wives the freedom to tell them where they are not like Christ. But I want you to know [pointing his finger at me] that I wholly disagree with you. If my wife were to try to tell me about areas in which I am not Christlike, she would get a mouthful right back in her face!"

It was obvious that the meeting was not the place to make any attempts to reason together. I realized it would be foolish to offer any opposing viewpoint. He had made his statement. He had made up his mind, and there was nothing to add. Since that was not the first time someone had reacted in that way to what I was teaching, I had learned to detect the difference between someone asking for clarification and someone wanting to tell me what he thought. There was a pause as I waited to see if he had anything else he wanted to cover. Basically, the meeting was over. I expressed my thanks to him for taking the time out of his busy schedule to meet with me. There was some shuffling about among his staff, and so as we rose to leave, I looked at each member and conveyed that it was a pleasure to meet him or her. We then left.

Outside, my friend asked, "Why didn't you say anything?" He added, "Why didn't you defend yourself?"

"I didn't need to," I answered. "He wasn't there to listen. He wanted to make it perfectly clear where he stood. I wasn't going to persuade him of anything. And the others in the room were going to make up their minds based on whether or not they agreed or disagreed with him. He made his case, and based on what he said, the others had to decide which side was right. If he was to be judged wrong, I'd let him convict himself."

It was obvious to me that he was infuriated that I would say a husband could give his wife, an inferior person, the freedom to share how she felt he was affecting her.

We also need to recognize that taking a theological stand that women are inferior is in part tied to our understanding of the temptation of Adam and Eve in the Garden of Eden. Have you noticed how quick everyone is to place the blame on Eve for the fall of humankind? As proof, doesn't everyone offer Genesis 3:6, asking, "Well, wasn't it Eve who took of the forbidden fruit?"

One day Danny Ben Gigi, a Jewish friend who is also the professor of Hebrew at a university, was reading this passage in Hebrew to a class he was teaching. He expressed that it illustrated how women are such a source of grief for men, and how it proved that men must be on guard against the trouble women can cause them. Later, I brought up the topic again, asking him if he realized that Adam was standing right there watching Eve eat of that fruit.

"No, no!" he protested. "That's not the case."

I opened my Bible to Genesis 3:6 and read, "She took of its fruit and ate. She also gave to her husband *with her,* and he ate." I asked, "What does that mean?"

My friend replied, "I'll tell you what it means. He was in the area somewhere. He was 'with her' because they were man and wife."

"No, I don't think so," I said with a smile. "The language is clear. He was '*with* her.' He was standing right there, watching."

My friend opened his Hebrew Bible and seriously examined the language. He was not a born-again believer, so he was only operating from his typically male-influenced thinking. That told him that when the Bible says Adam was "with her," it meant that he was in the general area; they were "together" as man and wife. He was not without her; therefore, he was with her.

Danny Ben Gigi was clearly struggling with his traditional thinking, but he was also a sincerely honest man when it came to translating God's Word. After serious deliberation, he looked up and said, "You're right. There's no doubt. That's what it says. Adam was there with her. He was standing right there watching her eat."

Both he and I agreed that Eve was not to blame. Adam was. Careful reading shows that the command not to eat of the fruit was not given to Eve—it was given to Adam: "And the LORD

God commanded the man, saying, 'Of every tree of the garden you may freely eat; but of the tree of the knowledge of good and evil you shall not eat, for in the day that you eat of it you shall surely die'" (Gen. 2:16–17). When God came to the garden to confront this violation of His command, *He went to Adam* and asked *him,* "Have you eaten from the tree of which I commanded you that you should not eat?" (Gen. 3:11). God didn't go to Eve and ask her because He knew to whom He had given the command. God knew that He had given Adam the command and that Adam was responsible for what happened.

Adam's response was typical of men even today. He didn't say, "You're right. I ate. I disobeyed You." Instead he adopted the male defensive stance. He not only blamed Eve—he ended up pointing the finger of blame at God because God gave Eve to him: "The *woman* whom *You* gave to be with me" (italics mine). He might as well have added, "If only You had not created her, everything would have been fine." And I'm sure that if anyone else had been around, Adam would have blamed that person as well. But he was limited; there were only two people to blame, Eve and God.

That scene portrays the nature of men. We don't accept responsibility easily at all, especially in relationship to our wives. We don't want to be held responsible for their reactions. At that point our defensive juices are really flowing, and it's convenient for us to emphasize that they have their own free will.

Even in our description of that scene, we reveal how deeply ingrained our concept of the inferior woman is among men. Theologians included call it the temptation of Eve instead of the temptation of Adam and Eve.

If one side of the coin is the inferiority of women, the other side is the role of the man as "the boss" in the home. Thus, the fourth male prejudice is that

4. MEN ARE SUPPOSED TO BE "THE BOSS"

If women are inferior and not too smart, others have to step up to take care of and protect them. That's us, the men of the world. We operate as though we're destined from creation to be "the boss." Wasn't Adam created first and then Eve?

We even use descriptions like, "The home is a man's castle." A castle clearly needs a king, and we nobly accept being the king of the castle.

That's what aggravated the pastor so much in the example I gave earlier. The biblical teaching that the wife is part of God's accountability structure to help us become Christlike is astonishingly threatening to men everywhere, especially men in spiritual leadership roles. As they see it, it threatens their leadership role in the home; in fact, it *establishes* their spiritual leadership role.

The role of boss means that the husband can disregard his wife's needs while abundantly taking care of his own. For example, a "Christian" farmer had two sons for whom he consistently purchased the latest tractors and field machinery. He drove a nice truck. But he refused to install plumbing in the house, making his wife carry water from a well several hundred feet from the house while he had luxury-level equipment.

As you read on, traditional thinking, which portrays the man as the boss in the home, is going to be undermined by scriptural teaching—but the genuine spiritual leadership of the man is going to be reinforced. Men will be asked to stop thinking of themselves as the boss, the king, the emperor, or possibly even the dictator. Instead, they will be asked to earn positions of leadership in the home by dying to self (putting self last, and others first, including the wife). This does not mean ignoring responsibilities as husbands—it means reevaluating attitudes.

I am constantly astonished that men in spiritual leadership roles never seem to have read Philippians 2:3–4 in the context of their responsibilities in the home. I provide the verses here:

Let nothing be done through selfish ambition [a bossy attitude] or conceit, but in lowliness of mind let each esteem others better than himself. Let each of you look out not only for his own interests, but also for the interests of others.

When I confront men with the need to give up the throne, they often ask questions that illustrate the following attitudes: "Is that wise? Can a man's kingdom function if he steps down from being the king?"

Implied in those attitudes are issues like these: "What happens to me if I step down? Would my wife assume control in our home? How can I trust my wife not to become arrogant and/or rebellious? Surely, somebody has to be in charge?"

What they mean is, "Is it safe? Who will protect my kingdom?"

This attitude really reveals how unbiblical we have become: "Is focusing almost exclusively on myself, requiring that I become Christlike *first,* a necessary aspect of seeking the kingdom of God and His righteousness?"

My experience has been that when a man makes a commitment to step down from his ego-controlled throne and yield his throne to Christ, there is a remarkable change in the dynamics of his home. Only when he becomes Christ's representative on that throne can he rightfully occupy the position he thought was his automatically.

God's will is that every man first remove the beam from his own eye, purging himself of un-Christlike attitudes and behavior, before assuming any position of spiritual leadership in the home. That beam may be one of the four male prejudices already mentioned—or it might consist of all four of them. Only when we as men provide Christlike examples, becoming role models attuned to Christ's ways in our relationships with our wives, can we begin to be the powerful, yet loving, influences God wants us to be. For too long we as men have tried to rule in our homes through words only, forgetting the following words of admonition:

> But be doers of the word, and not hearers only, deceiving yourselves. For if anyone is a hearer of the word and not a doer, he is like a man observing his natural face in a mirror; for he observes himself, goes away, and immediately forgets what kind of man he was. But he who looks into the perfect law of liberty *and continues in it,* and is not a forgetful hearer

but a doer of the work, this one will be blessed in what he does (James 1:22–25, italics mine).

Contrary to popular notions, most wives do not want to occupy the throne in their marriages. A wife wants her husband to be her spiritual leader, but she is designed by God to feel secure only when she sees that her husband is not the final authority in their marriage, that he is looking to God for direction and guidance. Only then can she be confident that her relationship with her husband will be based on scriptural principles and not on her husband's personal preferences, which she recognizes can be prejudiced or selfishly motivated. Rather than argue with her when a husband discovers that his wife truly feels that he is prejudiced or selfish, he should be willing to learn what he can do to change in order to restore her confidence in him.

From God's perspective, becoming Christlike is more important to a man than developing a home government in which the husband is established as king. And more important than being the boss is having the character traits of mercy and justice. God notes the benefits of that thinking in Proverbs 20:28: "Mercy and truth preserve the king, and by lovingkindness he upholds his throne."

God has always called husbands to a deeper commitment to Himself. The Christian community seems to have wandered so far away from the idea that Christians must be like Christ that it's as if this is a new calling. As men, we need to continually examine ourselves ever more closely to see how these prejudices have affected us. And then we must determine that we will not allow ourselves the freedom of making any excuses for the sin revealed in our lives.

Special Alert: By now you may be saying, "If my wife's reproof is God's principal method of testing how Christlike I am, where does that leave the Holy Spirit and His Word?" And if you are a single guy, you may wonder how God's testing for Christlike responses comes to you. So let me establish some underlying principles guiding me as I write this book.

1. As men, single or married, we all have the Bible, God's Word, as light onto our path. His revelation in Scripture, as illuminated in our minds by the Holy Spirit, provides primary guidance for Christlike attitudes and behavior at home, on the job, in society, at church. That guidance is reinforced by everyone He sends into our lives as a spiritual mentor.

2. God, however, created Eve to become Adam's life companion. He says that in marriage a man and a woman become one flesh. In that one-flesh relationship, God has given our wives a unique helper role for us as their husbands. Our wives are used by God in *many* ways, but a key role He has given them is to help us mature into Christlikeness. And in this book you will learn why that is, how it works, why we as men resist it so strongly, and what an incredible difference cooperating with God makes in all areas of life, especially in our primary relationship, marriage.

3. And how does God minister to women? That's what you'll discover as you read this book!

Maybe this chapter has challenged some long-standing notions that have motivated your actions in the past. By now you may have recognized that what you thought was a normal marriage, the normal Christian lifestyle, is not at all normal to God. I suggest that if that is the case, you are about to discover some interesting insights as you read this book and attempt to implement its ideas in your home. A common phrase in the sports world is, "No pain, no gain." That is true as well as we seek to become Christlike in the marriage relationship.

You might take the time now to place your desires for your marriage before the Lord in prayer. Ask Him to give you the motivation to follow through on self-denial, to give you the perseverance needed to become a Christlike person and husband.

4

HUSBANDS THAT WIVES LOVE TO LOVE

Have you ever asked yourself, "Have I been the kind of person my wife has been able to love?" If you have, you certainly are in the minority. And if you've asked your wife, "Have I been the kind of person you love to love?" you are in an even greater minority.

You see, because of the four male prejudices described in the previous chapter, a husband usually wouldn't bother to ask that question. Whether he's a lovable husband is irrelevant if a husband believes that his wife is so mysterious that he can never really get to know what's going on inside her. Why bother to ask that question if he is convinced that she, not he, is the problem, if he considers his wife inferior to himself, and if he believes he is right simply because being the boss makes him right?

Most wives are desperately trying to love their husbands. But the typical husband doesn't know what it means to open up his heart and let his wife in. The typical wife thinks her husband is deliberately resisting her and is convinced he won't let himself be loved. When a wife sees that her husband has discovered her need to know what is in his heart, and that he is genuinely concerned about becoming the kind of man that she can truly love, she will be ecstatic. I find wives willing to forgive almost anything if their husbands let them into their hearts to be loved.

The reality of this situation came home to me with renewed force when I was counseling a couple new to our counseling services. In counseling with the husband, I discovered that he was struggling with severe immorality. At the time the Lord was really getting to him because the man recognized that he was destroying his family, his marriage, his children's trust in him. He felt ashamed to be around his children because he was so afraid they were going to discover his immorality.

I talked to him about learning to face himself, to recognize that his shameful sins were the evidence of the real "him." I asked whether he could thank God for saving him, whether he could consider how terrible it would be if he were not a Christian and had nowhere to turn for help and forgiveness.

A PAINFULLY HONEST LETTER

The man related that his life was a distorted mess: "I don't know how to explain or express it. Could I write a letter about what has been going on in my life, where I am, and how awful things are?"

I assured him, "Absolutely."

So he wrote a letter that really revealed what had been going on and how he felt about himself. What he shared was, as he put it, truly gross.

"So what do I do now?" he asked.

I had already met with his wife, which had given me a chance to evaluate her character, so I said, "I want you to share it with your wife."

"I can't," he insisted. "It's too gross. Believe me, she'll hate my guts."

"No, I don't think so," I responded. "She knows that something is keeping you and her from being one. She just doesn't know what it is. And because of that she can't join you as your helper as you fight this evil in your life. She is, however, the kind of wife who will stand by your side. That's why you need to share it with her."

He pleaded, "Would you do it for me? I can't be there."

As we talked, I discovered that he didn't think even God could possibly love him, much less his wife. He had always believed that nobody loved him because he'd been taught that he was no good. I let him know that I would meet with his wife and be with her as she read his letter. Then I said, "I believe God is going to teach you what real love is through your wife."

He started weeping at the thought. He was sure that she couldn't possibly love him, that she only hated him.

His wife came in for her counseling session. I prefaced his letter by telling her that her husband felt very threatened, that he was convinced she was going to leave him. I concluded, "Now if that's what you feel you have to do, I understand. I don't blame you. That's just another thing we'll have to work through."

I told her I had a letter from her husband, and I was going to let her read it so she would understand what his enemy was. I explained that she could help him fight it. As she got into the letter, she began to weep. Her tears were not just at his unfaithfulness in their marriage, but at the thought that he would share the knowledge of his immoral activities with her, that he would let her into his heart at those depths.

I continued, "I let your husband know that God was going to teach him what love is through you."

With tears flowing freely, she said, "I've always wanted to do that for him. I've always loved him. I've never not loved him. But I didn't know he didn't know how to let me into his heart. Now that I know, it makes my heart go out to him even more."

PERSONAL TRANSPARENCY WINS BACK THE WIFE

When I met with them together, I said to the husband, "Though she is deeply affected and is feeling defiled by the revelation of your gross immorality, your wife's heart went out to you because you opened your heart to her."

He was overwhelmed. He said to her, "How could you possibly love me? How could you possibly care for me? How could you possibly want to have anything to do with me?"

She responded, "I've always wanted to love you, but you kept me out of your heart. You have not let me into your heart."

They had been alienated for nearly a year, hardly talking to each other, except for saying mean, bitter things. That weekend, after she read that letter, saw his transparency, his brokenness, his willingness to humiliate himself, and his attitude, she opened her heart to him even more.

They came to see me after that weekend. I said to the husband, "One reason the Lord has let you go through these things is to let you know how much your wife is committed to you. The time is going to come when your flesh is going to rise up again, and you are going to need something that is so dear, that has ministered to your heart so deeply, that you can reflect on it and say to yourself, 'Dare I risk what I had that weekend for what is presenting itself to me now?'"

His vulnerability opened her heart to him. Actually, he didn't know he was vulnerable or what being vulnerable was. But he had a living example, and he could use that as a point of reference in the future, remembering how good it felt. He told me later that their time together had been the richest weekend ever in his life. That weekend was the foundation from which they could spend years building intimacy and richness in their marriage.

If you happen to be a woman reading this, you are probably wondering what diseases he brought into his relationship as a result of his promiscuity. His wife asked me that question as well: "What is he bringing home to me and exposing our family to?" I told her that he was no longer fearful about her finding out. He was willing to take the necessary tests to see if he had been infected with venereal diseases or AIDS.

"But what do I do until the tests prove conclusive?" she asked.

"This is a good time to trust God," I told her. "God says that all things work together for good to them that love God—and He means it. We don't know what the good is yet, but if anything has already happened, He wants to convert it into something good for us. And rest assured, your husband is willing to—and has agreed to—abstain from sex until the test results are in. His whole thinking has changed—he isn't thinking of meeting his needs now because of his concern for you."

Men, women have an enormous capacity to love their husbands—if we will genuinely open our hearts, repent of our sin, and take positive steps to heal the relationship. Wives do not always respond as quickly as in the above example, for some have built up barriers of intense dislike, even hatred. But love does break through the barriers that have been erected once a husband becomes vulnerable.

DESIRABLE QUALITIES IN A MAN

So what are the qualities the wives I talk to look for in their husbands? I'll highlight them in this chapter. You may want to mentally tape them on the mirror of your mind because I'll get back to one or another of these qualities repeatedly throughout the rest of the book.

A major quality a wife is looking for in her husband is that

1. He Can Walk in and out of the House without Causing Damage

A man does not have to stop at a bar on the way home to inflict damage when he comes into the house. Our wives and children experience damage in ways we men never think about.

The first clue to whether your wife thinks you are walking in without causing damage may be found when you ask yourself, "What do I typically say and do when I walk into the house after a hard day at the office?"

A wife often tells me, "He walks in like he's the only person who's done any work. He'll say, 'Why is the house always like a pigsty? When is supper ready? Can you quiet the kids? They get on my nerves. Where's the newspaper? Why can't I even sit in my own chair when I come home without having to shove off some toys or books?'"

Although he aims this stream of questions at the wife, he may stop long enough to yell at the kids, "Turn down the TV! Are you kids deaf or something?" No wonder the dog runs for cover—he could be thinking, *I'm next.*

Maybe your home situation doesn't strike you as that extreme. Okay, good. But before you conclude that you don't have any problem in this area, ask your wife if you ever have a negative effect on the home—even if it's only occasionally negative. I'm sure you will want to fix that. Usually, it's hard for a wife to be completely honest with her husband about the negatives she observes in his life, but so many privately tell me amazingly similar stories when I focus on the attitudes a husband conveys from his heart.

No, you don't have to take home flowers every day, though it wouldn't hurt to try it sometime. Then, if your wife faints, or if she asks, "What's this all about?" you might take a hint that she's suspicious.

When was the last time you made your wife your priority as you entered your house, embracing her, giving her more than a glancing peck on her cheek? When was the last time you asked, "How did your day go?" And then you stuck around, concentrating on her answer, even if it took a while and disrupted your schedule. When was the last time she felt your heart reach out to her with a question like, "What was the toughest thing that happened to you today?"

If you are Christlike and convinced that she is more important than you are (see Phil. 2:3), your first concern when you walk in the house will not be that your needs are met. You will be concerned that your wife and children know that you are thinking of *them* first when you walk through the door.

Even if a wife isn't used to considerate treatment and doesn't know any better, God considers it causing damage when you are demanding, critical, selfishly insistent on having things your way, questioning the housekeeping, cooking, and her appearance in a demeaning way, always negative and complaining about your children's habits and lifestyle. You are causing damage when you demand respect, when you treat your family members like they're your servants or slaves and you're the boss or the king in your home. You may consider yourself the king, but your subjects won't love you if you're that way, even though out of fear they may not show it.

Can you imagine Jesus like that? How would He behave if He came to your home after eight hours at a pressure-filled job? Now compare that with how you behave.

A second quality that every wife looks for is that

2. He Will Open His Heart to Her

I've already suggested that most men don't know that they are not letting their wives into their hearts. If you are like most men, you may think you are letting your wife into your heart by letting her into your thoughts. Even if she may not be able to put it into words, a wife instinctively knows when her husband is letting her only into his mind, not into his heart.

Women sense whether or not we are letting them into our hearts by attitudes, words, and actions. One day I was talking to a couple when the wife said that she did not want to think about her husband meeting her needs anymore. For years she had longed to know that he needed her, but she considered it totally unlikely that he would ever express such a need, so she was giving up.

She reported, "When I asked, 'How did your day go?' he would indifferently, almost resentfully answer, 'Okay.' And that was it. End of conversation."

She was sensing an evident lack of interest, an unwillingness to become conversational and include her in his day.

And that hurt her deeply. Simply put, he was not letting her into his heart, whether he meant to convey that or not.

At times when he was doing something, she would ask, "Can I help you with that?" Acting as if she were a nuisance, he would respond, "No, I'll do it myself." She felt he was telling her, "I don't need you." He was making her feel excluded, and that did not let her into his heart.

Yet, there were times when he did need her, so he would ask her to help him.

"Yet when I began to help him, all he did was complain, get upset and impatient with me. He made me feel as if I could do nothing right," she said.

Again he was making her feel inadequate and excluded from his life. His attitudes were killing her inside, but he didn't recognize what he was doing to her. You see, she knew how much she needed him (that is, his acceptance of her was vital to her), but she could only conclude, "He doesn't need me." And that caused her to feel that he did not want her getting into his life and heart. So in her desperation to feel needed, knowing that she had some value, she began looking for fulfillment elsewhere.

Trying to stop the hurts caused by such insensitive men, many women try tennis, swimming, jogging, women's Bible studies (either as participant or as leader), various social groups and clubs, and/or volunteer services to needy people. Not that every woman involved in these activities has an insensitive husband, but it is one way women try to find the significance their husbands should give them—if only they would open their hearts to their wives.

We'll revisit this concept again and again. Meanwhile, let's consider the third quality a woman looks for in the man she loves to love.

3. He Is Sensitive to Her and Other People

A woman loves a man who has tear ducts that work. That may sound strange if you have been raised with the macho image of the Wild West cowboy, if you were told as a boy, "Men don't cry."

Yet crying is the result of an emotion. You can tell a lot about the condition of a person's spirit through his emotions. If you see joyful emotions, then you know the spirit is joyful. If you see grieved emotions, then you know the spirit is grieved. That's what the Scriptures say in this proverb: "A merry heart *makes a cheerful countenance,* but by sorrow of the heart the spirit is broken" (15:13, italics mine).

Because of our insensitivity, most of us men are far more adept at breaking our wives' spirits than creating in them merry hearts. And most of us don't realize how insensitive we are. Because we don't understand our own hearts, we don't understand what it means to open our hearts to them. That's why one of my tasks as a counselor is to help men understand more about their own hearts, their own emotions.

I start with trying to help a man understand more about his emotions—to realize he has emotions, even if he is unaware of them. So as I am talking to him, I keep alert for any signs of emotions. When I notice that he is experiencing even slight emotions, I will say to him after he finishes his sentence, "Just a couple of moments ago I saw you emotionally affected. Do you know what you were experiencing?" Almost without exception, a man will get a puzzled look on his face. I have to remember the topics, so I can go back over them and refresh his memory on what we were talking about.

Going back to the topic—again he is emotionally affected. So I say, "Right now you're being emotionally affected." Hesitantly, he will say, "Y-e-a-h. . . ." I will ask, "What emotions are you feeling?" And he still isn't able to identify them—he doesn't have a clue.

So I reflect on what emotion I would be feeling if I were him and if I were in the same situation, experiencing what that situation would do to me. Then I name an emotion and ask if he can identify with it. I watch him really digging deep inside himself, finally saying, "Y-e-s. That feeling is there." But it's not clear yet, so I describe another emotion, and I ask him if he is feeling that emotion. Digging even deeper into himself, he looks at me with a bewildered expression and responds, "Y-e-a-h, that's there, too." I name two or three more, and it's

obvious I'm causing him to really struggle as he tries to identify his feelings. Finally, I ask him, "Would you have thought
about how you were emotionally affected if I had not taken
you back and asked you to identify *your own emotions*?"

"No," he admits.

Emotions are difficult for most men to register because
they are experienced for only a couple of seconds.
Repeatedly, I have to take men back and introduce them to
their own emotions as part of the process of validating emotions. As a man experiences his emotions and gives them
credibility, he begins to see their value. He is ignorant about
his own emotions, and thereby ignorant about his wife's. But
to get into her heart, to appear sensitive to his wife, he has to
value her emotions and honor them as valid.

Beyond that, I have to help a man see that his lack of
awareness of his emotional condition makes it almost impossible for him to recognize how insensitive he is in the eyes of
his wife. A man may be aware of insensitivity in others long
before he recognizes how insensitive he is.

An Emotional Paradox

Sharon was being tormented by the insensitivity of her husband, Mark (not their real names). One day Sharon's friend Marie
devised a plan to help Sharon. Marie would illustrate to both
Mark and Sharon a difficult and harsh marriage situation she
knew of—and that example was to be a hint to Mark about how
harsh and insensitive he was. Sharon readily agreed to the plan.

The stage was set, and Marie started sharing about a pastor whose wife was expecting a baby. He was totally uncon-
cerned about meeting his wife's needs to have the nursery
ready ahead of time for the new arrival. As the story unfolded,
Mark became more and more agitated and irritated at this
"monster" of a pastor.

Actually, the pastor's actions are quite common. Most men
go on their merry way even during the stressful times of pregnancy, revealing a remarkable degree of insensitivity to the
needs of their wives.

Mark, however, was extraordinarily upset with the pastor.

"He should be brought before the governing board of the church," he protested. "A man like that should not be in the pastorate."

All that time Mark was totally unaware of the look on Sharon's face, which Marie could easily read as, "I can't believe you can get so upset about someone else's insensitivity and still be so insensitive yourself."

One goal of the small group meetings we have with couples is to help interpret for husbands what their wives are saying. In addition to the group meetings, we meet with individual couples in their homes. On one such occasion, a husband asked to be shown how he could improve his attitudes and responses toward his wife. He was insensitive to the devastation his attitudes and responses were causing.

Later I was helping him examine the things he was doing to his wife while he was doing them. Even though he mentally saw what he was doing, he had a hard time adjusting to the idea that anything was wrong with what he was doing—especially since many of the actions were, in his mind, typical of men and thereby acceptable in marriage.

Over the next weeks this husband had time to observe some of the attitudes and actions of the other husbands in the group. Reflecting upon what he had seen in the group, he said, "I can't believe some of the things these guys say and do to their wives and not know it. Do you really think that they don't see what they are doing?"

I nodded affirmatively. He was quiet for a few moments. Then with an inquiring look of concern on his face, he asked, "Could I also be blind to ways that I am hurting my wife, and that it's just as clear to others what I am doing? Are they watching me, too, and wondering how I can be so insensitive?"

"Yes," I said as I nodded my head sympathetically. And what a blessing to watch the Holy Spirit deal with that man's spirit, causing him to see and understand in his heart the destructive effect of some of his ways.

It is possible, with the Holy Spirit's and your wife's help, to become more sensitive to her needs and the needs of others.

We'll discover how that can happen to you in a later chapter.

Another quality that a wife loves in her husband is that

4. He Is Thoughtful Enough to Remember the Things Important to Her—and Is Creative and Imaginative in Doing Them

Did you drive by a field of wildflowers recently with your wife in the car? While you were driving by, your wife may have commented on the flowers she really liked. Did you pay attention enough so you could remember which flowers appealed to her in a special way?

Now you are returning home from three days on the road and you drive by those flowers. What do you do when you see them? Let me suggest that if you want to be a man your wife loves to love, you will stop, pick several of your wife's favorite flowers, and take them home. We're talking about taking maybe ten to fifteen minutes out of your whole life to do this.

So let's say you stop and pick the flowers and walk in the door with them. What do you think will happen? After she faints and you revive her, she might ask, "What are these for?" You say, "They're for you." She faints again, and you revive her and tell her, "Honest, honey, they're just for you."

How do you think she will really be affected? Okay, maybe she will remain suspicious the first time, but you pull another surprise like that, and she will be saying to herself, "Wow, Jim has really changed. I like it. I love this new Jim."

Inspired by a book on marriage he was reading on the plane to a convention in Orlando, Florida, a friend of mine took off time to walk down the road to the Walt Disney Village. There he purchased five little surprises that he knew his wife would love. Because the convention was short, he sent the package and a card with his expression of love by Federal Express.

Despite attending many conventions, my friend had never gone out of his way to do something thoughtful like that before, though he had occasionally brought home a surprise gift. He felt so good about his new approach, and got such a warm reaction, that he began haunting card racks wherever he traveled. He'd drop unusual cards expressing his love and affection in the mail whenever he was on the road to a convention.

Wives *love* thoughtful husbands like that. It helps take the worry out of knowing their husbands may be with some attractive women at conventions.

So when was the last time you remembered your wife's birthday and did more than peck her on the cheek and wish her a happy birthday? When was the last time you remembered your wedding anniversary—without being reminded repeatedly—and you planned something special to celebrate?

"That gets to be old hat," you say.

Not to women, it doesn't. They just love to be remembered by thoughtful, creative, imaginative husbands.

A fifth quality that a wife loves in a husband is that

5. He Does Things with Her—He Is Inclusive, Not Exclusive

Ever heard your wife say, "We never do anything together"? You defensively replied, "Oh, yes, we do. Didn't we have dinner last Thursday at our favorite restaurant, and on Sunday we went to dinner with the Smiths?" And she said, "That's not what I mean. You just don't understand."

So you buy season tickets for the local university's artist concert series to prove to her that you are willing to do something with her. About a month after attending the second concert, she again complains, "We never do anything together." And you just explode and walk out of the room muttering, "Women!"

Most of us husbands don't realize that our wives want to be included in everyday activities that involve give-and-take from the heart. Going to a concert is nice, but that can happen without our having an inclusive attitude that lets them into our hearts. That's why many wives can be satisfied with taking a long walk with their husbands in the park. It involves more than participating in an activity together.

I was working in our yard one day digging up Bermuda grass so I could put in roses as a border around our driveway. I dug up the dirt and removed all the Bermuda from it. It was time to put in the edging that would act as a barrier to keep the very aggressive grass from creeping back into the rose bed.

Just then I realized that I had forgotten to buy the edging, and that it was too late to go to the hardware store. Watching, Nancy remembered some brick wall top caps that the previous owner had left in the backyard. She asked if they would work. She explained that they could be set on edge and attractively curve around the border while keeping out the grass.

"That's a *great* idea," I said. And by my *enthusiastically* acknowledging she had a creative solution to my dilemma, I brought her into my heart. Accepting her idea meant that I admitted that I did not have all the great ideas—and that made her feel more confident about herself. Additionally, we both had ownership in that rose border, and every time she or I walk by it, it's a reminder of our togetherness. I had included her, not excluded her. I think the thing I enjoy most is that I've convinced her that she has the freedom to offer suggestions when she is with me, and I will be receptive.

I'm the first to admit I had to train myself to be open to Nancy's involvement. As a man, I was used to doing things myself, my way. So I had to literally tell Nancy, "Whenever you see me making decisions that don't include you, and whether or not you are going to be involved in it, please let me know your thinking."

While working on the car one day, I came into the house and informed Nancy, "I'm getting ready to go to the store to get some parts for the car."

She asked, "Do you still want me to tell you when I see examples of how you make decisions without including me in your thinking?"

"Yeah," I said with curiosity and hesitation.

"If you were including me in your thinking, I think you would have thought, *I need to get some parts. While I'm out, I wonder if there's something Nancy needs?* Then I could have said, 'Yes, I need some laundry soap. Do you have time to pick some up for me?'"

I have to admit that my flesh wants to react with, "Great, I'm supposed to check with you now before I can do anything." But I know that's my flesh's noninclusive attitude of selfishness. More times than I can count now, God has blessed me through Nancy by revealing un-Christlike attitudes in my heart. My tendency is to be much more exclusive than I realize.

Most of us don't think of our wives as God-given, valuable assets, worthy to include in our problem-solving processes. One of the ways it shows is that we don't share our serious problems at work. For example, the part you manufactured for a major manufacturer didn't meet specs, and you got your head in a vise. And the person you hired for supervisor of office services is just not turning out to be a good hire, and it's eating you alive. But you think sharing those problems would reveal you as a failure, and you don't dare appear less than perfect, even though it's eating at you.

Although your wife may not understand all the complexities of life on the job for you, she wants to be included, especially if something is eating you alive. There are a number of reasons why you should share them with her:

- She is negatively affected when the man she loves is hurting.

- She feels accepted when you are open to her ideas. Sometimes someone not involved in all the complexities of the problem is free to see a solution that no one else would have dreamed of. Remember the truck that was about six inches too high for the tunnel entrance and was going so fast that when it hit, it was wedged quite a way into the tunnel entrance? All the engineers were standing around trying to figure out how to remove it. All efforts had failed. A little boy began tugging on a man's pant leg, trying to get him to listen. The man impatiently said, "What?" And the little boy suggested, "Why don't you let the air out of the tires?" Astonished that they hadn't thought of it, they let the air out and were able to move the truck back out of the tunnel.

• Finally, and most important, she can provide prayer support.

So let her show her love for you by being there for you emotionally and spiritually.

A wife loves the husband who believes that she is intelligent enough, that God is intelligent enough, to use her to help him become more effective because he is more inclusive.

Finally, a wife loves to love a husband who demonstrates that

6. He Believes They Really Are One

What with the excitement of the wedding and the pleasure of the honeymoon, few men concentrate on God's perspective about the requirements of marriage. Even though we read in Genesis 2:24, "Therefore a man shall leave his father and mother and be joined to his wife, and they shall become one flesh," the typical man thinks about "one flesh" in the sexual context. But since it comes from God, becoming one flesh has to mean much more than having good, frequent sex or even making babies.

Wives know instinctively that there is more to oneness. And they love to love men who understand what it means in everyday life, and who practice it on a regular basis.

We just finished examining inclusive *thinking.* Now let's add to that dimension the idea of being one flesh through inclusive *decision making.* That may run counter to the "I'm the boss" attitude so common among even Christian men, but I think it's consistent with God's perspective of oneness.

I'm convinced that the concept of oneness involves these principles: two halves fused together, making one. They are unable to properly function separately; each requires the other for success. Let me give an example of the reasoning I think is required to make oneness really accomplish God's purposes: "I do not make any decisions without letting me know what I'm thinking. Therefore, since my wife is 'me,' I'm not going to make decisions without letting 'me' know what is going on in 'my' thinking!"

Including wives in the decision-making process so improves their sense of security that it is also reflected in all aspects of intimacy.

ONENESS IN DISCIPLINING CHILDREN

An area in which husband and wife need oneness is in disciplining their children. A husband who disciplines the children without ever discussing it with his wife tells her (whether he intends to or not) that she and her thinking are unimportant to him. Maybe her half of their oneness feels that he is being unnecessarily harsh, but because he never considered including her in the disciplinary policies, she feels alienated. She certainly is not able to exercise her God-given different perspective.

Nor, if necessary, is she free to express her desire to protect the children and help him avoid the rejection she senses her husband is developing in the children. His harsh actions are damaging the children and her; thus, their relationship, intimate or otherwise, is adversely affected. Resentments build up that destroy any sense of oneness that may have existed.

ONENESS IN DRIVING HABITS

Another type of alienation occurs when the husband drives at speeds that make his wife feel that her safety is threatened. She may protest, but he inconsiderately says, "I'm not an unsafe driver!" True, he may never have had an accident, but he is still scaring her half to death. Again the sense of oneness is not functional because he did not consider her sensitivities in the decisions about his driving conduct.

ONENESS IN MAKING FINANCIAL DECISIONS

Family financial decisions are another area in which God does not exclude wives. Yet most husbands don't consider their wives when it comes to financial decisions. And many wives don't feel the freedom to express their hearts by asking, "Do you know how it makes me feel when you don't consider me in respect to finances?" Instead, they often wait until they feel so alienated that they explode with comments like, "What am I supposed to do if anything ever happens to you? I know nothing about our finances. For all I know, I could be in great jeopardy!"

It is not surprising when the husband gets defensive and scolds his wife by saying, "You're not in jeopardy. You don't have anything to worry about!" Yet with that reaction, he further denies her the oneness God wants him to build with her. Without an explanation he is still out of the will of God.

Maybe you, like me, are a risk taker. And your wife, like Nancy, tends not to be a risk taker. If Nancy sees me disregarding her and the family, then she gets nervous and is really uncomfortable about that. When I began involving her in the decisions, she started understanding what my thinking was and often saw the value in some of the risks, becoming more of a risk taker as well. Still, on some occasions Nancy was able to help me recognize some important cautions, reducing the risks I took.

Nancy says, "At one time I was really scared about our financial security. But today I'm confident that when a husband finally involves his wife in the decision-making processes, there are fewer chances for negatives. Making the decision together makes us feel closer because we've taken the risk together."

Oneness in Including God

The most important factor in all of this is that our wives know we are including God in our decision making. When I'm making the decisions instead of seeking guidance from God, something deep within Nancy's spirit starts gnawing at her. Her inner caution makes her nervous. It's as if God makes her feel those cautions so my other "me" will prompt me to get back with God. When she hears me praying about a situation, observes me searching Scripture for direction, and shares her thoughts as I include her in the discussion, looking for her perspective on the options, she feels much safer about a decision. And so do I!

Now when Nancy sees me making decisions without asking her, she knows I'm being exclusive. But she has come to realize that I don't do it because I want to; it's just natural to me. I naturally think exclusively. Involving her in the decision lets her know that I am being more inclusive. She is also the kind of good help meet who might say if I were to ask her what she is thinking, "I guess I'm wondering what God is thinking."

At one time that comment would have bothered me. I'd defensively think that she was implying that I don't include God. Or, worse yet, I'd feel guilty because I got caught. So I'd have to answer, "I had not thought to include God." Or I was able to assure her that I had, and then she felt a lot more secure. You see, she knows God is not selfish, so she feels more confidence when she is aware that I've not excluded Him. She also knows that He will help me be unselfish.

There you have them. Six attitudes and related actions that make women really love their men. In one way or another we'll touch on them again and again because they are so foundational to discovering the mind of a woman.

5

"DON'T TELL ME I'M THE KEY TO THE PROBLEM"

One of the lessons God had to teach me before I could help other men was how to see myself from His frame of reference. Once I began to learn that lesson, I began to see how destructive my ways could be to a relationship.

My wife, Nancy, believed I knew exactly how destructive I was to her spirit. She was sure that I understood clearly the difficulties I was creating, but that I refused to accept the responsibility for what I was doing. From her perspective, I was living in denial and not accepting the reality of how un-Christlike I was treating her as my wife.

The reality is, I didn't have a clue that things were as bad between us as Nancy thought they were. If anything, it was obvious to me who the troublemaker was. It was Nancy. I figured that her problem was that she exaggerated everything—and even invented troubles. Like Adam, I felt that my wife was the real problem.

I've been blind to many lessons God has prepared for me. So I've missed identifying many circumstances from which He wanted me to learn major lessons. Instead of seeing God's hand in my life and learning the lessons, my blindness typically made me resent, overlook, or react negatively to them. And that was true of my relationship with Nancy.

You see, God says of us:

For the hearts of this people have grown dull.
Their ears are hard of hearing,
And their eyes they have closed,
Lest they should see with their eyes and hear with their ears,
Lest they should understand with their hearts and turn,
So that I should heal them (Matt. 13:15).

Some people have responded, "That's referring to unregenerate people, so it doesn't apply to me." Those folks were not the first to miss the relationship implications of that verse, the need to listen and use our eyes if we want to develop good relationship skills. Many Christian men coming into my office are easily diagnosed as relationship ignorant, and like me, they are in need of help.

THREE INSIGHTS

As I learned to listen to what God was trying to teach me and paid attention to what wives were telling me, I gained three insights:

1. Husbands do not generally understand the minds of their wives.
2. Husbands are inclined to be blind to their own faults, and yet extremely alert to their wives' failures, and they are very quick to condemn them for their faults.
3. Husbands don't always know how to evaluate the circumstances in their marriages from God's perspective, so they miss the opportunity to use those circumstances as build-

ing blocks. Few men know how to make the change from just seeing what is happening to also seeing what God is trying to teach them through what is happening.

I'll refer to these three problems repeatedly, but at the same time I'll offer ways to overcome them in your life.

God has furnished us a blueprint, His Word, as an invaluable aid for men who are seeking to become Christlike and build, or possibly rebuild, their marriages. Perhaps a word picture from Scripture will set the stage. The psalmist describes us this way: "Behold, I was brought forth in [a state of] iniquity; my mother was sinful who conceived me [and I, too, am sinful]" (Ps. 51:5 AMPLIFIED).

What that tells me is that I started life with a major obstacle to becoming Christlike—sin had clearly influenced my very being from birth. But that's not all—I was up against it at another level even after I became a Christian, according to the apostle Paul in Ephesians 6:12: "For we are not wrestling with flesh and blood—contending only with physical opponents— but against the despotisms, against the powers, against [the master spirits who are] the world rulers of this present darkness, against the spirit forces of wickedness in the heavenly (supernatural) sphere" (AMPLIFIED).

Although the following is not a totally accurate analogy, I use this particular illustration to convey the point of those Scriptures. Imagine a baby being born. Waiting right there is an evil presence, and if you could see it, it's in the process of entering in and uniting itself with this newborn baby. This evil presence has the power to become the controlling influence in this new life. Actually, this possession occurs at conception, and the evil influence exhibited in humankind is known as the sin nature, or lower nature.

While the child is growing up, he will have no awareness of the power and influence this evil has on his life. Neither will the child sense that the presence is undesirable and harmful. In fact, since this has happened to everyone, the child does not see himself as being different from anyone else. The child may think about God, but he will not consider whether or not he is the person God wants him to be, free from the control of evil. Nor is he likely to consider that his life should be led by the Holy Spirit.

This evil spirit has joined each person because he wants each person to be with him in hell. Therefore, God sent His Son, Jesus Christ, to make it possible for us to be saved from going to hell. We are saved by agreeing with God that we have this sin nature and that we are sinners in need of forgiveness. Christ died for our sins, and God raised Him from the dead. We need to believe that Christ is our Savior and trust Him with the balance of our lives.

Next, we need to let the Holy Spirit be the chief influencer in our lives. But evil still wants to control us, so the next goal of evil, after being forced out of our spirits by God's Spirit, is to influence us even after we have made a faith commitment to Jesus as our Savior. The apostle Paul put it this way:

> For I know that in me (that is, in my flesh) nothing good dwells; for to will is present with me, but how to perform what is good I do not find. For the good that I will to do, I do not do; but the evil I will not to do, that I practice. Now if I do what I will not to do, it is no longer I who do it, but sin that dwells in me. I find then a law, that evil is present with me, the one who wills to do good. For I delight in the law of God according to the inward man. But I see another law in my members, warring against the law of my mind, and bringing me into captivity to the law of sin which is in my members. O wretched man that I am! Who will deliver me from this body of death? I thank God—through Jesus Christ our Lord! So then, with the mind I myself serve the law of God, but with the flesh the law of sin (Rom. 7:18–25).

The evil one does not want anyone to see his desperate need and invite Jesus to become his Savior. Also, the evil one wants others to see no changes, no joy, no purpose or value in being a Christian. That's why—now that we are Christians—we must look at and examine the contrasts between Christ and ourselves. We must let the Holy Spirit help us make the changes that will show others what happens when Christ is not only our Savior but our Lord as well.

Remember, since the influence of evil in our lives is not something we can see (that is, not as we can see another person), we don't easily recognize evil's influences. Then, too, because this evil (or sin nature) is common to all of us, and isn't noticeable as, say, a grapefruit in a pile of apples, we don't suspect that it is with us. As a result, we don't put ourselves on guard against it.

To prevent the spirit of evil from successfully convincing others that accepting Christ as Savior does not make any difference, we need to be willing to examine our lives in the light of Christ and the scriptural principles that lead to Christlike living. Becoming Christlike requires that we let the Holy Spirit be our boss. This will result in a wonderfully fulfilled, meaningful life, benefiting not only ourselves but also all those around us.

By contrast, a person who lets the spirit of the evil one lead his life will experience a frustrated, meaningless life, full of destruction—especially in the marriage relationship and the family. That sin nature in us is our enemy and the enemy of God.

By now you know that I believe that every enemy of God should be fought and defeated. Since Satan was defeated when Christ rose from the dead, we face a defeated enemy pretending as though he were still in charge. We need to claim the victory Jesus won over the evil one, thus realizing the victory ourselves. That will not happen, however, if we live in ignorance about our sin nature and its manifestations in our lives as men.

RESPONSES ILLUSTRATING THE FLESH'S DEFENSIVENESS

I've mentioned that we as men have a terrible time recognizing and admitting that we are not Christlike, that we are the key to solving relationship problems. The most common response illustrating this is an innate focus that says, "Wait a minute. She's gotta be Christlike, too. She's not perfect, either." That, my friend, is the flesh, the sin nature, instinctively responding in defense of itself when there are problems in the marriage relationship.

I was discipling a senior pastoral staff member of a local church, teaching him what the practical application of Christlikeness meant in his everyday life. When he and his wife came in, she brought attention to his habit of being impatient with the children after arriving home from work, insisting that he be left alone and that his needs be met first. She added that she and the children had been waiting all day for him to get home.

"But I've been under enormous pressure all day long," he protested. "The last thing I need is to come home to you needing me urgently."

In that statement alone, that pastoral staff member revealed that he is not truly Christlike, for Christ said, "Come to Me, all you who labor and are heavy laden, and I will give you rest. Take My yoke upon you and learn from Me, for I am gentle and lowly in heart, and you will find rest for your souls" (Matt. 11:28–29). If Jesus took that attitude, then even a busy pastor ought to reflect that attitude to his family as well.

It's as if Christian men believe these verses apply only when *they* are experiencing Christ's relief from stress. Some might agree this would be a Christlike attitude—unless, of course, they've had a pressure-filled day at work, or things just haven't gone right and they're exhausted. Then being Christlike doesn't apply! Instead, they get to take their burdens home, and their families have to minister to them—by not needing them. This would mean that since every day is full of pressures, men are free from ever having to concern themselves about applying these verses in their relationships in the family.

Or does that Scripture mean precisely what it says? And that if those family relationship demands being made on a husband are not catching God by surprise, then God is allowing those events to take place. God is at work. He is using that man's family. They are instruments in God's control, being used to reveal how much that man has learned or needs to learn about Christlike attitudes in his responses.

Anyway, having to face the responsibility for his attitudes toward his family, the pastoral staff member was really getting wound up, getting more and more angry in defense of himself. His flesh instinctively responded as he reacted to his family's "unreasonable" demands. As things escalated, he started using some pretty graphic language, quite out of character to his position. Wanting to redirect his thinking, I asked the following question: "Would you have ever believed that you, *as a Christian leader,* would use *that kind of language* and say *those kinds of things* about your wife and family?"

In stunned shame he said, "Never!"

I pressed further, "Would you have ever believed that *your flesh* has that much control over you?"

"Never!" he repeated.

I said, "Would you have ever believed that your flesh is that dominant in your life, that God *had* to use these circumstances to get past your superficial natural Christian responses in order to reveal your flesh's existence and its control over you?"

Overwhelmed, shaking his head in disbelief, he responded hesitatingly, "Never, never."

You see, we are able to remain ignorant about our being at the core of the problem because of our fleshly nature. Typically, our sinful nature has never been cross-examined in terms of our ability to portray Christlikeness in our marriages. We have never been tried to the point of having to go through the fire of actually illustrating Christ to our wives *under pressure.* So when that fire comes, and it is pointed out that the flesh is in control of our responses instead of Christ in us, the flesh's response is to become defensive and try to avoid exposure. We try to shift the focus with statements like, "Well, she's not perfect, either. I wouldn't have gotten angry if she hadn't gotten in my face." Those are all excuses provided by the flesh as a strategy for maintaining its freedom to exercise control and thus discredit Christianity.

The Scriptures tell us that the Spirit wars against the flesh. But until he experiences the type of confrontation just mentioned, the typical man coming to me is not aware of any war. Without that frame of reference, when asked, "Do you sense a war going on inside you between godliness and ungodliness?" the man responds, "No. Maybe some struggles about life, but a war between good and evil? Not really." There is not a sense of war.

So what is this war the apostle Paul is writing about in Galatians 5:17? "For the flesh lusts against the Spirit, and the Spirit against the flesh; and these are contrary to one another, so that you do not do the things that you wish." Is this war something just a few people experience, or is it the typical experience of Mr. Average Christian?

If it's typical, why do so few people sense a fierce battle taking place inside themselves? Why do they not sense it unless they are confronted about everyday issues that expose bad attitudes—right in the middle of those attitudes? It's because the everyday attitudes in our lives are just that, everyday attitudes, natural and common to the flesh. That's why God has to use our everyday experiences, like feeling the need to rest when we get home. Then upon walking in the door, we find a wife who is at her wit's end. Or our kids make demands on us when we're worn out. Suddenly, we discover how much the flesh is still in control—and we also discover that we don't know what a Christlike response is!

Another reason a man may not sense a war in his inner being is that he is not aware of God's expectations of him spiritually—other than that he has acquired the title "spiritual leader," which most men believe comes with the territory. Acquiring that title gives him the authority (if he had a mind to) to have a plaque made that might read SPIRITUAL LEADER, HEAD OF THE HOUSE, or BOSS. Too many Christian men live under the assumption that the moment they are married, the title and its accompanying authority are theirs.

We believe we are in charge, physically and spiritually, when we don't have a clue what it means to be in charge of our wives' spirits. But Christ would *know* precisely what that would involve. So, to *know* Christ would mean we would have to be like Christ. We would also, as Christ does, have an understanding of what is involved in operating within God's economy. Since we do not have the inner security that comes from knowing God's perspective about our leadership role and all of its requirements, we are easily threatened by the concept of giving our wives the freedom to express themselves. That's true especially since it means evaluating our behavior as husbands about whether or not we are illustrating Christlike attitudes and behavior. The average Christian husband cannot handle his wife questioning his character. He does not feel free to let her ask such things as, "Do you realize that when you spoke like that to _____, your words were offensive?"

A truly Christlike husband would insist on responding positively to that question. He would want to hear it as a genuine expression of interest in his improvement, helping him to gain greater credibility. He would not conclude that his wife was trying to put him down or to question his leadership.

Our wives see us with eyes that we cannot see ourselves with. And yet we rarely accept their assessment, even when others might agree with them. So we remain ignorant and don't work on our problems, leaving ourselves with a huge credibility gap in the eyes of our wives—and among those who have drawn the same conclusion about our character, but are unwilling to take the risk of informing us.

If we recognize that our salvation has requirements, that Christ is to live in and through us, and that becoming like Christ is to be our highest priority, then our behavior will begin evidencing that priority. As we gain Christlikeness, our witness will become credible. And as our wives become living illustrations of what it is like to have a joyful relationship with their husbands, it will further enhance our testimony.

LET'S GET REAL!

A common Christian notion emphasizes the need for a woman to always have a quiet spirit before she approaches her husband. She can come to him only if she conveys a positive, uplifting manner. A man who buys this philosophy usually rationalizes, "If my wife would just approach me in a nicer way, I would have a Christlike response. If she would stop being so offensive toward me, everything would be fine."

Imagine if you would, a desperate woman approaching her husband with a soft, uplifting appeal. Keep in mind that this wife is to portray a pleasant look and a soft-spoken gentleness in her approach. She says, "Sweetheart, there's something I regretfully submit to you because I'm sure it conveys a terrible spirit of ungratefulness in me for all you've done, but being crushed, my spirit is dying within me. (*Continued gentle smile, speaking softly.*) I didn't know a person could be so emotionally violated in a relationship. (*Still examining herself for respectfulness in her attitude.*) Although I know it is my problem, the hate I have for you is overwhelming. And because our relationship is deteriorating daily, the love I had for you when we were married has died. (*Still maintaining a relaxed body posture and casual tone of voice.*)"

If your wife said that to you, how believable would that be? Those words, spoken in that manner, would be totally incredible. Somehow or other, in that situation, a wife's expression of hostility and bitterness conveys much more reality. It's much more convincing. I'm not saying that hostile bitterness is acceptable, but if you're going to learn how to honestly face the facts, those are the facts!

As a man, tell me you've never been mad at God. Tell me that when you are angry and reactionary, you don't speak in negative terms to Him or anyone else. And when you were angry with God, did He reject you, or did He, in full understanding of your distraught condition, minister unconditional patience and love to you?

That's why it is such a farce to try to sidestep personal responsibility by saying, "She's the problem."

NOT EVEN THE PASTORS

My associate, Eldon, whose story I told in chapter 2, is a former pastor. He recognizes how difficult it is for pastors to

accept that they need their wives' help toward Christlikeness.
And Satan is definitely determined that they will not become
more Christlike in their attitudes and behavior toward their
wives and toward the church, any more than he is going to
stand by and let anyone else become an example.

We had a promotional meeting with thirty-five pastors in a
western state. We started with Eldon giving his testimony,
revealing how for years he hurt his wife's spirit deeply, even
while having a successful television and pastoral ministry. He
shared how he had learned to understand his wife, and that
through God's ways applied in his own life first, he had
brought healing to his marriage.

We expressed the Bible's challenge in which we men are
commanded to become Christlike for our wives. We also
offered, as a follow-up to our seminar, a course in which we
promised the men would learn how to understand the mind of
a woman. We invited them to attend as our guests. But not
one pastor responded.

Because of that typical response, I've wondered if a thousand pastors were offered the promise to genuinely understand their wives, and if they were invited to accept the
challenge to become an illustration of Christ as validated by
their wives and families, would only a few respond?

Pastors have boldly announced to me in front of their
wives, "We don't need this. We have a good marriage." And
then I watch their wives look downcast, telegraphing, "There
go my hopes." And when I've had the chance to meet with
their wives, they've said, "He knows we have problems. I told
him *we need this*. I've even threatened to leave him, but I
guess he doesn't care."

Those pastors are like the rest of us men. They, too, think
their wives are exaggerating and are inventing problems. As
Eldon says, "If a man thinks he knows, but doesn't even know
that he doesn't know, he certainly won't have the motivation
to learn. You're not going to teach him anything."

Ignorance, along with the flesh's self-preserving nature,
makes a formidable foe. If we do not accept the responsibility
for providing Christlike spiritual leadership, we will also be

incapable of receiving the messages God is trying to convey to us through our wives. Not living with our wives in an understanding way carries two consequences: we do not receive God's messages for our spiritual growth, and we make it difficult, if not impossible, for God to regard our prayers (1 Peter 3:7). And then we wonder why our prayers are not effective.

Do you still struggle with the idea that you're the key to your relationship problems? Then move into the next chapter with me for further clarification.

6

HOW TO KNOW IF YOU'RE THE KEY TO THE PROBLEM

I wouldn't be surprised if by now you're saying, "Does this guy think that the wife can do no wrong, that she's always right, no matter what her attitudes are?"

Of course, a wife's attitudes and behavior are not right all the time. They may be wrong a lot of the time. I'm not, however, going to try to address that now. Instead I'm trying to convey that I have discovered that being my wife, Nancy is unable to control the way I *affect* her. (A wife *does* have a choice about her response to the effects. But I am dealing with only the effects here.)

Why? Because, as God's representative, I have been given the responsibility of illustrating Christ to my wife, giving her an example to follow. That's the message of Ephesians 5:25–29. God has provided me with a tangible, physical means of evaluating whether or not I am portraying Christ! When I am not caring for Nancy as Christ would, she must be adversely affected. When I am caring for Nancy as Christ would, she must be positively affected.

There is a reason Nancy cannot prevent her emotions from being affected by the un-Christlike attitudes I have toward her, why she cannot overrule how her inner person, her spirit, and her emotions are affected by me. If she were able to exercise control over her emotions, I would lose the gauge God has provided me to evaluate my capacity to portray Christ to my wife.

Here's what my wife, Nancy, says, "Even when I'm faithfully praying every day, when I'm in the Bible diligently searching what the Holy Spirit has for me, I am emotionally affected in a negative way when Ken does or says something to me that does not reflect Christlikeness. Even though I purpose that I will not let his negative ways hurt me, they still do. They put me in a mood that is not of my own making. It's as though I'm powerless to determine whether or not I will be affected. When he's not Christlike, I don't enjoy being interdependent and susceptible to him."

WOMEN KNOW WHEN THEIR ATTITUDE IS WRONG

Many Christian women have confessed to me, "The way I react to my husband is awful! I know when I'm reacting I'm wrong. I don't understand it. No matter how much I purpose that I will not let him affect me so negatively again, I cannot restrain myself from reacting to him. And I feel so ashamed because I know I'm being ungodly."

I'm sure this statement may sound radical to you, but a wife really does not have a choice about the effects her husband has on her emotions. Again, please note that I am talking about *effects*—not the wife's responses. In God's scheme, a wife is compelled to reflect to her husband how he is or is not being like Christ. From the beginning of creation, the woman was identified by God as help for the man. In God's masterful plan the woman was designed as a road map for the man. By the way her husband affects her, a wife is God's means of revealing the course he is on. Is he on the road to Christlikeness or the road to un-Christlikeness?

Now that's what I call proof of a loving God! He knows how blind humankind is about godliness. That's clear from Proverbs 16:25: "There is a way that seems right to a man, but its end is the way of death."

Our natural state is described in Romans 3:10–12:

> As it is written:
> There is none righteous, no, not one;
> There is none who understands;
> There is none who seeks after God.
> They have all turned aside;
> They have together become unprofitable;
> There is none who does good, no, not one.

Because of that, God provides men with customized gauges that allow us to constantly measure our character and check our attitudes, seeing if we are on track or not.

IMPROVING MARRIAGE NOT THE REAL MOTIVATION

Some readers might think, *Ah, that's what it's all about. I should be motivated to be like Christ so I can have a better marriage!*

No, no! If that's the conclusion any man draws from reading this book, then I've failed to convey the real motivation. Every man's motivation to improve his marriage should be based on the fact that his marriage relationship helps him measure whether or not he is becoming more Christlike.

Being Christlike means richer fellowship with the Father—
that's the greatest achievement a man can attain, a deeper fellowship with God through Jesus Christ.

The flip side is that when I am in fellowship with the
Father, I will provide Christlike leadership for my wife and
family. I will be credible as I exercise my God-given role of
spiritual leadership. My wife can observe my example and
say, "You know what? I've always wondered how a Christian
was supposed to _____ (conduct himself or respond to
life in a certain way). Now that it's clear to me, I can follow
your example."

Seeing me focus on building my relationship with God, my
wife will be motivated to enhance her relationship with God,
that is, she will also be illustrating Christ. Should she still
struggle over flaws in her behavior or attitudes, she will be
much more receptive and respond more positively to me as I
reach out to help her. Because she knows I am aware that I
have not arrived, that I know I'm not perfect, she will recognize that I am humble in my approach to her as a fellow
learner.

When I am working on myself, letting the Holy Spirit be
active in reshaping my attitudes and behavior, Nancy knows
it's safe to develop a genuine level of trust. She believes in my
commitment to become more and more like Christ and to do
His will. Because she must be affected by the attitudes in my
heart, she senses when my selfish attitudes are dropping
away, and she is inspired to the point of thinking, *My husband
is of true spiritual leadership material. I can follow this guy.* And
isn't that what all of us men want—wives who will admire and
follow us?

IT'S AMAZING TO WATCH

I have repeatedly seen—and am constantly amazed by—
how quickly a wife is positively affected by a change in her
husband's attitudes. One day a couple in my office illustrated
this dramatically.

The wife was angry and making no bones about it. Her vocal inflection, her posture, the way she leaned away from her husband, and even her facial expression exhibited hostile anger. She spat out words in a tone that I would describe as venomous, "He loves his family more than he loves me! I hate him! I hate him! He's always treating his family better than me!"

Her husband, clearly not understanding her heart and what she was trying to communicate, squinted his eyes in disapproval and snapped, "Why do you say that? Why are you always trying to cause trouble between us, trying to make me choose between my family and you? What you're saying simply is not true. I married you, didn't I? That ought to prove something to you."

I interrupted, "Whoa, whoa, stop! Is what you're saying now accomplishing what you want it to?"

"No," he admitted.

"Would you like to see what happens when you do it right?" I asked.

"Yes," he responded with a puzzled look on his face.

"Would you be willing to let me put words in your mouth?" I asked.

"What do you mean?" he questioned.

I answered, "Will you repeat what I say after me?"

He agreed, so I started, "The first thing I want you to say to her is, 'It's obvious that I have impressed you in some way that I care more about my family than I do about you.'"

He repeated what I said, but he was looking at me. So I redirected him, "Look at her." He turned to look at her (it was obviously very difficult for him) and questioned me, "What was that I was supposed to say?" So I repeated my statement. After he copied my words, I continued as though I were him, talking to her. He repeated every statement word for word, as follows: "I believe it is very hurtful to you when I act as though my family is more important than you are to me. And since that is how I have impressed you, I can see why it would make you very upset with me.

"I want you to know that it is not right that I have impressed you that way. It is not what God would want me to do. I want to learn how to be the kind of person who causes you to believe I care as much about you as I do about my family, if not more. And I recognize that I have not done that. It's obvious to me that I don't know how to do that, but I want you to know that I have every intention of learning."

STILL NOT CATCHING ON

Having finished, he looked over at me. By looking at me, he revealed that he had missed, and was still missing, what was taking place right before his eyes. He was oblivious to the most important thing he should have noticed—how what he had done had affected his wife. I wanted him to be encouraged with what had taken place. Wanting him to gain new understanding, I guided his attention, saying, "Look at your wife. What do you see?"

He turned and examined her face, reporting, "Peace." Drawing him into more observation for more understanding, I added, "Isn't that interesting? Even though she knows I put the words in your mouth, they still brought peace."

As though that was her cue, she erupted again. The accusations continued, "Well, it won't last! We'll get in the parking lot, and it'll be gone! He'll be the same old rat again!"

She was not far off. He didn't last until the parking lot. Right after she erupted, he reverted to his old nature, blurting out, "Now why do you have to do that all the time?"

"Whoa, whoa, stop," I said. "Let's not go down that road again. Will you let me put words in your mouth again?"

"Yes," he replied, recognizing he was not doing too well on his own. So I offered a response, with him repeating it after me: "Obviously, you don't trust me very much. Obviously, my character and conduct haven't provided you with enough confidence that you can trust me any longer than the time it takes to get out to the car. And that isn't right. I know that Christ would not have impressed you that way. I will have to become more like Christ so you can have more confidence and will be able to trust me longer."

By now, his wife had her head resting on his shoulder, looking up in admiration at him. Wanting to emphasize and prove my point, I asked him, "Is this not evidence to you that your wife is a responder, that she will follow your lead? That what it says in Ephesians 5:25–29 is true (and I paraphrased), 'If a man will learn to lay down his life for his wife like Christ, that through the washing of the Word he will present his wife holy, without wrinkle, spot, or blemish, but glorious.' Is this not living proof of that formula?"

He affirmed, "It sure is!"

To emphasize the lesson I believe God was teaching him, and also to encourage him, I asked, "Can you see the difference between the way you usually try to solve your problems and the solution you used here today?"

"Absolutely!" he said with a smile.

Like all of us, this man needed to learn that if he approaches his wife in a godly manner, she will be emotionally affected; she will respond—even though she is violently angry and is full of hate for him. If he ministers to her as Christ would, she cannot help herself; she will be emotionally affected; she will respond—God has decreed that she will (Gen. 3:16; Eph. 5:25–29).

A REALISTIC CONCEPT

We have no problem believing that our Christian testimony is supposed to have an effect on the lives of others. We have great confidence that God will powerfully influence others through our lives, especially as we illustrate Christ. It's not unusual for people to blame themselves when a non-Christian friend dies without receiving Christ as Savior. So why is it so unrealistic to accept the responsibility for the influence we have on the lives of our wives? Didn't God ordain us to be spiritual leaders?

Incidentally, the problem of the man in the preceding example was not his wife! His problem was revealed through his wife. His actual problem was that he didn't know how to respond to his wife with Christlikeness. And nothing will bring out a man's true nature like marriage. It will reveal precisely what his abilities are in handling relationship needs.

As long as we're at it, let me introduce you to some more radical thinking. Many wives are suffering emotionally and physically. Although it may not be a part of most husbands' conscious thinking, if they were asked to explain why so many wives are sick, they might answer that it's the result of women being members of the weaker sex. Unless supernaturally smitten, a husband would be unlikely to believe that he could be the cause of some of his wife's illnesses. No man would suspect that his un-Christlike attitudes and/or behavior could bring on his wife's physical and emotional symptoms. I'm not saying that is *the* reason for *all* of the diseases women experience, but many more times than not, that is exactly why so many wives are suffering.

Let me share some examples where un-Christlikeness produced emotional, physical symptoms that changed dramatically as a result of a husband becoming more Christlike.

A Wife with Unexplained Hair Loss

In our first meeting at a seminar Lance, a medical doctor, got right down to business. He explained that his wife was losing her hair, and that was causing her great emotional stress. He described all that had been done trying to cure her, but nothing was working. After a brief conversation, I started asking him some questions.

"Do you have children?"

"Yes, we do."

"Would your wife say that you do or do not help her with the children?"

He figured she would say no, that he was little, if any, help. His reasoning was, of course, that since he was a doctor—and everybody knows how demanding a doctor's work is. . . .

"Was there a recent pregnancy?"

"Yes, there was," the doctor said.

"Was it an unwanted pregnancy?"

"Yes. We already had two children."

Let me insert that although there may be only two children, sometimes wives feel like they have three children, what with the demands put on them by their husbands. It's like having another child around the house.

I suggested that his problem was not to find a way to keep his wife from losing her hair, for that would not eliminate her emotional struggles. Rather, that as a Christian woman, his wife was emotionally struggling over her attitudes:

- Toward the pregnancy—not wanting this gift from God.
- Toward her husband—how could she be so ungrateful? She was thinking, *I'm angry with my husband because he's too busy for me or the children, but I feel so isolated, unimportant, and lonely.*
- Toward God for letting all this happen, even though she had prayed for relief from her weariness with the children. She had prayed about her husband's workload, jealousy toward his patients. You see, contrary to his conclusions (as well as those from other doctors), she was not losing her hair and becoming emotional. Instead her emotional struggles were causing her to lose her hair.

He was willing to accept that suggestion, especially since nothing else seemed to work. So I gave him a project to help him see his wife as someone God had given him to care for as God's representative. He would need to see her as a priority and set aside time for her, caring for her as Christ would. Instead of sitting down and watching television, he would need to give the children priority and spend time with them, which would also give his wife some relief.

Within six months his wife was emotionally stabilized and had stopped losing her hair. The doctor was not only the key to his wife's ailment; he had more healing power than he ever dreamed possible.

A WIFE WITH FAINTING SPELLS

Another wife had severe fainting spells. To keep her from getting hurt, someone had to be with her constantly to catch her in case she fainted. She couldn't drive her own car, go grocery shopping, prepare dinner, or do almost anything else by herself.

When she and her husband came into my office, she was a nervous wreck. She couldn't sit still, moving about constantly. When she sat down, her skirt wrinkled, so she had to straighten it out. The strap on her purse was crooked, and since it was sitting on the floor, she had to bend to straighten it out. That action wrinkled her skirt, so she had to straighten it out again. Then she noticed her blouse was not perfectly arranged, and on and on and on.

Centering on the suspicion that her behavior was the product of a wife feeling totally unacceptable, I asked some questions. It became apparent that this man's wife felt she could do nothing satisfactorily for her husband.

- He questioned the wisdom of her purchases at the grocery store.
- He scolded her choices about what she fixed for meals and even how she set the table.
- He challenged her judgments about driving and timing.
- He was constantly reacting negatively to her decisions.

This wife basically felt that she could not do anything right. Anytime she had a decision to make, she knew it would be unsatisfactory to her husband. She was so uptight about being such a failure in the eyes of her husband that rather than face more emotional rejection from another "wrong" decision, her body would compensate by fainting.

I had to teach the husband not to be so critical and negative. He had to learn how to see his wife as Christ would see her, and begin to praise her for things she was doing. Need I remind you how that can minister to a wife's spirit and bring healing? And it did in this case as well.

The above illustrations are compiled from real-life situations. They represent attitudes, psychological conditions, and physical conditions demonstrating that a husband can be the key to the problems his wife experiences.

Physical and emotional problems are not the only area in which men can be the key to the solution. God has even blessed husbands with the capacity to heal attitude problems as well.

A Wife with Attitudes of Spiritual Superiority

This woman gives the impression that she thinks that everybody but her falls short of knowing what true Christianity is. Few people seem to have what it takes to measure up to her standards. She spends a lot of time reading and studying Christian materials, and she comes across in a very authoritative manner. Because of her reservoirs of insight and her in-depth studies, she comes across as a know-it-all.

When I see a woman like this, I recognize that she must have a wounded spirit. Her spirit has not been cared for to the degree that she recognizes and accepts her value as a person, especially in the eyes of God. Instead, she senses that her value as a person is gained by taking a strong stand for righteousness. She is certainly not free to recognize or focus on herself as a sinner, like the rest of us, because she knows that's an unacceptable condition.

Again, this problem can be traced to the spiritual leadership in her home. Usually, this woman's husband winces when he hears his wife talking—he either subtly or blatantly reacts negatively to her. Others recognize his disapproval and feel free to join him in his rejection of her. The rejection can take many forms: outright disagreement, ridicule or laughter, ignoring her comments, or people distancing themselves from her.

Let's say that she brought these characteristics into the marriage with her. Does her husband have a practical understanding of how Christ would minister to her? Does he specifically understand what illustrating Christlikeness to her requires, no matter what the circumstances are? Does he recognize what qualities God might want to build in their marriage through her? Obviously, the answer is no. Otherwise he would have been ministering to his wife, and she would not be acting that way. Surely, we believe Christ would know how to minister to this woman and bring her healing. Doesn't the example of the Samaritan woman prove Christ's capacity to minister to even a truly disreputable woman?

Typically, this wife tries to find value by straightening out everyone else, since her husband has not ministered to her. As a result, she continues to focus on everyone else's inadequacies. This conduct is proof that her spirit needs to be cared for. She needs to be relieved of her feelings of inferiority, insignificance, and worthlessness, which will free her from the need to prove that she has some value.

A Wife who Displays a Stubborn, Strong Will

Most people feel sorry for this woman's husband because it looks like she manages everything in their home—even him. She is always making plans, and he seems to be swept along. She is known as one woman who is going to have her way, no matter what. She is also seen as a woman who strongly reacts to and resists men.

Most men don't look past this woman's attitudes and actions to ask, "Why is she like that?" They just negatively react to this woman—which is not what Christ would do. But it is Christlike to see into the heart of such a person.

If people were able to see into her spirit, they would most likely see a woman who is unwilling to submit to a man in anything because no man, from her perspective, has proven himself trustworthy. She has basically concluded, "I have never had a man in my life who was concerned about what is best for me. So since I have not had that experience, I can trust only one person in my life. Only one person has consistently shown concern over what is in my best interest—me! I will have to watch out for myself. I will have to protect myself. If I don't take care of me, no one else will. Why should I worry about anyone else, since no one ever worried about me?"

As a discipler, I have the duty to illustrate 2 Timothy 2:2 by first challenging myself to Christlikeness. When I do that, I can discover un-Christlike attitudes and ways in my heart first. I can also learn what is required to experience the victory of exchanging my ways for Christ's ways. Only then can I help other men recognize any un-Christlike attitudes and ways within their hearts and teach them how to have victories as well.

With victory over un-Christlike attitudes as the prerequisite, I would like to emphasize two different attitudes. The first one reveals the typical male attitude toward this type of "independent" woman, illustrated with these words: "You are stubborn and you are strong-willed. Your Christian testimony, to say the least, is suffering. You had better get your act together."

The other attitude I believe illustrates more Christlike attitudes and is expressed in these words: "How may I become the kind of person who would inspire you with greater confidence? How can I prove that I am concerned about what is in your best interest?"

This second attitude demonstrates the following: "I know that God is not surprised that you are in my life, so I can trust that God wants me to learn through you, not only how I may become more Christlike but also how I may discover what is the best way to minister to you."

Let me amplify the need for me to be watchful about learning of un-Christlike ways in my life as a prerequisite to helping others. God can, and often has, chosen Nancy as the means through which He would teach me. I remember one evening Nancy and I were having a heated discussion about something she had done. She complained, "You never tell me I need to change in my own best interest. You just tell me to change because you don't like it."

That statement utterly boggled my mind! As I slowly shook my head from side to side, the look on my face must have also said, "What in the world are you talking about?" She answered, "When you don't like something about me, you just tell me, 'I don't like that!' You don't tell me you don't like it because you see that what I'm doing will make me look bad in other people's eyes. You don't tell me because you recognize that I am presenting myself in a way that will make me look bad—and you don't want me looking bad before other people. You just chew me out because you simply don't like it. Period! You never tell me how much I need to change because the improvement would be in my own best interest."

What a revelation! I would never have considered my motives as I reacted to Nancy. Is it any wonder that when we affect our wives so negatively, they begin to resent us and develop their own philosophies about how they should handle life? They don't look for input from their "spiritual leader" because he is not acknowledged as such. I'm so grateful to God for teaching me that insight through Nancy. I gained insight into much more Christlike attitudes and motives when it comes to correcting people—doing it for their best interests. Isn't that the very reason Christ died for us? He put our best interests ahead of His own.

A Wife who Is Considered Domineering

Everyone notices when a wife bosses her husband around, constantly telling him what to do or say. She doesn't even try to hide it. So people say, "That poor guy. His wife sure dominates him."

But here again, as is frequently the case, this situation is accepted at face value. What no one knows (and certainly wouldn't accept if she were to give her side of the story) is that her husband is so unmotivated, especially in his marriage, that he doesn't offer any input about anything. No suggestions, no opinions, no ideas, no nothing! He may have them, but he is not committed to anything outside himself.

In reality, what we're seeing here is a husband who is neglectful of his God-given role. He is not doing anything that demonstrates Christlike leadership, for he cannot remain uninvolved in his relationship with his wife if he is to offer

Christlike leadership. He may think he is being a Christian martyr—laying down his life—because he never stands up for himself. But he is really practicing concession, not leadership!

This wife has no leadership. So why wouldn't she conclude, "If anything is going to improve around here, I'll have to be the one who gets it done"?

Case in point. Tom (not his real name) came home from work every evening, grabbed a beer, and sat down to watch television. Come Friday, he dutifully handed over his paycheck. As far as he was concerned, he had completely fulfilled his responsibilities. By turning over his paycheck, he had, he felt, earned himself the freedom of another week of unhampered beer drinking and television watching. Proudly, he would say, "What more could a man do for his family than to give up his freedom and go off to work for the little lady and the kids?"

As the years passed, this wife watched the house get smaller and smaller, since the family was growing larger. She wondered how to solve this problem. She went to her husband, asking him, "What do you think we should do about our crowded situation?" He avoided all responsibility by saying, "Don't ask me. They're your kids and it's your house. I do my part. I go to work and bring home the bacon. What you do from there on out is your problem."

Sometime later she again tried to involve him in finding a solution by asking, "What do you think about building a room addition?" He again shirked involvement, "You want a room addition? Go ahead. Just don't bother me about it."

So she drew up some rough plans, which he refused to review. She started checking with some builders. From there she started getting bids. When she had enough bids for comparisons, she went to Tom and showed him what it was going to cost, looking for his approval and help with the decision. He scolded her, "Hey, I told you not to bother me with your problems. If you want to do it, then do it. Stop bothering me with these things."

Continuing as best she knew how, she engaged a contractor and the work began. Still trying to get Tom's approval, she looked for ways to save money. Being a resourceful woman, she decided there were several parts of the job she could do herself. She could do the painting. And if the contractor would cut and put in place the drywall (on the walls only, not the ceiling), she could finish putting in all those nails that the city code called for. Then she could tape and paste it. Thinking he would be pleased, she went to Tom to share the good news with him (when will she ever learn?). In anticipation of his pleasure, she smiled as she said, "I'm going to do the drywall myself and save some money. What do you think?"

He snapped, "Hey, I told you not to bother me. If you want to do it, do it, but get outta my face, okay? Can you get the picture? Stop bothering me!"

Eventually, it was finished. Visitors commented to Tom as they toured the house, "Wow, look what you've done!" And Tom grudgingly responded, "Don't look at me. I didn't want the thing. She did! That's her baby. She decided that's what she wanted, and she got it done. And since she wanted it and I didn't, she knows better than to bother me with that stuff."

Now, what do you think is going on in the visitors' heads?

"Well, you poor guy. You don't even want something, and your wife goes right on and gets it done anyway. Boy, am I glad I don't have to live with a domineering wife like that."

So the public perceives her as a domineering woman when in reality she has tried desperately to involve her husband. He has refused to exercise his role of Christlike leadership in their marriage—and she gets the blame. Of course, there are many other ways in which we men are failing to understand and apply Christlike leadership in the home.

A Wife who Appears to Lack Confidence in the Spirit of God and Is Unsure of Her Salvation

It's not unusual for women to be fearful. It's also not unusual for unsympathetic husbands to scold their wives with statements like, "Hey, I thought you were a Christian, so why don't you stop fearing everything and trust the Lord more?" They might even think that they are being good spiritual leaders by pointing out their wives' failures.

Yet what do those words convey about leadership? Instead of being Christlike, they are demeaning and condemning. They will only make a woman feel unacceptable and result in more insecurity—and insecurity increases fear in a woman. Even when she was caught in the middle of failure, Jesus did not demean or condemn the adulterous woman in this way (John 8:2–11).

Another kind of fear is seen in the lack of assurance about salvation. The typical solution offered to someone who doubts her salvation is to explain again (more emphatically this time) the plan of salvation. Usually, that will make the person feel even more insecure. Since that is not the right solution, it will not remove her doubts.

After the first attempts to reassure her fail, a salvation-plan presenter who is more expert is sought. Perhaps an evangelist is introduced, or the pastor may get involved. At times a respected Christian leader or friend is brought in to try to help this person gain assurance of her salvation. After repeated attempts to produce results fail, it is easy to grow impatient and conclude that the person is clearly resistant to the Spirit of God.

One man I was counseling had a wife who doubted her salvation. She had frequently been subjected to presentations of the plan of salvation. By this time she was in worse shape than when she first started having doubts. After a couple of hours of discussion with her, I could see what her problem was. She had defined it in three passing comments. The first two were to be expected, but the last one provided the answer. Her statements were as follows:

1. "If the Spirit of God were really living within me, how could I possibly doubt my salvation?"
2. "I'm so confused."
3. Her final statement clearly revealed her defeat and despair: "It's easy to see how God would send His Son to die for y'all. Y'all are good people, but I'm not like y'all."

Her problem was not doubting her salvation—that was only the manifestation of her problem. Her real problem was that she felt absolutely worthless. Actually, her first line of reasoning made sense. But even Peter the apostle had trouble with doubts and unbelief (Matt. 14:25–32). So that did not constitute proof that she was unsaved. Her second statement was evidence of Satan working to destroy her, since Satan is the author of confusion (1 Cor. 14:33). Her third statement explained the condition of her spirit and indicated that it was a spiritual problem—that is, a problem that her spirit was struggling with.

As a means of "healing" her, I discipled her husband! He was the key to his wife's problem. I talked with him about caring for his wife's spirit. I had to teach him how to become alert to positive character qualities in his wife's everyday actions. And then I had to teach him how to express in words of praise to his wife the things he was learning to notice.

After about six months of teaching him to see his wife's value, and then teaching him how to express to her the value he was just discovering (even though it was there all the time), both of them noticed that she had stopped doubting her salvation. She was "healed" because her husband implemented Christlike leadership. Basically, her healing was the result of her husband applying Matthew 11:28, for she had been heavy laden from laboring over her insecurity and doubts. Because he ministered to her spirit, he had brought on the rest found in emotional security.

A Christian Wife who Has Lost Interest in Christianity

This is a fairly common condition, even among couples in which the husband is active in the church. The common denominator is that the husband has not learned how to minister to his wife's spirit. A Christian wife who feels uncared for may prayerfully plead with God, asking, "God, please help me to be the kind of person that my husband will love." So this wife starts looking for ways to gain her husband's love.

Try as she may, he remains typically male—un-Christlike. So she prays harder, goes to Bible studies, joins church committees, and volunteers for all kinds of activities. She is trying to prove to God that she means to be a good Christian. And everybody else recognizes what a dedicated Christian woman she is! She is trying so hard to be the perfect wife, trying to avoid anything that might make her seem like a squeaky wheel to her husband.

Does her husband understand her desperate search? Does he realize how hard she is trying to do whatever it takes to influence him (and God) into letting her feel loved by her husband? No. So she starts losing hope. Finally, she concludes that neither her husband nor God cares about her desperation, and she says, "It doesn't pay to trust in Christianity. Neither my husband nor God cares about me!" If she has been taught that her husband is her spiritual leader and that God will take care of her, and she feels unfulfilled as a wife, a woman, and a Christian, where in the world is she supposed to go?

All too often husbands approached about their responsibility in this matter will react by saying, "Hey, don't come to me about it. She's her own person. I'm not responsible for her Christian walk!"

That's typical thinking. But let me relate another example of what can happen when a skeptical wife has a husband who is dedicated to Christlike spiritual leadership.

After our Phoenix presentation of the Life Partners "Discovery Seminar," we offer a three-year discipleship course. This course guarantees, among other things, that upon completion, a man will understand the mind of a woman. We are so sure of this that we promise that his wife (who knows him better than anyone else) will confirm that as a fact. His wife will also be inspired to follow his leadership since he will illustrate the Christlikeness that inspires confidence.

After one such Discovery Seminar, we announced to the alumni that there would be a follow-up discipleship class. A man I'll call Bret decided that he would sign up for himself and his wife, whom I'll call Barbara. Bret was a determined student. Even though his flesh rose up frequently in its attempt to avoid being "put to death," he persisted in his fight to defeat his flesh. He was committed to learning how to minister to his wife's spirit as Christ would.

Barbara was a sharp and learned Christian woman. And as is often the case, she far outdistanced her husband in the study of Scripture and other spiritual pursuits.

Six months into the discipleship program each student was asked to share in class how he or she had been affected so far. When Barbara's turn came, she said, "When Bret signed up for this program I thought, *Now what could you guys ever teach my husband that could possibly inspire me to have any confidence in him? There's no way he could learn enough for me to see him as my spiritual leader!* But the last three weeks have been the most spiritually significant days of my life.

"I have never felt as close to God as I have lately because of what has taken place in our relationship. I would never have believed it possible that feeling a greater closeness with my husband than I have ever felt with anyone else in my life could also make me feel a greater closeness with God. And yet, *I know* in my heart that is exactly what is happening within me."

What evidence do we need before we will realize the enormous power God has entrusted to us men? We are the key to solving relationship problems!

A Wife who Has Lost Interest in Her Personal Appearance

Over the years this wife's appearance has gone downhill. Her husband has finally convinced her that he doesn't care about her, so why should she care? She starts putting on weight, which is often indicative of an emotional factor.

But let's say that she can't help it, that it's a glandular problem. It's still an opportunity for a husband to examine the attitudes within his heart. Her weight gain is not a surprise to God. God is not watching over the marriage, and all of a sudden, He discovers she is gaining weight and says to Himself, "Oh, boy, I didn't plan on this!"

So how a husband responds shows him whether or not he has Christlike attitudes. If he starts to get irritated and critical about her weight, he is beginning to reveal un-Christlike attitudes. However, let's suppose this husband is feeling compassion for his wife. Let's suppose he reassures her by saying something like this: "I know this is a struggle for you. My greatest concern is that you will think this affects my love for you. Let me assure you that I am committed to love you for the rest of my life."

If you face this situation, don't fall into the trap of thinking, *Now that I've told you what I think, don't expect me to tell you again. If I ever change my mind, I'll let you know.* Saying this once will never solve the need. You will need to reaffirm your commitment and love often—preferably daily.

Now back to the nonglandular weight problem. One overweight wife told me the reason she was not motivated to lose her excess weight. Not too long after getting married, she started experiencing emotional abuse from her husband (and a husband cannot be the one who decides what is or is not emotional abuse to his wife). As time went on, she became more and more defeated. She turned to sweets (subconsciously looking for something enjoyable in life), and she started gaining weight. She also noticed that as she gained weight, men stopped paying attention to her.

She grew more and more discouraged. She felt guilty about her weight and thought about losing it. As she thought about herself being trim, she remembered how men used to notice her. So she decided that losing weight would be dangerous for her because then she would enjoy the attention and probably do something she would be sorry for.

We were grateful to have the opportunity of working with her husband, and were able to minister to his need for greater understanding. One day she asked, "I wonder what it would take to get rid of my weight?"

Again, notice the effects of his commitment to Christlikeness—he is the key to solving this relationship problem. You might ask, "What was he doing that was so abusive?" Well, he was very busy with the demands of his work. He was too tired to spend time devoted to his wife. His exhausted condition caused him to snap at his family, which said to them, "I don't like you." Little things like that piled up, communicating un-Christlike insensitivity.

A Wife who Is a Poor Communicator

This category covers a range of verbal uncertainties. A wife may talk too much, or she may not talk enough. She may ask too many questions, or she may show almost no interest in what her husband does. Almost always I discover that these verbal uncertainties have grown as a result of her husband's not knowing how to tap into his wife's spirit. He doesn't know how to listen to his wife's words and realize that she is communicating much more than mere words. He needs to listen to her heart and understand what it means to affirm her as a person, as Christ would. Communication improves dramatically when a husband becomes more interested in what is in his wife's heart than in what she is saying.

The clearest symptom of a husband's not listening to his wife is when she says, "You don't understand me," and he responds, "Yes, I do, too. I heard every word you said." She experiences that response as a defensive action. She sees a husband who is unwilling to accept her words as an expression of how he is affecting her heart.

The typical husband doesn't know that the way to minister to her spirit would be to put his arm around her and say, "I apologize. Help me understand what you mean. I want to know what is involved in caring for you in a way that causes you to believe I do understand and care for you." Then he will have begun to verbalize the situation from her perspective.

Remember the husband who said to his wife, "I don't really love my parents more than you!" All she experienced from him was defensiveness. But when he apologized and acknowledged the situation from her perspective, she believed he was concerned about how he was affecting her. She began to see that he really wanted to minister to her spirit.

A Wife who Experiences Excessive Depression

A severely depressed person is illustrating the following principle: "Life is overwhelming me, and I can't find any answers. No matter what I've tried, nothing works." Every source of this person's energy is being depleted. She is struggling so hard to manage life that her system wants to shut down. Depending on how far advanced her case is, it may already have shut down, or at least it is not functional.

If a man is experiencing this depression, then his condition is God's way of alerting him to the fact that he is not familiar with the specific answers that God has for everyday, specific situations.

If a wife is experiencing this depression, then her condition is also God's way of alerting her husband to the fact that he is not familiar with the answers that God has for specific situations. This husband has not been able to build his wife's confidence in him through the resolution of life's issues, showing that God's ways provide answers.

We all know that God allows evil and tragedy to come into our lives. We also know that God can use any of life's events to teach us. It doesn't make any difference what the events or problems are; God understands and has answers. For example, a new couple to our church were sitting in a Sunday school class I was teaching, and they heard me quote Romans 8:28: "And we know that all things work together for good to those who love God, to those who are the called according to His purpose." I added, "There is nothing that happens to us that God cannot use for our good. Nothing! And when we understand why He has allowed something to take place in our lives, it will free us to rejoice over what He has taught us through the event."

They waited after class to talk with me. They explained to me that their son, a young man, had been killed in an accident a year earlier. That loss caused them such severe depression that they couldn't get free of it. They told me that they couldn't imagine being free and rejoicing over any lesson learned from it—they couldn't imagine God using such an event to teach spiritual lessons.

I knew I couldn't explain what God wanted to teach them through the tragedy at that point; they were not able to hear it yet. So I told them that I would need to teach them some principles before they would understand how to have eyes and ears that could receive the special blessings God wanted them to have out of the tragic event.

A year and a half passed before I could share the blessings with them. During that time, I introduced them to their own human spirits. The husband discovered how dysfunctional his spirit was, how basically he was emotionally dead. Eventually, I was able to show him how his wife and children had suffered from his inability to identify with their emotions, which meant he didn't identify with their spirits, either.

I helped him realize that the tragedy caused him to become emotionally overwhelmed. He was flooded with emotions so overpowering that he couldn't escape them. We talked about how God let the event serve the purpose of awakening his spirit; God was not willing for him to remain spiritually dysfunctional, since "God is Spirit, and those who worship Him must worship in spirit and truth" (John 4:24).

Those were all totally new concepts to them. Their eyes were opened to aspects about relationships that they had never dreamed about. The concepts introduced him to relationships with God, his wife, and his family that were beyond his grandest imaginings.

The son who had died had accepted Christ as his Savior, so his eternal condition was secured. Finally one day, after much preparation, I explained why God may have been willing for the life of their son to come to a conclusion. I reminded them that God was willing to redeem us with the life of His own Son. I related to the man how even though he had accepted Christ as his Savior, for which God had given life to his spirit through the indwelling Holy Spirit, his spirit was still virtually comatose. It was quickened, but no one ever discipled him with a focus on his spirit. He was never shown how to put his flesh to death, bringing his spirit under the leadership of God's Spirit. So he was not able to have a Spirit-to-spirit relationship with God. His wife was not able to experience the joy and fulfillment of a spirit-to-spirit relationship with him, either. So, to make him aware of his spirit and allow God to continue the building process in his spirit, which meant bringing maturity to his spirit, God gave the man's son the extreme honor of being the price for awakening his father to his own spirit so that his father and God could have a rich Spirit-to-spirit fellowship.

It had never occurred to that mother and father to see their son's death in that light. Then although their hearts were aware of grief, they could rejoice and thank God even in the tragedy!

What an honor for their son! But again, it was the father, the husband, who was the key to resolving the problem of depression. God wanted to get to the husband's heart for the solution to their depression.

A Wife who Shows Symptoms of Emotional Instability

This wife often seems to be angry, crying, fearful, or in the middle of some emotional trauma. Let's say it's from childhood abuse. That way we can say for sure that it was not the results of her husband's failures. Yet if Christ were this woman's husband, He would never dismiss His responsibility to her by saying, "You were a mess before I ever met you. This is not My fault, so don't expect Me to be responsible for fixing you." Does Christ say in Matthew 11:28, "Come to Me, all you who labor and are heavy laden, and I will give you rest—unless it's not My fault"? No!

No Christian husband can ever excuse himself from being Christlike to his wife. As illustrated, there may be perspectives that are foreign to him, and they may prevent him from understanding how to apply God's solutions. But as long as his wife has needs, he must *diligently* search for solutions. He may never give up on her, just as Christ never gives up on us. As the spiritual leader of his home, a husband is the key to resolving problems and bringing the abundant life to his home.

We've just gone through several examples that reveal biblical perspectives for victorious living in everyday relationship situations. There are more!

7

THAT MYSTERIOUS, INCOMPREHENSIBLE WOMAN

Have you ever noticed what the conversation is about when a group of men get together? There's the weather, the successes or failures of their favorite sports teams, enthusiasm or groaning about politics, discussion of hobbies like golfing or hunting, or what's new in cars. Seldom do men talk about relationship situations unless it's something about the kids' failures or achievements.

When, for example, was the last time you were hanging around a group of guys and heard them bragging about whose wife was the greatest? You see, talking about marriage is almost taboo. The closest most men come to conversation about relationships is to complain about, ridicule, or joke about their wives or women in general. And when you hear a guy running down his wife because she is going to leave him or divorce him, how often do you hear men's conversations turn to helping the guy find a solution?

Unless the talk is about sex, men consider the subject of relationships with women so mystifying that most of them don't contemplate it as a topic of conversation. It's not that men think about relationships with women and then pass by the subject. It's that men don't consider relationships important enough to surface as a topic for conversation.

PROBLEM SOLVING FROM A MALE PERSPECTIVE WON'T DO IT

One of the reasons men consider women mysterious and incomprehensible is that we are not trained to understand them. We certainly don't know how to solve relationship problems from a woman's perspective. We most naturally think mechanically, and so our approach to resolving problems is geared along mechanical lines.

A man may, for example, come home at the end of the day, walk in, hang up his jacket, and ask casually, "So how'd it go today?" His wife might respond, "This has been a horrible day! I feel like I'm going to fall apart." As a man, he automatically thinks, *Sounds like she's run-down and out of energy.* His solution for her most likely becomes, "Have you taken your iron pills?" Whatever pills they might be, iron, vitamin B, or something else, he thinks that's the solution to her problem. Meanwhile, her eyes roll heavenward as she blurts out, "Why do I even bother talking to you? You just don't understand anything."

Defensively, he shoots back, "That's the thanks I get! You have a problem, I offer help, and you get mad at me." So he decides, "If that's the appreciation I get, then forget it." He might conclude, "What an idiot I am! Why do I even bother trying to understand women?" Meanwhile, she is back in the kitchen, trying to keep the kids under control during final supper preparations.

Suppose that instead of following his first mechanical impulse, offering the quick mineral or vitamin remedy, he gives her what could be called a "husband vitamin pill." Instead of trying to solve what *he believes* is the problem, how about if he considers a new approach? Suppose he decides to put his arm around her and say, "I'm sorry you had a rough day. I really do care. And I want you to know I love you, and I'm here for you. Since your day has been so stressful, how about if I look after the kids while you finish supper preparations?"

After reviving her (why wouldn't she faint?), how do you suppose a wife might respond to that tenderhearted thoughtfulness? Based on personal experience, her response would be so appreciative, it would warm her heart with love.

If your wife, however, has felt neglected for a number of years, don't expect your new behavior to bring on a conversion experience, producing within her a positive new impression of you. Don't expect her to act as though all the transgressions of the past are instantly forgotten because one day you behave differently. If you expect her to respond to you as though everything is different between you now, then I suggest you're the one who is mysterious and incomprehensible.

On the other hand, even if things have been ugly between you and your wife for a while, your response to your wife as I've just suggested will affect her positively. You may not see the results you'd like to see right away, but your persistence in responding in a Christlike manner will bring long-term positive results.

It's so typical to respond with something like, "Did you take your vitamin pills?" that we don't realize that the response is actually condemning to a wife. We are saying in effect, "You don't seem very smart. If you were, you would have taken your vitamin pills." No wonder wives feel like throwing things at us.

That's a simple illustration of how our problem-solving attitude can get us into big trouble with our wives over minor exchanges. And because we repeatedly come up with those innocent, yet demeaning, comments, our wives clam up. As a consequence, they distance themselves emotionally from us. The greater that emotional distance, the more mysterious and incomprehensible our wives seem to be.

HIS SOLUTIONS INCREASE THE DILEMMA

Because of the mechanical orientation toward life, men approach relationship needs as mechanical problem-solving opportunities. Husbands apply *their* mechanical solutions to the problems that develop between them and their wives.

When a man's solutions don't work, he becomes frustrated. Occasionally, he may seek help from professionals. When most solutions suggested by counselors don't seem to have lasting results, he may conclude that there are no answers, so he gives up. After all, if the answers they have don't work, there must not be any answers to marital problems. So he accepts for himself the "mysterious, incomprehensible woman" reasoning and excuses himself from pressing on for a solution. Too many men conclude that they are going to have to accept a miserable marriage or get out.

Unsolved problems in the home, especially those between him and his wife, frustrate a husband. Continued frustrations will wear down his endurance, eventually causing him to lose interest in the marriage and stop caring for his wife. Yet the visible problems in marriage are not the real difficulty—not knowing how to solve the problems is what wears a man down.

Instead of using the "mysterious, incomprehensible woman" rationale, I suggest that we consider our problems with our wives as a doorway to new levels of understanding. Yet *we need to see our problems from God's viewpoint* before we will consistently see the doorway that leads to blessings open up. And we have to learn that skill because God's ways are not naturally man's ways.

God points out the historically independent nature of man in the book of Judges. When left alone, "everyone did what was right in his own eyes" (Judg. 21:25). That's the natural inclination of every man. The wise writer of the book of

Proverbs presents the contrast between the human and the divine perspectives: "Every way of a man is right in his own eyes, but the LORD weighs the hearts" (21:2). Notice, the Lord's focus is on the importance of the heart. He does not merely notice what is obvious to the eyes (ways). He emphasizes the value of the weightier matters, the emotions, the feelings of the spirit (the heart) where, incidentally, women tend to operate.

A similar statement in Proverbs 16:2 highlights God's ability to evaluate the inner person, the spirit: "All the ways of a man are pure in his own eyes, but the LORD weighs the spirits." If that is the way of the Lord, then men must also seek to achieve that ability through the awareness the Holy Spirit can provide.

As far as relationships are concerned, doing what is right *in our own eyes* will likely increase the problems in our marriages, since *our* ways will not provide answers that minister to the needs of the spirit.

When a man doesn't seem to be able to get a handle on his wife's emotional responses, that is, her inner feelings, the natural male response is to resort to demeaning, verbal, or even physically abusive behavior. The resulting silence or lack of resistance can falsely lead him to believe he has solved the problem. However, instead of solving the problem, reducing the tension and stress, he has multiplied dramatically the intensity of the problem.

I am constantly astonished at the number of men who do not have the slightest suspicion that they have created many of their husband-wife problems. They are created by acting on what "seems" right.

I am thinking, for example, of the young pastor who early in his career was the cause of his wife's alienation from his ministry. One Sunday morning I watched her make a decision, based on his response, that it was not safe to care about his reputation. She backed off and let him gain a reputation of being irresponsible and unreliable.

He talked with a couple for quite a while after church let out. His wife waited in the car with the children, knowing he had made an appointment to meet with some other people at his house for lunch at twelve o'clock. It was twelve when she first started trying to remind him by stepping out of the car, getting his attention, and then pointing at her watch. He not only didn't check his watch to see what time it was; he kept talking.

At 12:30, after making several more futile attempts to generate a response, and thinking he may have forgotten the previous engagement, she calmly walked over to him. She stepped discreetly behind him and whispered over his shoulder a reminder of his appointment. In full sight of all those present, he turned to his wife and in a slow, you-will-not-force-me-lady spirit said, "I will be there when I am finished." Her head instantly dropped in shame. Keeping her eyes on the ground, she walked away, totally humiliated.

He was aggravated because, from his perspective, she forced him to set her straight in front of everyone. He hated it, but it had to be done. She had to know her place. He had to show her who was the boss. Why did she do those things?

I'm ashamed to say, "I know exactly how he felt. I've been there. I've done those things." My heart aches when I remember those days.

Consider the opportunity the pastor missed. Think of the testimony to Christlikeness he would have given us all if he had thanked his wife publicly for caring about him and the people who were waiting at his house. Imagine the inspiration he could have given us—while building a reputation for promptness—if he had said to the couple, "You know what, my wife has helped me remember that I've got another commitment I must keep. I'm going to have to get together with you at another time." They would have understood and seen him as a man of his word, since their conversation was not about an emergency situation.

Once people saw his wife reminding him, the pastor switched to a contest mentality: "Who's gonna be seen as the boss?" He totally misunderstood her motives and misjudged almost everything from that point on. He did what he thought was right, and most of the men in the Christian community would agree with what he did. And like most of the men who think that way, he lost not only his wife's respect but also her commitment to preserve his reputation. He suffered that loss not from that one offense but from his continued demonstration of offensive attitudes.

We will benefit from our relationship problems only as we change the way we evaluate the problems we face. That will happen only when we begin to reflect on our circumstances from God's perspective rather than from our own. Then our understanding will keep us from feeling as though we are victims of life.

GETTING GOD'S PERSPECTIVE

In the book of Romans, the apostle Paul provides some foundational thinking from which we can start to discover God's perspective. He writes, "And we know that all things work together for good to those who love God, to those who are the called according to His purpose" (8:28). This verse is especially true when applied to what is going on in marriages.

When your wife is so upset that she is crying and is angrily accusing you of not caring how she feels, you can be sure that is one of the "all things" supposed to be working together for good in your life. When she is so fed up with your behavior that she leaves the house for a long walk, and you wonder if she'll ever return, that, too, is one of the "all things" working for your good.

If we accept the Bible and say that we believe it means what it says, then we must also accept the reactions of our wives as one way in which God is working "all things" for our good. And in direct proportion to the understanding of that truth, each of us will be on the path to understanding that mysterious, no-longer-incomprehensible person, his wife. We will also be ministering to our wives' spirits in ways that will give them the confidence that it is safe to open up their hearts to us.

In several passages the apostle Paul mentions Christlike attitudes that minister to our wives. One call to Christlikeness is found in Philippians 2:5, where he exhorts us, "Let this mind be in you which was also in Christ Jesus."

Did you catch the significance of that statement? We can actually have the mind-set that was in Christ Jesus when He was on earth. Notice, too, that the determining factor for having the mind of Christ (aside from salvation) is whether or not we will *let* it take place. Since He demonstrated that He understood people, even women, then (if we will let it or allow it) recognizing we can have His mind should generate a lot of hope that we, too, can understand people as He did.

How do we demonstrate the mind of Christ? Look at the earlier verses (Phil. 2:2–4):

> Fulfill my joy by being like-minded, having the same love, being of one accord, of one mind. Let nothing be done through selfish ambition or conceit, but in lowliness of mind let each esteem others better than himself. Let each of you look out not only for his own interests, but also for the interests of others.

None of that will take place as long as my flesh, my natural man, remains strong. If my flesh is in control, then Christ is not in control. I manifest Christlikeness in direct proportion to the level my flesh is being crucified. And I can be sure that my flesh is *absolutely not* going to stand by idly and let me become Christlike. That is why it is impossible without the mind-set of Christ to fulfill the command of Ephesians 5:33: "Nevertheless let each one of you in particular so love his own wife as himself."

Assuming, then, that a man really means it when he says he wants to be obedient to the Lord, that he recognizes that God requires that he love his wife just as much as he loves himself, and that he can have the mind of Christ, what can a man use as a gauge to determine how accurately he is illustrating Christ to his wife?

Here are some prerequisites to demonstrating Christlikeness:

- If he is to be like-minded with Christ, and if He understands how women think, then a man must also learn to understand how women think.

- If he is to love as Christ loved, then a man must learn how to totally give of himself for the betterment of his bride, like He did.

- If Christ is in accord, or cospirited, with God, then a man must learn what it means to be cospirited with his wife. And his relationship with his wife is proof positive of whether or not he has a working knowledge of cospiritedness.

- If Christ's goal was to be one with God, then a man must learn how to demonstrate oneness with God in Christ through oneness with his wife.

- If Christ did not seek to promote Himself or His interests, but found His importance in glorifying God, a man can practice not promoting himself or his interests by preferring his wife. She in turn will be his glory because he is obedient to God (1 Cor. 11:7).

- If Christ valued us so much that He did for us whatever God required of Him, a man must do the same as a husband who highly values his wife.

- If a man is to portray Christ before the world, he will concern himself with the betterment of others, especially his wife, as Christ did. He lived an exemplary life for a man to follow.

When he does these things, unique attributes will begin to show up as evidence of Christ living in a man. For example, remember when Jesus was on earth, He had the unique ability to perceive others' thoughts? We read in Luke 5:22 that "when Jesus perceived their thoughts, He answered and said to them. . . ."

"Wait a minute," you're saying. "I think you're going too far now. I have never been able to read my wife's thoughts, and I know Christ is living in me."

Let me then ask, "Would your wife say that in your relationship with her, you have exhibited the Christlike attitudes listed above?" Because if you have not, your flesh is still exercising control, and a man's flesh is unable to have the mind of Christ. But when the Holy Spirit is truly exercising greater control over your attitudes and behavior, I can guarantee you that to the same degree He is in control, you will be able to read your wife's thoughts. And the longer you exhibit the mind of Christ, the more effective you will become in reading her thoughts and ministering to her spirit.

DISCERNING MY WIFE'S SPIRIT

An experience at home confirmed this principle and made me aware that it is possible to know, without my wife saying a word, her innermost thoughts within a given situation. One Saturday when Nancy and I were painting the living room, a friend came by to invite me to go with him to K-Mart. Determined to learn how to be a considerate husband, I said, "Just a minute. Let me check with Nancy." I went inside and asked Nancy what she thought about me going to the store with my friend. She said, "Sure, that's okay. Go ahead."

I went back outside and told my friend, "You go on. I'm going to stay here. Thank you for asking me to go with you, though."

When my wife heard the door open as I reentered the house, she was surprised. "I thought you left to go to K-Mart. Did your friend change his mind about going?"

"No," I replied. "I didn't go because you didn't want me to."

With a slight smile, she asked, "But how did you know that? I thought I had hidden how I really felt."

True. She had done a good job of trying to conceal her true feelings from me. But because I had been working hard at my commitment to become more and more Christlike, I was developing a sixth sense for understanding the attitudes of her heart. Now I'll admit it was not easy to develop the ability to detect how she was really feeling. In fact, it required more of me than I thought I would have to pay to learn it.

You see, I had to learn how she really felt in her spirit, and that meant repeatedly, sincerely, listening to her—even when I thought there was no need to consider her perspective because I felt confident that I was right about whatever I was saying or doing. Gradually, she began to feel safe about revealing what she was thinking and feeling in her spirit.

Too often a man doesn't place enough value on his wife's spirit. He doesn't recognize that God wants to teach him through his wife to become sensitive to the spirits of others. When a man doesn't recognize and receive the messages being sent to him through the spirit of his wife, he fails to benefit from these learning opportunities.

Maybe, like me, you received signals from your wife, but you ignored them as worthless, thereby missing signals that God was sending you through your wife. God is trying to make you more sensitive, especially to areas in your life that your wife sees need improvement.

As long as we're on the topic of learning from our wives, let me give you a valuable tip. I have learned that women do not like to *appear* to be the boss in the home. A wife would rather not be asked questions in front of others that make it look as if she is the one making the decisions. It is possible to learn her opinions without creating an embarrassing situation for her. Try to reserve your questions until you are alone with her, or at least make sure your questions do not draw attention to her or the answer.

WOMEN SENSITIVE TO HOW THEY ARE PERCEIVED

Most women are concerned that they will be thought of as stubborn, strong-willed, or dominating if they state their true feelings or wishes. They also may fear that expressing themselves truthfully will result in a fight. So they often stop speaking up. I'm convinced they are more willing than men to surrender their rights. In our situation, my wife and I were supposedly painting the living room together, and if I had gone with my friend, she would have been left to do it alone.

I know I could have gotten away with being upset with my wife at not wanting me to go with my friend. I could have been resentful and decided that she was being selfish about my time. It would have been easy to tell her I felt like she was trying to run my life, and I did not like that. But I would have been the loser, wouldn't I?

I am convinced that God wants all husbands to stop being losers, especially in our relationships with our wives. He wants us to be able to perceive the spirits of our wives and of others. He wants us to keep the problems in marriage from intensifying and compounding. He knows that if problems are permitted to grow and fester, they can destroy a marriage.

Let me repeat it! If a husband is to be the spiritual leader, his spirit must be sensitive to spiritual things. He must be sensitive to God's Spirit prompting his spirit. Before he can minister effectively to his wife, he must also be sensitive to her spirit. A man should become so alert to the spirits of others that he can discern the emotional state of another person— sometimes even over the phone. And when that happens, it has enormously positive effects on his marital relationship and on relationships at the office or factory, in his church, and in his neighborhood. (We'll get into the impact on other relationships in chapter 14.)

PROBLEMS REVEALING NEED FOR SENSITIVITY

In the previous chapter we covered symptoms that reveal a problem husband, a husband who is not living with his wife in an understanding way, who is not demonstrating Christlikeness in his attitudes toward her, who is not being encouraging and supportive, as Christ encourages and supports the church through thick and thin. I have discovered that all of these problems reveal a lack of sensitivity, a failure to minister to a wife's spirit.

"Right," you may be saying, even a bit sarcastically. "I've got to take all the blame for what's wrong. But if you knew my wife, you wouldn't say that I had failed. She had those problems long before I met her."

Granted. But let me ask you how long you have been married. When I ask that, husbands may say, "Ten years," with a puzzled look on their faces, wondering why I asked the question.

"Okay, you've been married ten years. Has she gotten better or worse since you married her?" I ask.

What would your answer be? Without fail, the husbands reply, "Worse." If that is your answer, then my next question is, "If you are the spiritual leader in your home, and the job of a spiritual leader is to bring the one you are responsible for to spiritual maturity, then why has your wife gotten worse instead of better?"

Maybe, just maybe, you are the problem after all. Wouldn't it make sense to learn ways to discover whether you are on the right track or on the wrong one—especially if you could discover it without anyone, not even a counselor, having to say anything to you? And being able to correct the problem in your home yourself would be genuinely satisfying, wouldn't it?

THE SECRET TO UNDERSTANDING YOUR WIFE

There is a secret to understanding the spirits of others that women practice often, usually without knowing it. And you can discover that secret.

Next time you are with couples, try this little experiment. Ask a husband a question about his wife. Then watch him closely as he answers you. Now turn to his wife and ask her a question about him, watching her closely as she answers. You might ask the husband, "Do you think you spend as much time talking with your wife as she would like?" Then ask his wife, "Does your husband give you quality conversation time so that you can share your innermost feelings?"

Did you notice anything special about them as they answered? In my experience, when you ask the husband about his wife, he will usually look only at you. But the wife will be watching her husband's responses closely while she is answering you. Why do you suppose the wife was watching her husband so closely?

You might be saying, "That's because she's afraid of him, afraid of what he might say or do once they leave to go home." That may be true in some instances, but let me assure you that what you saw both the husband and the wife do when you asked a personal question is typical.

When we as men answer a question about our wives, we typically answer as straightforwardly as we would a question about the car or our tools. Women, on the other hand, are watching for attitudes, for how the person they are talking about is reacting to their answer. They observe the spirits of people by noticing the action in the eyes, the facial expressions, and the voice tones. As the wife in your experiment will have shown you, she was watching her husband closely to see what his response to her would be. And she can do that only if she observes the changes in his facial expressions, his body language, and his eyes.

I grant you, a wife will often base her answers on what she feels her husband would be willing to hear her say about him. That's because it is so very important to a wife that her husband does not reject her. Sometimes it is easier for her to live with an answer that is not the truth than with his rejection.

On the other hand, as the husband answered you, he was watching you more than his wife. You see, what you and others think of him is more important than what his wife thinks of him. In most cases, he is not even thinking about how his words or ways might affect his wife.

Most men do not realize that everyone has a spirit, and that they must be careful not to wound or damage the spirits of others—especially not the spirits of their wives. Wounding the spirit of a person, your wife included, is a good way to crush and inwardly destroy a person, as the writer of Proverbs reminds us in Proverbs 18:14: "The spirit of a man will sustain him in sickness, but who can bear a broken spirit?" Is it any wonder that a wounded wife withdraws and becomes "mysterious and incomprehensible"? That she may in time become the husband's enemy because of repeated wounding?

Let's consider another common situation. You are leaving after visiting friends or relatives and your wife says to you,

"You turned them off," or "You offended them!" or "They were not listening to you." Did you believe her, did you ignore her, or did you respond defensively? I used to ignore my wife, that is, I did until I learned how much I was hurting myself by not paying attention. Wives notice things that we men do not usually notice. And because we are not aware of how we are affecting others, especially the spirits of our wives, we create all kinds of problems for ourselves.

WOULD YOU LIKE TO BECOME SENSITIVE?

Having a sensitive spirit is essential to a healthy Christian life. It is the unseen spirit that is able to draw close to the unseen Spirit of God. The spirit does not have flesh and bones (Luke 24:39). It's like the wind; you know it's there, but you can't see it (John 3:8). We can only be as close to God as our spirits are alert to God's Spirit. It is through our spirits that the Holy Spirit communicates with us: "The Spirit Himself bears witness with our spirit" (Rom. 8:16).

Why do you think Jesus was able to lead a sinless life? Was it only because He was God? Or was it that even though in becoming a man He had emptied Himself, His Spirit was still in direct communication with the Holy Spirit of God? He was able to know and do the will of God. Jesus said, "For I have come down from heaven, not to do My own will, but the will of Him who sent Me" (John 6:38). On another occasion, He said, "I do nothing of Myself; but as My Father taught Me, I speak these things. And He who sent Me is with Me. The Father has not left Me alone, for I always do those things that please Him" (John 8:28–29). Jesus' Spirit was in such constant contact with His Father that He reflected the sensitivity of the Father.

I've already indicated that it rarely occurs to men to think that others have a spirit in them that can be encouraged or wounded. We don't even think about ourselves as having a spirit. The first step, then, is to become genuinely aware of the concept of a spirit: God's, ours, and others'—and this will often require a major shift in our thinking.

If you accept the fact that you and others have spirits deserving attention, the next step is to stop resenting your wife and what she is saying and doing. Instead of seeing her as a problem, consider her as a mirror in the hand of God, revealing how sensitive or insensitive you are. Once you do that, it is amazing how much she can help sensitize you to the needs of her spirit and to those of others' spirits.

THE LITMUS TEST OF SENSITIVITY

You can gauge the sensitivity of your spirit by asking, "Am I meeting the needs of my wife's spirit?" How will you know it? Very simple. If your wife is unpleasant, difficult to live with, and frequently depressed and moody, then you are not ministering to her spirit. If your wife is pleasant, easy to live with, and able to handle the stresses of life confidently, then you are in all likelihood ministering to the needs of her spirit. Here's how the wise observer in Proverbs puts it: "A merry heart does good, like medicine, but a broken spirit dries the bones" (17:22). He put it another way in Proverbs 15:13: "A merry heart makes a cheerful countenance, but by sorrow of the heart the spirit is broken."

Becoming sensitive is like gaining a skill, like learning how to use a computer. When a husband decides to become sensitive to his wife's spirit, he will first become more sensitive to his own spirit's needs. Because his spirit's sensitivity is increased, he will be able to have increased fellowship with the Spirit of God, receiving more clearly instructions from the Holy Spirit and God's Word. That will inevitably increase his sensitivity to the needs of his wife's spirit.

Once I had recognized my need to develop personal sensitivity and I was aware of how the Holy Spirit worked in me to increase my sensitivity, I could begin to do some basic things to improve my understanding of the needs of another's spirit. I very deliberately went about learning to "read" another person's reactions.

If I wanted to become alert to my wife's spirit, I knew I had to learn to watch her eyes and facial expressions very carefully. Developing this habit was difficult because it was not the way I had ever observed others. Like most of you, I had been conditioned since childhood to avoid eye-to-eye contact. You see, if we as children saw that someone disapproved of us, we learned to look away instead of trying to change our ways.

DEVELOP A PARTNERSHIP WITH YOUR WIFE

Unfortunately for us men, we have let our wives know so often that we do not like their disapproval of our behavior that they will try to hide their true feelings from us. In my case, my disapproving looks had made Nancy feel that I was rejecting her as a person. In time she no longer wanted me to see her expressions of warning or caution, or her feelings of grief and anger. As a result, I totally missed out on the help she could have given me.

Even though most of the time Nancy was trying to protect my reputation, my insensitivity was causing her to suffer in her spirit. Because it hurt her too much to feel my rejection, she decided it was safer, caused her less inner hurt, to let me fail.

I remember a significant lesson God taught me through a poorly hidden look of disapproval from my wife. This lesson also made me aware of how delicate the feelings of a woman are.

We had been visiting a friend in his place of business. Several women were working for him. After we completed our business, we got into the car. I looked over at Nancy and noticed a severe expression of resentment on her face. As I turned the key to start the car, I asked, "What's the matter?"

"Nothing," she said in a tone of voice that implied, "Don't play dumb. You know what's wrong, and I'm not about to get into another fight with you by telling you."

Typically, I would have thought to myself, *Well, you had your chance, Toots!* Then I would have proceeded with whatever I was doing—and I was always the loser. This time, having learned to value what God wants to teach me through my wife, I insisted, "We will not move until I know what is bothering you." Finally, though she was still concerned what it might cost her in additional suffering, she said, "I don't like the way you were flirting with those women in there."

"Flirting?" I threw back in a high-pitched voice. "I was just being friendly."

She responded, "I'm a woman. I know what flirting is to a woman, and that was flirting."

Having become aware that God was helping me see the need to reevaluate my life and attitudes, and even though it was very difficult, I paused to consider her statement. Feeling it would be good to search my heart in this matter, I thought to myself:

Q. *What was your motive?*

A. *I was just trying to be friendly.*

Q. *How were you being friendly?*

A. *Well, I was being funny and wanting to be clever.*

Q. *Why did you feel the need to be clever?*

A. *Well, what's wrong with wanting to be clever and cool? Everybody wants to be thought of as neat. It's nice to be the center of attention.*

Q. *Why do you need to be the center of attention with other women?*

A. *Doesn't every man feel good about women paying attention to him?*

Yep, she's right—that's flirting! I had to admit to her that her evaluation was accurate. Since then I have tried never to act toward women in a way that my wife would interpret as flirting. I would of course try to never again rely on how I might interpret what is or is not flirting. My conscience is not always willing to judge me accurately. Without Nancy helping me, I might not have known the difference between paying godly attention to the spirit of a woman and paying special attention to the woman. That's one cause of jealousy.

It's a tragic thing to watch husbands flirt with other women in the name of Christian friendship and see wives suffer guilt feelings because they are experiencing jealousy. A wife often does not say anything about how she feels because the husband usually justifies his actions. He will turn the situation around and make her appear to be the culprit. It's as if he is saying to her, "How dare you have such unfair, unrealistic feelings?" And by doing that, he is wounding the spirit of the person he promised before God to love and protect at all costs—instead of ministering positively, as Christ would, to her spirit.

What have I said in this chapter? That we as men label women as mysterious and incomprehensible because it takes the responsibility off us to become truly Christlike in our attitudes and behavior toward our wives. It excuses our unwillingness to genuinely listen to their hearts, to try to determine how their feelings are being displayed in their eyes, facial expressions, and body language. Most of all, it provides a rationalization for not listening to our wives when they are being used by the Spirit of God to point out some of our weaknesses that God wants to deal with. But I have also said that it is possible to discover what is on the mind and in the heart of the woman a man married if he is indwelt by the Holy Spirit and begins displaying Christlike attitudes toward his wife. Finally, we have learned that although it may be painful at first, we can over time discover what will not and what will minister to the spirits of our wives.

You and I have to make the choice every day to minister in Christlike ways to our wives. When we do that, we'll gradually discover they are no longer mysterious and incomprehensible. After all, they never were mysterious to the Holy Spirit who is living in us.

In the next chapter we will discover what it means to genuinely care for our wives. By now you realize there are no easy solutions—being a servant never was easy. But the rewards are an incredibly improved marriage relationship, and that is worth all the effort.

8

HOW DO I MEASURE UP?

everal years ago a friend was teaching a men's class. To get a feel for what the men considered their weakest areas, he gave them a quiz. But he also sent home a quiz in a stamped, self-addressed envelope so the wives could complete it anonymously and return it to him. He received twenty-two out of twenty-four letters sent home to the wives, showing their genuine concern—while only half of the men completed theirs.

The difference between how the men perceived themselves and their relationships with their wives, and how their wives perceived their husbands' strengths and weaknesses, made for some interesting times in class. According to the wives, failure to communicate, outbursts of anger, and the inability to make decisions were reported as the men's major weaknesses, but those same weaknesses hardly showed up on the men's quizzes.

You may want to take the time right now to complete the "Attitude Self-Quiz" on how well you care for your wife and children. Read the Scriptures included for a thorough self-evaluation. If you want to really be vulnerable, let your wife evaluate how you completed it. There is nothing like getting her perspective as you move into this chapter on measuring up to what God means when He asks you to care for your wife! You see, no one is more concerned about the success or failure of your marriage than your wife. Every counselor I've talked to confirms my finding on this.

ATTITUDE SELF-QUIZ

1. Would your family say that your work habits make your work seem more important to you than your family? (See Prov. 15:27; Eccl. 2:4–11; 5:12.)

   ___Yes ___No ___Often ___Seldom

2. Would God be pleased with all that your eyes look at— and how long your eyes rest on it? (See Job 31:1.)

   ___Yes ___No ___Often ___Seldom

3. Do your children regard you as a wise teacher? (See Deut. 6:7; Prov. 15:2; 17:6.)

   ___Yes ___No ___Often ___Seldom

4. Does your wife feel that after your relationship with God, she holds first place in your life? (See 1 Peter 3:7.)

   ___Yes ___No ___Often ___Seldom

5. Do you seek your wife's counsel before you make decisions (as much as possible)? (See Matt. 19:5–6; Eph. 5:31; Phil. 2:2.)

   ___Yes ___No ___Often ___Seldom

6. Do you think your wife is too emotional? (See Prov. 18:14; 1 Peter 3:7.)

   ___Yes ___No ___Often ___Seldom

7. Do you look forward to talking with your wife with as much enthusiasm as you experience when talking with friends (or even strangers)? (See Mal. 2:14–15; John 15:15.)

   ___Yes ___No ___Often ___Seldom

8. Do you share your innermost needs with your wife so she can pray for and with you? (See 1 Tim. 2:1–2; 1 Peter 3:7.)

___Yes ___No ___Often ___Seldom

9. Do you welcome your wife's criticism of you as an opportunity to evaluate how you affect others? (See Prov. 10:17; 13:18; 15:31.)

___Yes ___No ___Often ___Seldom

10. Do you know the goals of each member of your family? (See Prov. 22:6; 27:23.)

___Yes ___No ___Often ___Seldom

11. Does your wife confide her secrets to you? (See Prov. 14:26.)

___Yes ___No ___Often ___Seldom

12. Do you get angry with members of your family? (See Prov. 14:29; 1 Cor. 13:5; Eph. 6:4.)

___Yes ___No ___Often ___Seldom

13. Do you think of your family members as persons God has given you to help you learn? (See Prov. 1:22–23; 1 Cor. 3:18.)

___Yes ___No ___Often ___Seldom

14. Would your wife say you put spiritual and emotional needs above your sexual needs? (See Matt. 6:33; 2 Peter 1:3–6.)

___Yes ___No ___Often ___Seldom

15. Do you feel that a home, money, or prestige builds security in a wife? (See Prov. 16:25; 24:3–4.)

___Yes ___No ___Often ___Seldom

16. Would your wife say that you understand her frame of reference in most matters? (See 1 Peter 3:7.)

___Yes ___No ___Often ___Seldom

A pastor once told me that a meaningful service to men would be to find a way to help them recognize the serious trouble toward which their marriages were headed. He revealed that twenty-five couples in his church had marriages on the verge of destruction. But he also shared that he didn't know how to get the couples to recognize that reality. He knew how defensive men can get when shown their faults.

The pastor was not saying that men purposely want to defend anything that is wrong. Instead, he was saying that because men can be insensitive to their wrong attitudes and actions, they will often blindly defend something that is actually wrong.

A year later, that pastor's wife left him! I had hinted before she left him that he might want to attend our seminar and classes. Because he, too, was defensive, I offered this idea under the guise of knowing to what he was sending his people.

Why do men become so defensive when we are asked to examine ourselves? The Bible reveals that no one likes to have his wrong ways exposed. We frankly do not like light shed upon our evil nature. Here's what the apostle John wrote about it:

> And this is the condemnation, that the light has come into the world, and men loved darkness rather than light, because their deeds were evil. For everyone practicing evil hates the light and does not come to the light, lest his deeds should be exposed. But he who does the truth comes to the light, that his deeds may be clearly seen, that they have been done in God (John 3:19–21).

In view of what the Bible says about us, is it any wonder that we resist coming into the light where we can be stripped of our defenses? Not until a crisis exposes our desperate condition do most of us men even question whether or not that's where we've been operating.

It's smarter—and much less destructive—to pay attention as the Lord uses our wives and children in daily situations to shine His light on our dark ways. It isn't necessary to wait until each situation becomes a crisis before we attend to it. But we will have to become willing to hear about our inadequacies. That's the purpose of the quiz. If you answered five or more questions in the negative, you are a candidate for learning how to care for your wife more effectively.

IT'S A MATTER OF CONTROL

In chapter 6, I revealed how significant a husband's attitudes, words, and actions are to his wife's spiritual, emotional, and physical health. That's because a husband has incredible (*and unrealized*) control over his wife's emotional condition, whether she wishes it or not. Many women fiercely resent how much their husbands affect them emotionally. That's why I keep emphasizing the extremely serious responsibility God has given us as men to become living illustrations of Christ as we interact with our wives.

My associate Eldon shares the following illustration from one of his counseling experiences. It indicates the control husbands have over their wives' emotional state.

"John came into the office for help. A professional painter, he dropped by regularly for almost a year. He had been divorced from his wife a second time, having remarried her after their first divorce. Their second divorce had been finalized when he showed up in my office.

"John's wife, Monica, whom I did not meet during the year of counseling, had been seeing another man, explaining that because of John's violent temper she was scared to be without an adult male in the house, even though she had three sons with her.

"During the counseling sessions, the focus was always on Christlikeness. That's all. Our focus was not how to win his wife back, but how to help him grow into the kind of spiritual leader that God wanted him to be.

"Toward the end of the year I received a call from his ex–wife. She was extremely angry and almost shouted at me, 'Is this the man who counsels my husband, John?'

"I said, 'Yes.'

"'I want to talk to you,' she said heatedly.

"About two that afternoon she came stomping into my office. She was fuming. She sat down and angrily said, 'How dare you counsel my husband and get him to change! After the life he has put me and the kids through for six years. . . .

I've been on food stamps. I've had to scrounge around for jobs, getting childcare when I did find a job. I've had to scrape and scavenge to make ends meet. Now, after putting me through hell on earth, John has the audacity to change.'

"Suddenly, she bent forward even more and shouted at me, 'Why didn't he change six years ago, so I wouldn't have had to go through all of this?'

"I said, 'I don't blame you for being mad.'

"'You don't?' she exclaimed, clearly surprised.

"'No,' I said. 'After all the pain and suffering he has put you through, being scared at night and all that, and now he comes around a changed person.'

"John's wife, like all alienated wives we meet, did not trust the changes at first. But as the months went by, she saw that John had indeed changed, that he was Christlike in his attitudes and behavior toward her and the boys. About seven months later I had the joy of reuniting John and his wife in marriage. That's six years ago, and the marriage is holding this time.

"The sons saw such a dramatic change in their dad's attitudes that they came to me for counseling as well. One of the sons is in college now, but when he comes home, he still drops around to talk about walking in God's ways."

John's control reached further than he could have imagined it would. And he knows now that control doesn't have to manifest itself in negative ways only!

TIMELINE OF A MARRIAGE WITH AN UNCARING HUSBAND

Did you complete the "Attitude Self-Quiz"? If so, you know by now whether you could be identified as a caring or an uncaring husband. I appreciate the discipline you exercised in following through with that task.

I provide the following scenario as a timeline to evaluate the status of a marriage. Maybe it can help you determine where yours is.

1. A man and a woman get married, anticipating happiness.
2. Gradually, the husband seems to forget or overlook little things that demonstrate thoughtfulness. Or he may actually never have learned what things represent thoughtfulness to a wife.
3. The wife is hurt by this neglect, but she is willing to give her husband the benefit of the doubt, concluding that his oversight is possibly due to his being tired, too busy, or under distracting pressures.
4. Like most wives, she doesn't say anything about what is going on in her mind since she doesn't want to seem too picky.
5. As time goes by, he becomes more insensitive to his wife. It's becoming clearer that he is basically self-centered.
6. Time offers no improvements. He becomes extremely selfish in his attitudes and behavior.
7. Her reminders of how he used to be more loving, with requests that he show her more love, are met with expressions that reveal his lack of interest. It is obvious to her that he does not share her enthusiasm for maintaining a mutually joyful relationship. He seems to project an attitude of independence: "You live your life; I'll live mine." Or he may project an attitude of indifference: "Everything seems fine to me. Why are you always looking for trouble?"
8. Though she is searching for ways to restore or even build the oneness that is so vital to her emotional well-being, he determines her need to talk about their problem is simply nagging.
9. Her spirit is wounded even more now. She interprets his attitude toward her as personal rejection.
10. She quickly recognizes that he is more concerned about her response to him sexually than he is about her emotional responses. He is not living with her in an understanding way, and when she tries to explain her needs to him, she finds he really does not want to hear her concerns.
11. She feels disloyal and guilty because she is reacting negatively to him and his insensitive manner toward her. She

does not like the feelings of anger that arise when she thinks about him.

12. She may become openly unstable emotionally.
13. Realizing their marriage is in trouble, she asks him if they can get help. Having seen her emotional instability, he responds, "I don't need any help. You're the one who's having the problem. If you want some help, get it for yourself, but don't try to include me in your problems."

This scenario has been described to me by many women who wanted me to counsel their husbands. It reveals far more than how a marriage is doing. It also reveals why I say that husbands control their wives' emotional well-being. The emotional condition of wives is tied to how responsive and caring their husbands are.

You see, a husband's refusal or inability to responsibly manage his role as spiritual leader will only add to his wife's emotional instability. Numerous wives I have talked to have questioned their sanity, for they felt like they were being torn up inside, being shredded emotionally by the lack of emotional responsiveness on the part of their husbands.

WIVES ATTEMPT TO FIND THEIR OWN SOLUTIONS

Where is a wife to go when her husband refuses to minister to her spirit and makes her feel rejected? What can she do to fill the gaping wound in her spirit caused by the increasing distance she senses between them emotionally? Lacking genuine spiritual leadership, and being severely affected by the disharmony, she will set out to discover what is wrong.

Wives who feel increasing desperation about their relationships with their husbands will develop their own theories about why their husbands are unresponsive to them. They will then conclude what it will take to survive in their marriages. Meanwhile, uncaring or insensitive husbands (not involved in meaningful communication) will grow increasingly baffled by what they find at home.

1. The No-Problems Wife

This wife may resign from being an active participant in the marriage; she may become a passive member who routinely performs her duties but evidences no joy or excitement. This passiveness will add to the guilt feelings she has been experiencing. She knows that giving up is not the answer, but her spirit is drained by the continuing struggle to maintain her marriage.

Typically, the no-problems wife feels that she has become part of a charade, that she and her husband are playing games, that she has become a liar and actress, pretending everything is fine in her marriage when she knows it is not. She begins to feel used sexually by her husband while performing her wifely duties.

Astonishingly, few husbands are aware of what is happening. They don't know that their wives have given up on their marriage. They may think things are looking up—their wives have stopped complaining.

At some point the wife decides to end the farce. She tells her shocked husband that she is tired of playing the marriage game, and that she is leaving. If the husband pushes for an answer, the wife may say, "You wouldn't understand anyway." Sometimes she will admit to having found someone who is interested in her, but that is not the case all the time.

Don't think this wife is leaving her marriage with joy. She is, I find, guilt-ridden almost to the point of despair. But she is determined to make the new situation work because she believes it can't be worse than what she is leaving behind.

I'm not saying this is right—I'm only explaining what happens. And there is help for this marriage if the husband will submit to self-examination in order to learn how to die to the self that has kept him from exhibiting Christlike care. It may take up to a year and a half, but the impact of a husband's deliberately demonstrating Christlike love and care is astonishing.

2. The Dying-Inside Wife

One of the deepest longings of this wife is to know that her husband needs her. Instead, this wife recognizes that her husband is indifferent toward her. To a woman, that is the same as personal rejection.

Such rejection will severely wound this wife's spirit. Sooner or later her wounded spirit will start to affect her emotions. She will start to show signs of being emotionally disturbed. She will begin to seek help, possibly in books on marriage or on emotional well-being. Reading books that identify her problem and offer solutions will allow her to keep her unstable condition a secret a little longer. She will not, however, experience lasting emotional satisfaction since her husband is still not caring for her spirit. So she will eventually feel the need to come out into the open, seeking more help.

Each time this wife finds a new approach, she will think that she has received "sure cure" instructions. She begins to implement the action suggested with great anticipation because she thinks, *Now I have answers that will allow me to rise above my emotional dependency.* But her hopes are dashed again and again because the steps she's supposed to implement that are supposed to be designed for emotional freedom don't work.

Why should they work? The steps to emotional freedom in these books are typically designed for her, not for her husband. Yet her emotional hurts are the result of her husband's insensitivity, his continuous (and frequently unrecognized) rejection of her as a person and wife. Her husband has the disease, but she is taking the medicine.

That reality doesn't prevent this wife from blaming herself for failing. She thinks she is overreacting. She feels guilty for taking his indifference, his perceived rejection, so personally. As a result of this continuing treatment/failure cycle, her emotions will usually become increasingly unstable. The cycle of gaining hope, then having it dashed by the reality of her husband's insensitivity, seems unending.

At some point the dying-inside wife discovers that not only is her husband disturbed about her emotional instability, but her friends are concerned about her as well. They are wondering how a husband can be so patient and tolerant under such trying circumstances, living with "that poor, sick wife." What has been happening to her has made her appear as an emotionally unstable wife, while he is seen as very stable. This additional rejection by her friends increases her guilt and sense of despair.

This wife's guilt and wounded spirit will probably result in physical symptoms of one kind or another. The possibilities are endless, since every wife will have a different physical manifestation of her emotional stress. Visits to the doctor result in attempts to treat the physical symptoms; however, her physical symptoms are the product of her wounded spirit.

In her case the wounded spirit is the cause of the physical symptoms, and you cannot medicate the spirit of a person. That's why the person receiving medication for emotional conditions frequently experiences no relief. She doesn't realize lasting relief because her spirit received no attention for healing. In fact, often the medication has to be monitored and increased over time because it's not bringing resolution.

I've seen dramatic healing take place in wives whose husbands learned how to care for their wives with Christlike attitudes of support and encouragement. Even wives on medication have reached the point of no longer needing the medication—their husbands' demonstration of Christlike attitudes and behavior brought healing!

3. The Silent, Spiritual Wife

This wife has heard teaching in her church, on radio, and on television emphasizing that it is unspiritual for a wife to have any expectations of her husband. Because she doesn't want to be unspiritual, she stops openly expecting her husband to demonstrate husbandly (Christlike) characteristics. Inwardly, however, she continues to long for her husband to demonstrate Christlike love for her. Because she still really wants him to appreciate and admire her, she feels unspiritual—and that only adds to her sense of guilt.

This woman may be active in the church, in women's ministry. Yet her friends are not sensitive enough to notice that her spirit is being crushed. You see, her mouth is not speaking words of discontent. People with whom she associates assume that everything is fine, not realizing she is in agony in her spirit. A quiet mouth doesn't mean there is a quiet spirit.

No one has to verbalize that it is eccentric or unusual for a wife to want her husband to be alert to her as a person, to demonstrate to her in words, actions, and especially in attitudes that he needs her, too. Yet this wife has been taught to consider it eccentric. Outwardly, she appears to be placid and undisturbed, but inwardly, she is being destroyed by emotional turmoil. More and more she feels like a hypocrite, since she is pretending that everything is fine when she knows it isn't.

Very often this woman is considered a spiritual giant; she seems to have it all together spiritually. In fact, she considers herself a hypocrite despised by God. And since she is so good at covering up, she must keep up a positive front. She cannot let people know the truth. She cannot cry out for help, especially if she is a pastor's wife. She not only feels trapped—she is trapped.

When this woman "blows," the top really pops off. And again all the sympathy is for the husband, who is being embarrassed by an unstable wife. Some of these wives try suicide. Others walk away from the marriage and distance themselves from anything Christian. As I have indicated earlier, help is as far away as her husband—if he will develop a Christlike, caring attitude. I have never known that "cure" to fail.

4. The Strong-Willed Wife

This wife is generally more outspoken than a lot of women. Each day, as her marriage experiences become more hurtful, she grows increasingly resentful and bitter. She typically discusses his offensive attitudes and behavior with her husband, but that usually builds resentment on his part. You see, husbands have been taught in our churches that a wife's outspokenness is based on an inner refusal to be submissive.

This woman refuses to suffer in silence, to take the "spiritual" route. She starts letting others know about her husband's failures. She may be embarrassed initially as she reports how inattentive her husband is to her—almost everything takes priority over her. He is preoccupied with work, the needs of others, or pastoral duties. But she feels it's worth being embarrassed if that will cause him some humiliation as well.

As time goes on, her intentions may be to tear him down, to get revenge. I'm not saying this is right, but it is a fairly common response and reveals a problem that needs resolution.

This wife will have to learn to live with being branded a strong-willed woman as a result of honestly speaking out about her husband's irresponsibility and hurtfulness. And that label will only be reinforced as her husband expresses the general opinion of "churchianity," that she is unsubmissive.

There is also a sure "cure" for this wife's condition. Because Christ is the Great Physician, and a husband is to be like Him, he will administer the medication of appreciation, encouragement, and unconditional (agape) love. And over an extended period of time, a husband will see healing take place. I have never known it to fail.

5. THE I-GUESS-I'M-NOT-SO-BAD-OFF WIFE

I have discovered that wives have an incredible capacity for unselfish and loyal attitudes and behavior. Many think they are too demanding by wanting things to be better in their marriages. They will settle for marriages that fall far short of what they could be while having a longing within that the marriage relationship would be improved. Some have a secret hope that something will happen to dramatically improve their marriage.

You're skeptical? You've heard too many complaining wives? Let me illustrate what I have found rather frequently.

After a seminar, I met with a couple. There was a very comfortable feeling between us. Following some friendly conversation, we talked specifically about their marriage. As usual, the wife was the first to break the ice.

"I feel kind of ridiculous for wanting to get together with you. I guess it's because we don't really have any situations in our marriage that are desperate. Even though our marriage isn't exactly terrific, it isn't terrible, either. Maybe that's why I feel guilty and ungrateful. I feel that I'm expecting so much from my husband," she said, evaluating herself. "My husband is really a good man."

Wanting to let her know that I understood how she was feeling, I asked her if I could express what I thought she was going through emotionally. I hoped I could express her feelings in such a way that her husband would gain a new look at his responsibility as a Christian husband. She gave me permission. Looking at her, I said, "You are saying to yourself, 'When I look around at other marriages, I see that I'm really not so bad off, even though our marriage seems to be missing something spiritually. My husband is a good provider. He has good friendships. He's never left us. He's a reliable businessman. He's a good father. He doesn't neglect the children. He never physically abuses us. He makes sure that we attend church regularly. He helps out when the church needs him. He reads his Bible. What more can I expect from him?'"

She nodded her head as if to say, "You're right."

Again speaking for her, I said, "What more can I expect from him? Perfection?"

Realizing that those had been her thoughts, she dropped her head down as if she were ashamed of herself. Then I began speaking for myself, so I added, "What can you expect from a Christian husband? That he be like Jesus—perfect?" She lifted her head slowly as she began to understand the point I was making. Looking at me with a slight smile, she said, "Yeah, I see what you're saying now."

I continued, "Is it such a terrible thing for a wife to be

unwilling that her husband settle for anything less than what God desires for him? Christlikeness! If God designed a wife to help her husband be successful, would He design her to be satisfied with anything less than helping him become success- fully Christlike?"

This story has a happy ending. Her husband realized that he should accept that she had an honest need, that her long- ing for him to be Christlike was legitimate. So he challenged himself to quit playing at being a Christian and get serious about discovering what God was showing him through her— to learn how to be more sensitive to her spirit and to the Holy Spirit. That desire alone lifted a great burden off his wife; that alone gave her hope. She recognized that Christlikeness must be achievable because that is also the goal of the Holy Spirit, and she could trust Him to finish the good work He had started in her husband.

A Wife Settling for Less

Let me give another example of a wife settling for less because she was making faulty comparisons. This wife's father never bought her anything other than what he felt was absolutely essential (does that sound like a lot of husbands or not?). He made her feel stupid, ugly, and unwanted. He also hit her with his fists. With this role model, she entered marriage.

This woman's husband never hit her. He did buy her clothes—tight-fitting ones to show off his wife's figure. He was trying to prove to others what a man he was—just look at the trophy he had bagged. He often used her as his source of humor, hurting her spirit repeatedly. Yet even though she didn't feel good about what her husband was doing, she didn't dwell on it. After all, compared to living with her father, she had never had it so good. That faulty comparison meant that she wasn't about to challenge her husband to be Christlike.

I find it heartbreaking to talk to the wives experiencing the syndromes discussed here. They typically don't want to believe their husbands don't know how much they have hurt them as wives. They typically think that their husbands just don't care about how they are destroying their wives emotionally. Yet when I talk to the husbands, I discover they don't even see or know what they are doing to their wives.

It is difficult for me to convince a wife that when her husband asks, "What did I do?" he really doesn't understand what he has done. Because his offenses are so obvious to her, a wife is unwilling to believe that the offenses are not obvious to her husband. That's why a wife can become bitter.

Wives experiencing this turmoil in their marriages often develop a strong feeling of hopelessness. That's why the wives described in this chapter tried to devise their own conclusions about what was going on, thinking they could also try to develop methods of survival in their relationships.

Wives who come from homes with a stable family life, or who have a great deal of personal confidence, can survive longer than others. Even though they may experience severe damage to their spirits and develop emotional scars they will carry for the rest of their lives, these more confident wives seem to be able to manage longer. Even though they are suffering, such women try to carry on in their Christian growth, leaving their immature husbands far behind spiritually. By default, these wives become the spiritual leaders in their homes.

TAKING ALL THE BLAME?

By now, you may again be ready to throw this book in the trash. You cannot agree that you should be held responsible for marriage problems or for your wife's emotional health. If that's what you're feeling, you are perfectly normal, for this is what I hear constantly: "It sounds like all the blame for unsuccessful marriages is being put on the man, and I cannot accept that. That's not right! A wife doesn't have to react wrongly toward her husband. The grace of God is sufficient for wives as well."

Agreed, the grace of God is sufficient for women as well. That's why I believe they don't give up on their Christianity when it looks like even Christianity can't motivate their husbands to be like Christ.

Let me remind you that a wife is not oblivious to the fact that her hostile, angry, irrational responses are not godly. She feels guilty because she believes she is not responding to the grace of God, which she understands is sufficient for her. If you, for example, asked her in the middle of her anger, "Do you know that your anger is wrong?" she would say, "Yes, you idiot, I know I'm wrong." She may even be spiteful enough to refuse you the satisfaction of hearing that she realizes she is wrong, for that is part of the nature of anger. You see, her knowing that her responses are wrong is also part of what is eating at her. It is heaping inner guilt on her and making her spirit even heavier.

Yet what is your purpose: *to focus on her shame or to care for your wife's spirit?* Do you think you will minister to her if you merely get an admission from her that her responses are wrong? If you do, you are unwittingly giving Satan an opening in your life, letting him use your shortsightedness to distract you.

Isn't your goal to build your marriage relationship so that its central focus is Christlikeness—letting your wife know that no matter what, she can trust you to respond with a Christlike attitude toward her? If that is the case, then there is hope for you, for the Holy Spirit is ready to help you go beyond blaming to personal evaluation, to recognizing your own needs and discovering responses that become testimonies of Christlike attitudes and behavior.

I'd like to emphasize the need to get past the tendency to point the finger of blame at what we perceive is "wrong" and move on to the more beneficial territory of ministering to the need represented by the "wrong."

Imagine a friend coming into your house bleeding from a stab wound and getting blood on your favorite carpet. Would you scold your friend for getting blood on the carpet? Would you justify the scolding as necessary because "after all, a carpet really was not made to be bled upon, was it?"

Wouldn't it be more cruel if the one who did the stabbing (even accidentally) was also the one doing the scolding?

Wouldn't it be better to find out how to eliminate the stabbing, which would also eliminate the resulting blood on the carpet?

My job is to help husbands see how they are stabbing the spirits of their wives. You see, if husbands stopped stabbing the spirits of their wives, they would no longer have to scold them because their emotions are bleeding all over their marriages. Husbands could stop the emotional bleeding and set about healing the damage they have done. That's a decision men can make!

God, through Isaiah and the apostle Paul, is telling us, in essence: "Husbands, because your ways are not My ways, use Christ's unselfish love for humankind as your example of how to love your wives" (compare Isa. 55:8 with Eph. 5:25–29). If we do this, we will cause our wives to become spiritually mature through our loving and confidence-building examples.

One husband asked me, "Are you trying to say that a perfect husband makes a perfect wife?"

I replied, "I don't think we have to worry about that possibility."

He persisted, "If Jesus, being perfect, had a wife, are you saying that since He was perfect, His wife would have been perfect?"

I sensed a not-too-uncommon attitude of scorn toward women, so I said, "Since Scripture commands me to make my first priority that of actively seeking how to become Christlike, a better question might be, 'If my example, Christ, had a wife who was miserable, rebellious, strong-willed, and angry, would He have stopped being Christlike?'"

This man realized that this response put his need for Christlikeness in a new perspective. From that point on, he made the goal of Christlikeness his priority.

MEN ARE ACCOUNTABLE

Let's compare going into marriage to signing a contract to join the army. Once we have signed that contract, we're committed. If more is expected of us in the army than we expected, too bad. The same holds true for the commitment we made at the altar. The only difference is that in the army, we can be forced to follow through on the commitment or be court-martialed. In marriage, our wives cannot force us to keep our commitment—and we husbands know that.

Yet as you've learned in this book, God holds us as men accountable for the success of our marriages. The position of husband carries with it the charge of being spiritually responsible. And my responsibility to and relationship with my wife are to be just as Jesus' responsibility to and relationship with the church.

One pastor said to me, "Whenever I heard the expression 'laying down your life,' I always equated it with being willing to die for my wife. I imagined it being like a marine jumping on a grenade and being killed to prevent his friends in the foxhole from dying. And of course, I have always said, 'Yes, I would be willing to die for my wife.'

"But you're talking about something else here. You're talking to me about learning to put my wife first in our marriage, about trying to meet her needs, even before meeting my own needs. And if it comes to a situation where it's a matter of opinion between my wife and me, I'm to give her opinions priority over mine. In other words, I'm to put consideration for my wife before my own needs in our everyday living. Boy, that's going to be rough."

Another man said, "I feel like you are asking me to lose my identity, as though I'm not supposed to be me anymore."

"Exactly," I replied. "That's what becoming Christlike means. I'm not me anymore because I'm being conformed to the image of Christ, as Paul so eloquently states in Galatians 2:20, 'I have been crucified with Christ; it is no longer I who live, but Christ lives in me.'"

Isn't that what the apostle Paul means in Philippians 2:1–3? There he writes,

> If you have any encouragement from being united with Christ, if any comfort from his love, if any fellowship with the Spirit, if any tenderness and compassion, then make my joy

complete by being like-minded [Christ-minded], having the same love [as I have for you], being one in spirit and purpose [Christ and I]. Do nothing out of selfish ambition or vain conceit, but in humility consider others better than yourselves (NIV).

As I try to live by this word of God and make it part of my everyday life, it will free me from being preoccupied with the faults of others, including my wife. These attitudes will help me think of others as persons God is using to teach me, to show me, regardless of their methods, how to become more Christlike. And shouldn't my wife become the first living verification of how I live out these attitudes and the resulting behavior? If I exhibit this behavior at home, if I truly care for my wife, then I will also demonstrate that caring attitude at church, in the neighborhood, and on the job.

Looking ahead, what would you say is possibly the most common expression of a wife's concern? Could it be jealousy—ways a man makes his wife feel like others are more important to him than she is, especially other women? That's what I learned in "A Lesson from Secretaries Week."

9

A LESSON FROM SECRETARIES WEEK

It's astonishing how much we as men can learn from one incident if we are open to correction. One incident can open up a whole world of understanding about how our wives function.

Ever get into a flap with your wife over Secretaries Week—specifically, what you are expected to do on Professional Secretaries Day? If so, you'll understand what happened to me when I was working for a large Christian organization. We had fifteen young, single secretaries that the boss wanted to honor by taking them out for lunch. There were four secretaries per car, so we got everybody taken care of and took off for the restaurant.

One complication. My home, which was only a couple of blocks away, stood between the office and the restaurant. There I was, driving down the street with a carload of single young women when I saw her. Wouldn't you know that of all days to do it, my wife was out mowing the lawn. Even worse, there she was standing right next to the street as we drove by.

Since they all knew my wife, my carload of young women cheerfully yelled, "Hello!" and "Hi, Nancy!"

Get the picture? It was a perfect setting for jealousy to flare up. Nancy recognized the green-eyed monster immediately, so she tackled the issue head-on.

"Don't get jealous now," she lectured herself. "He's only following orders. He can't help it. Jealousy is wrong."

But all that rational thinking didn't help her. So she prayed, read her Bible, and continued to argue against jealousy. She determined she would not let her feelings show when I got home. Half an hour before I arrived, she felt that she had herself under control.

When I walked in after work, all her good effort came undone. She literally blew up in my astonished face. I didn't have a clue about what was going on, so I stood there with a questioning look on my face that said, "What did I do?"

While working through what the issues raised by this incident meant, I had to realize that she was expressing the honest feelings in her heart. I had to accept that something about my character and attitudes had caused her to feel insecure; I had somehow communicated to her that she was not a priority to me. Then I had to let her know that I saw this as a learning opportunity, teaching me how I had been affecting her opinion of me, instead of discounting what had happened as inconsequential—and demeaning her by treating her jealousy as the focal point of our (her) problem.

SITUATIONS THAT BREED JEALOUSY

Consider another situation where a man's typical response illustrates how totally oblivious we men can be to how we negatively affect our wives. A guy drives to a restaurant with his wife. All the way to the restaurant he is preoccupied and doesn't say a word. His wife wishes there were more conversation but does not intrude on his thoughts.

They enter the restaurant, and the hostess smiles and says, "May I help you?" He smiles back and starts carrying on a conversation with her. At that point something natural happens—his wife gets jealous. You may say, "What's the big deal? What gives her the right to react with jealousy?" The big deal is that her nonconversational husband suddenly comes alive when another woman enters the picture. He is more thoughtful, more courteous, and more interactive with the hostess than he has been with his wife since he came home from work. And his wife's spirit senses his attentiveness to another woman and reacts. Surely, we can recognize the contrast as preferential treatment.

Even an insensitive husband will notice something is wrong after they are seated. His wife will be cold, unwilling to talk, demonstrating body language that says, "I'm offended and disgusted with you." The husband might ask, "What's wrong with you?" Typically, a wife will say, "Nothing!" If he is committed to correcting this problem, he will persist in trying to find out what is bothering her. Yet no matter how sincere the attitude of his heart and the tone of his voice, he'll probably get an earful: "I'm sick and tired of you paying more attention to other women than you do to me!"

At that point there is no glossing over the fact that unless the husband swallows the pride that is bound to come to his rescue, neither husband nor wife will enjoy dinner. So how does a husband swallow his pride? He must believe his wife's expression of emotional pain. He must accept her evaluation of how he affects her. Only then can he say, "I'm sorry I've hurt you. That's terrible. As my wife, you should always sense that I am paying more attention to you than I am to anyone else."

Notice, as is usually the case, that a wife has to get jealous before her husband recognizes how he is not being as attentive to her as he is to the hostess, the waitress, or almost any other woman. Unfortunately, it's another price a wife has to pay as God helps her husband learn how un-Christlike and distorted his ways are.

Many other situations can breed jealousy. For example, you and your wife are at a party. She meets a friend and starts talking, so you drift away. You start telling jokes, and soon you have a small crowd around you, including a couple of very attractive women. You are feeling really good about it, since you enjoy the attention more than you would ever admit to your wife.

Your wife happens to glance your way and her attention is drawn to your focus, which seems to be on the women, who are laughing and smiling as you appear to be entertaining them. At that point all the Christian resolve a woman can muster may not be enough to prevent her from becoming jealous.

Or think of a man's relationship with his mother. Jealousy may make itself known through statements like, "I hate your mother." Of course, a man will question, "Why do you hate my mother?" The wife will likely give examples of how he shows preferential treatment to his mother.

I'm thinking of a situation where a wife said, "On Mother's Day, you made sure that your mother got to sit at the head of the table and was waited on first." He retaliated, "Well, it was Mother's Day!" His wife defensively said, "I'm a mother! In fact, I'm the mother of your children. But that doesn't seem to carry any weight with you!" He illustrated his deafness to her spirit by saying, "I'm not going to stop loving my mother just to make you happy!"

I informed him, "Your wife is not trying to force you to make a decision to love either her or your mother. Your wife is crying out to you from her heart, letting you know that she is grieved because you pay more attention to, and you are more responsive to, your mother than you are to her. May I encourage you to see God at work in this situation? God requires that a man leave his father and mother to become one with his wife. A man is commanded to lay down his life for his wife, not his mother. You could use your love for your mother as a source of measurement, allowing you to have a means of contrasting the love your wife experiences from you with the love she sees you demonstrate to your mother. Could your goal be to love your wife at least as much as, if not more than, you love your mother?"

The objective is always to be Christlike.

Another source of jealousy is the way a husband responds to his pets. His dog or cat can do almost anything and he is tolerant, but he is intolerant of almost everything his wife does. He always has time for the pet. It can jump onto his lap and be petted gently with no impatience. But his wife can't get that kind of gentle attentiveness.

A man's relationship with his brothers and sisters can also lead to jealousy. The husband is, from the wife's perspective, consistently more considerate to his brothers and sisters than he is to her.

A man's job or his involvement with sports can generate jealousy. Things that can say to a wife that she is not most important to her husband include the following:

- Seeming to be more concerned about his friends' thinking, and about being with them, than with his wife.
- Choosing to play softball, basketball, hockey, or cards, or getting involved in politics several nights a week, while not finding time for a date with her.
- Spending 80 to 90 percent of his free time doing things around the house or watching sports events on television.

WHEN TEASING WOUNDS A WIFE'S SPIRIT

Some men seem to take a perverse delight in making their wives squirm with jealousy. I was counseling a couple because what he thought was great fun was tormenting his wife. He was only teasing, he insisted, but the tears streaming down her face told a different story.

Here's what happened. While the couple were watching television, a commercial showed a female flight attendant pampering a male passenger. The wife was not a very secure person, and knowing her husband was leaving on another flight soon, she turned to him and asked if the flight attendants really paid that much attention to the male passengers. The husband, thinking it would be great fun, assured her that they certainly did. Then he started building a story about how much special attention he had received in the past.

This "fun" wounded this woman's spirit as she thought of her husband permitting other women to pay such special attention to him. She was overcome with jealousy, since like many other women, she felt she could not compete with the Miss Universe types or other ideal women. She wondered if she was going to be able to keep her husband, and her self-image eroded in the process.

I've discovered that even the Miss Universe types feel insecure about their ability to attract and hold a man. So teasing designed to make a woman jealous can be destructive even to the most attractive woman.

I've asked my wife, Nancy, to share about jealousy from her perspective.

"There are times when I have to deal with jealousy, and there are times when I don't. As a woman, I watch his eyes and just naturally read his body language. When Kenny gets out of his car after work, for example, we all know whether he's sad or happy by the way he walks. The kids will say, 'Dad's really upset today.' Or I'll say, 'Dad's really dragging today.'

"It's the same with jealousy. There are times when girls come into the office, and it doesn't bother me a bit. But there are other times when he might sense something is different about them, and I'll say, 'Kenny, that girl was flirting with you.' And he'll say, 'You're kidding?' And I'll say, 'No, I'm not. She was.'

"Back in the days when Kenny was painting signs, there was a girl who wanted to spend all her time around him, but not in a sexual sense. She just liked being with him because he was interested in helping her husband learn how to care for her spirit. So her wanting to spend so much time around him was not a problem to me.

"Most of the time when a wife gets jealous, it's because of the way her husband looks at a girl or the way the girl looks back at him for attention. And the wife sees that he doesn't recognize what he needs to do to make it clear to the other woman that he is not interested or available.

"Remember the story about when we first got married and we went into the business of his friend and Kenny was talking with all the girls? When we got outside, I told him, 'You were flirting with those girls.' He said he wasn't, but as he analyzed his inner motives, he realized that he was indeed trying to impress them and draw attention to himself."

Nancy is right. As men, we have a natural bent to want to impress the opposite sex. We quickly recognize that we can get their attention by being clever and funny. So if we work at it a bit, we can become quite adept at humorous banter that gets us lots of attention. But we don't realize the damage it does to the spirits of our wives.

JEALOUSY WREAKS HAVOC IN FAMILY EVENTS

Jealousy can wreak havoc in family events as well. A couple that had already separated came in for counseling. The husband's brother was getting married, and the niece had been asked to be the flowergirl. Yet the estranged wife was afraid that if she also was in the wedding party, it would give the appearance that everything was fine in their marriage (both to her husband and to his family). So she said, "I don't think it would be right for me to be in the wedding, but it's okay if our daughter is in it."

His brother's fiancée was miffed. So when the mother took her daughter into the room where everybody was getting ready, the bride told the flowergirl's mother that only the people in the wedding party were to be in the room. The flowergirl's mother said, "But she's my daughter, and I want to fix her up for the wedding." The mother was so steamed by the conflict that she determined to leave right after seeing the wedding party enter. And she did. Of course, everyone noticed since it was a small wedding.

At the wedding reception, the husband danced with the maid of honor. The daughter saw them and started screaming. She ran up to her father and said, "I don't want you dancing with her." She was terrified about what might happen as a result of her daddy's actions.

So the husband came back in my office and said, "How dare my wife cause all this chaos?"

I said, "Excuse me? What chaos?"

"My daughter is having a fit because my wife is . . . ," he started saying. I interrupted him and said, "Hold it. You don't sound like you are accepting any responsibility for this."

He countered, "What do you mean?"

"This is the loyalty you have to your marriage?" I exclaimed. "Your wife is mad and leaves, and you're enjoying yourself, dancing with the maid of honor?"

Trying to excuse himself, the husband said, "Well, it was just a special dance where the best man was supposed to dance with the maid of honor! My wife had left."

"Exactly," I said. "She was gone. You know that you don't have to dance with the maid of honor. You could have said, 'Listen, I couldn't do this to my wife.'

"Then you get mad at your wife because your daughter was terrified by what *you* did, and you shift the blame to your wife! From where I sit, it seems to me that you ought to accept the responsibility for your actions. The least you could express is, 'I have committed a wrong against my wife. Especially since we are already separated, the last thing I should be doing is dancing with another woman. And my daughter is God's reproof to me for something I shouldn't have been doing anyhow.'"

When I said that, the husband broke down and sobbed. He recognized his offensiveness as a husband and took responsibility for it. As a result of his brokenness, he and his wife got back together again. He was willing to die to self and accept responsibility for what he had done to the marriage. His awakening began when he realized that he had really upset his daughter and made his wife jealous.

THE SECURE WIFE

I don't want to give the impression that every wife spends most of her time being jealous. Some women are genuinely secure in their relationships with their husbands. If that is the case, then I know her husband understands what it takes to generate trust in his wife.

If my character is such that I create an atmosphere with my wife that is loving, caring, conversational, and fun, then that will become her frame of reference about who I am. So when I'm in a restaurant and I smile and talk with the waitress in a friendly manner, Nancy feels safe—as long as she has the confidence that I understand what impression I am making on her spirit and the spirits of others. If I am a polite, kind person at home, she expects me to be polite and kind elsewhere. I'm not behaving favorably to others. What she is measuring is the attitude of my heart to her and others.

A wife absolutely knows whether a husband is mindful of her by how he acts around her. For example, if I call up my wife during the day and ask how she is coming along, she knows I had to be thinking of her. If in the evening we are talking and I really pay attention to her, instead of cutting her off with, "It's late and I've got to get to bed," then she knows she holds a place of high priority in my life.

It's amazing what a regular phone call will do when a man is on the road. It illustrates his correct priorities—his heart has not forgotten his wife and the kids back home. He wants to keep his wife aware of his day because that refuels him as he lets her into his heart. It keeps a wife informed about the events in his day—and him informed about the events in her day—and indicates something far greater. It lets her know that she is important to him because he needs to touch base with her for his comfort. A wife feels loved when she knows that her husband receives comfort from their spirit-to-spirit relationship.

At one time I had to go to the mountains for a week to write. Before I left, Nancy had addressed and stamped postcards for me, so all I had to do was fill them in and drop one in the mail each day. I remember writing, "I got up this morning at 7:30. The sun was up and was beautiful. There were a couple of squirrels on the sun porch. I forgot to take the lid off the TV dinner I had in the oven, and it burned. I got most of a chapter written. The temperature is really nice. Miss you. Think of you. Look forward to calling you on the phone."

When I got back, my family said, "Man, that was the newsiest letter you ever wrote." And I'm thinking, *What? I thought it was just a bunch of stuff.* But it was meaningful to them because I was letting them into my day.

A wife must be affected by the attitude of her husband's heart—that's how God made her. That's why she can be his helper. But let's say that the attitude of a man's heart is not right, that he has learned how to mechanically do acceptable things. In that case a wife will eventually sense the husband's performance. She will say things like, "I don't know for sure what it is, but something is not right." She may not be able to put her finger on it, but she will sense that something is off balance.

When the wife in that situation starts probing, the guy wonders out loud, "I'm doing everything you wanted. What more do you want from me?" When his tone of voice indicates impatience, that's an indication that her radar is working fine. She might not yet have a clear understanding of what isn't right, so she might tell him, "I'm not sure I know." If he says, "When you know, let me know," and walks away, then it's obvious that the things he was doing before were only learned responses, not attitudes of the heart. God wants to expose attitudes within a man's heart, revealing either Christlikeness (for testimony) or the lack of Christlikeness (for improvement).

Jealousy is a natural outgrowth of a wife's insecurity. A husband who recognizes it for what it is will do everything he can to make his wife feel secure in the relationship with her. And living with her in an understanding way is certainly what Christ would do. He created such an aura of trust that people in all strata of life were drawn to Him. And a husband can so affirm and love his wife that she will not be distressed when he ministers to other women in genuine need. He will be doing it not to draw attention to himself but to draw attention to Jesus Christ, our wonderful Lord.

I've come to appreciate that in this one instance alone, the incident during Secretaries Week, listening to Nancy's heart taught me what causes a wife to feel threatened, resulting in jealousy. Just one of the benefits to me is feeling comfortable about reading the spirit of a woman. This helps me avoid any misunderstandings between myself and other women. What freedom!

In the next chapter, we will explore a topic most of us would rather avoid—how our character is reflected back to us by our wives, and how this provides motivation for commitment to Christlike attitudes and behavior.

10

THE CHARACTER ISSUE

Have you ever wondered why God seems to withdraw Himself from some men, while He blesses others? Why is it that some men's wives have a lot of problems, while others seem to always be on top of things? The prophet Malachi provides an answer most of us have never heard.

Malachi was the prophet during the time when several thousand Israelites were permitted to return to Jerusalem from captivity in Babylon. They had rebuilt the walls and were rebuilding the temple, but they were experiencing real problems. In chapter 2, Malachi is addressing the men of Israel about their problems. He says that their problems are the result of God's withdrawing Himself from them. God is permitting them to suffer for their attitudes and behavior. And as is typical of men, they seem to be asking, "What did we do that is so bad?"

Malachi, as God's mouthpiece, responds,

You ask, "Why?" It is because the LORD is acting as the witness between you and the wife of your youth, because you have broken faith with her, though she is your partner, the wife of your marriage covenant. Has not the LORD made them one? In flesh and spirit they are his. And why one? Because he was seeking godly offspring. So guard yourself in your spirit, and do not break faith with the wife of your youth (Mal. 2:14–15 NIV).

God let the men who were rebuilding Israel experience serious problems because they were mistreating their wives— and that was affecting God's plan that they have godly offspring. As part of God's design, the loyalty we illustrate to our wives (as those united to us in covenant with God) and our character are mirrored to us in the lives of our wives and our children.

Most men really do not want to hear this. We have all kinds of rationalizations about why our wives are the way they are, why our children are problems. But none of our reasons illustrate that we see our wives and children as reflections of our character. No wonder so many women report that their Christian husbands are calling them crazy, insane, weird, or sick—and so many children rebel against the Lord in their teens.

A man will complain to me, "When is my wife going to get her act together? I pray for her, but nothing happens." And in that pointed comment the husband reveals where he believes the problem lies—it's his wife. She is an ungodly, unspiritual source of turmoil, according to the husband. Some husbands even suggest their wives may be possessed by demons.

I know one pastor who determined the correct direction for his ministry by his wife's attitudes. If she disagreed with his thinking, he used that to verify that his thinking was in line with God's will. It was clear to him which way to go because his wife was so unchristian and unscriptural, so emotionally unstable, that whatever she reasoned or concluded, it had to be the opposite of God's direction for him.

Though that pastor's thinking may seem like an extreme example, he illustrates the thinking of many men who view their wives as the enemy. They react to their wives as someone other than the person they entered into a covenant with, which God called marriage. They act as though their wives are their enemy and the enemy of God. I'm not saying this is a conscious thought process, but it is a deep-seated, inner attitude reflected in their behavior.

CHARACTER ON DISPLAY

Case in point. The husband calls from the office and informs his wife that he is staying for an office party. She exclaims, "But you already promised your children that you were going to go with them to their birthday party!"

Her reminder rattles him. Having told everyone at the office he would be there, he feels pressure and attributes the pressure to his wife. He gets angry and responds to her as though she were his enemy, "Why are you doing this to me?" Even though he gave his word to his children, that is not as important to him as his word to his fellow employees. Despite her "coming against" his defective priorities, he angrily decides to stay for the office party. A man must make decisions as he sees necessary, he reasons misguidedly.

Now imagine if his wife were to respond to his rejoinder with, "But, honey, do you realize how this is going to affect our children? You promised them you would be at their birthday party, and now you are going to an office party instead. I'm afraid they are going to see you as a man who doesn't keep his word. They might even think that God is not trustworthy because they asked God that you would be at the party."

How would the typical husband react to this courageous wife? Most men I've known would have been outraged, thinking that their wives were trying to manipulate them. In some cases they would have gotten so angry they would have slammed the phone down.

We don't treat the commitments we make to our wives and children as seriously as God does, and that puts us in jeopardy. We lose God's blessing, and we sow the seeds of destruction—only too often resulting in taking a trip to divorce court as well as alienating children who end up wanting nothing to do with our God.

A DIVORCE COURT AWAKENING

I was sitting in divorce court one day with a man I had been discipling for a few weeks. With alarm he turned to me and said, "She's going to go for everything!"

"What does that mean?" I asked.

"She's going to go for everything," he repeated. "House, money, savings, everything. What am I going to do about it?"

"Nothing," I said.

"You mean, just let her take everything?" he asked incredulously.

"Yes," I said. And because I had been working with him long enough to help him see his marriage from his wife's eyes, I went on, "If you wiped her out all these years, if she's so angry with you that she wants to wipe you out, then let that be an indication of how badly you've hurt her. I mean, how can you possibly compensate her? The least you can do if you want to let her know you feel for her is give her what she asks for. At least that's some compensation."

"But she's going to take *everything*," he repeated.

"I understand. That's okay," I said calmly.

"She's going to take my retirement!"

"Okay."

"Well, it's *my* retirement," he sputtered.

"Okay, then give it to God," I replied.

"And half of my paycheck, too?" he queried.

"Okay. What's the difference if you want to start fresh with God anyway?" I asked.

"Man, this is really hard," he exclaimed.

"Yes, I know it is," I said.

After court he said, "Well, she really took everything."

"So what?" I countered. "You're starting over, fresh, new. If you become more and more like Christ and she comes back, you'll have it all back anyhow."

You ask, "What had he done to deserve that kind of treatment by her—and by you?" That question illustrates a greater concern for what is happening *to* him than what God wants *to teach* him about dying to self.

Here's what had happened. He had not come close to caring for his wife's spirit. He talked down to her, giving her no indication he was genuinely interested in her. He had business dealings that he never discussed with her, not seeking her opinion at any time. His attitude had been, "If I go bankrupt in my business, that is no concern of hers."

I remember asking him, "Oh! You're the only one going bankrupt? Was the money for your use only?"

"No," he admitted.

I asked, "If you go bankrupt, will your family not be affected?"

He replied, "Yeah, it will affect my family, too."

"Well, then, why shouldn't she be consulted?" I countered. "Since she will suffer bankruptcy, too, shouldn't she have a say in the policies that will determine whether or not you both go bankrupt?"

Through that conversation, he revealed a lot of characteristically male attitudes. They proved he really didn't know how to care for his wife from God's perspective. As a result she had just had enough. Like so many wives, she finally decided, "I've had it with him. I'm out of here!"

But this story has a happy ending. They were remarried six months after the scene at the courthouse. Why? Because he had begun to be concerned with how he affected her— from her perspective. And he had admitted to her, "I know that the way I've talked to you was degrading."

He also had to admit, "I didn't listen to you when you told me that I loved my parents more than you. I realize now that I did treat them better than you."

Those Christlike attitudes and actions, that character change, won her back, convincing her that he really could be loving to her and wanted to care for her.

A WIFE'S INSIGHT CAN INCREASE PROMOTION CHANCES

Have you ever wondered why you were passed over when someone else, who you know was not as qualified as you, was promoted? Because promotions are such a hallmark of success to men, you probably heard a dozen reasons that were supposed to explain why you were passed over. Most likely, none of them reflected on your character. Yet if you were to ask your wife, and she thought it was safe enough to tell you the truth, she could probably put her finger on some pretty significant character qualities that affected your promotion potential. That's because God made women especially sensitive to character issues.

I have to wonder how many men have been released during corporate downsizing because of character flaws their wives saw clearly and could have helped them overcome. Yet because too many husbands consider their wives too out of touch with the realities of their jobs, they refuse to see their wives as credible sources of input.

The impact of character (or the lack of it) is not limited to employment opportunities. Character is revealed through any of the circumstances life has to offer, be it through a job, social engagements, church, politics, or marriage.

Many men don't listen as their wives make suggestions about how they might improve. Arguments and fights usually result, with the wives being accused of being disloyal because they appear to be taking the boss's or the other person's side. Even when men lose jobs for reasons their wives tried to point out, they insist their wives were wrong in their assessment of their weaknesses. Many men are ruined financially and are suffering needlessly because they rejected cautions from their wives.

I remember that for years my wife, Nancy, didn't feel free to let me know about the problems she saw in my plans. She knew from past experience that I was stubborn and not a good listener, so she feared the consequences of being honest with me.

MEN ARE OFTEN BLIND TO DOUBLE STANDARDS

One of men's major character flaws that women comment on is our double standard related to anything that affects us.

A wife will say, "We need new sheets for the bed. Ours are really getting tattered." Her husband will reply, "We don't have the money right now. You'll have to wait until next month." Or he might say, "What have you been doing with all the money I gave you? No, you cannot have any more to waste!" Then he goes out and buys something essential like a special jogging outfit, another fishing pole, or a bigger carburetor for the boat.

A company president launched an all-out effort to cut costs in the company he headed. To make everyone supersensitive to the problem, he initiated drastic measures. Secretaries were not permitted more than one pencil. He had to personally sign every requisition for office supplies. The Christmas party was canceled, even though employees were to bring the food. However, as president, when the lease on his car came due, he went out and purchased an even more expensive car for his company and personal use.

A friend whose family finances were very tight put special restrictions on his wife's expenditures and then went out and purchased a motorcycle for himself. The reasoning he used to justify this expense to his wife was that the motorcycle was cheap. It had been disassembled, but it would "only cost a little bit to buy the parts necessary to put it back together again." Not wanting to appear that she didn't want him to have any fun in life, but against her better judgment, she agreed to the purchase. I couldn't help wondering how fulfilling it would have been to her if she knew that she was as great a source of joy to him as a motorcycle.

Two years later my friend's wife was still complaining about the pile of motorcycle parts in the corner of the garage. The motorcycle had never been completed. Of course, he didn't like those reminders, so his excuse became, "It will cost too much to fix it." Notice that the very reason he'd given for buying it in the first place (cost) became the reason why he couldn't fix it up and use it.

Do you think my friend was alert to his preferential treatment of himself? He wasn't—but he is now. He is learning to see his wife as a blessing from God while she is helping him see the attitudes and actions that will make him more Christlike. He is learning to see with his spiritual eyes, to hear with his spiritual ears, and to be a man of his word, reasoning things out before making decisions, and letting his wife be a part without pressuring her to agree to his wishes.

Women can tell of many situations like this—and some even more disturbing. Yet because husbands are unwilling to examine their faulty reasoning and admit to a double standard, wives finally quit reminding their husbands of their injustices. And because they won't listen at home, men carry this characteristic of unfairness with them wherever they go.

MEN ARE OFTEN BLIND TO HYPOCRISY

I'll admit that as a seminar leader and counselor, I get to hear mostly horror stories about men. Yet many examples point to the common problem of hypocrisy among Christian men, even leaders. Many men go to special men's prayer meetings, plead Christ's cause in a variety of settings, and admonish others for their lack of spirituality, then sit in church and pray noble prayers—while right beside these powerfully praying men are wives who are brokenhearted over the way their husbands are treating them.

Ralph, for example, prayed at church functions that more people would realize their responsibility to the reputation of Christ by following through on their commitments to the church. But when his wife reminded him that time was running out for him to prepare his reports for the missionary committee's meeting, he chewed her out for nagging him. And no, he didn't have it ready on time, even though his wife reminded him many times.

It seems that many wives wish their husbands wouldn't wait until the last minute to meet their commitments. They hear from others about their husbands' failures, and they get embarrassed. They don't want others to say negative things about their husbands; they want their husbands to be respected. But when husbands refuse to accept insights from their wives, the potential for self-improvement is minimal.

If a man says he wants to understand more about being a responsible car owner, he will prove it by discovering more about car maintenance. He will welcome instructions and criticisms. If he gets angry when someone points out that his car needs tires and needs the oil and oil filter changed, and that it needs to be washed and waxed as well, we might well question how serious he is about being responsible. Likewise, if a man says he wants to be a responsible spiritual leader in his home, yet becomes angry when he is shown what he can do that will allow others to see Christ in him, it's likely that his sincerity will be questioned. That is exactly what happens with many wives. It is not surprising, then, that some wives wonder whether the spiritual activities at church are a hypocritical front.

MEN ARE OFTEN BLIND TO SHIFTING RESPONSIBILITIES

Willie and his wife, Dee, had been putting many hours into the new business he had begun. After a couple of years, the business had grown to the point that they had to hire an employee, purchase additional equipment, or double Willie's time at work to "get them over the hump." The very job they were working on could help finance hiring an employee or buying the necessary equipment—but not before the job was completed. So the decision was made to work extra hours.

I cautioned Willie that a wife can recognize that a growing business will require an excessive number of hours to bring it to the point that it will serve the family rather than have the family serve it. By the same token a wife can see when a business is increasing to the point that additional help is needed. She can also realize that finances won't allow for it yet. So she is willing to let her husband do what is necessary to get past the problems presented by growth.

Yet if a man continues to maintain the extra hours as his normal work pattern, his wife will regret having made the sacrifice to help him get ahead. Getting ahead was, after all, supposed to benefit them both. Yet, as often happens, he ends up being pleased at the progress of the company, while his wife may be extremely unhappy. Then his wife is heard saying, "His job is the 'other woman' in our marriage."

Dee was standing with us as I explained this business trap. Willie, very willing to take steps to make his marriage successful, said to his wife, "If you see me starting to give this business greater priority than our marriage, you be sure to let me know."

I immediately realized he was shifting the responsibility for improvement to his wife, so I said, "Willie, it is good that you're willing to try to avoid falling into the trap I've just described. But I wonder if you know what you just did to your wife?"

A questioning look spread over his face, and Willie asked, "No, what did I do?"

"You have just made your wife responsible for your success or failure," I said. "You just said, in essence: I'm turning this responsibility over to you, and if you don't let me know when I'm starting to do the wrong thing, it will be your fault."

"I did?" Willie exclaimed, looking first at me, then at his wife, and then back at me with a genuine look of concern on his face. His wife said, "He does that to me a lot of times."

To alert Willie that potential problems in his marriage were his responsibility, I said, "There are probably thousands of electrical signals being broadcast into the air at any given moment: radio, television, CB, telephone. The only thing that keeps you from knowing what those signals are is whether or not you are tuned in to them. In the same way, many things taking place in marriage are signals for you as husband. It is your responsibility as the leader of your home to be tuned in to what is going on around you. You must be cautious of the things that will damage your wife and your marriage."

Speaking metaphorically, the writer of Proverbs reminds us, "Be diligent to know the state of your flocks, and attend to your herds" (27:23).

MEN ARE OFTEN BLIND TO SHIFTING PRESSURE

Another area in which a man frequently shifts responsibility is asking his wife to call back an angry bill collector to tell him "what's what." He asks her to do this, even though he was late in paying the bill, and she offered many reminders.

Men often ask their wives to take care of mechanical-type errands for them, ignoring that their wives might fear being able to handle the task. For example, a husband might ask his wife to purchase some materials—and then get upset that she doesn't want to do it or complains that she doesn't feel competent. Her reluctance is often due to knowing that someone is going to ask her questions she can't answer. She also knows from past experiences what is going to happen when she comes back with the wrong item, even though she did her best. But does his heart go out to her? Usually not. Usually, she just feels rejection. This is a mild example of shifting responsibility, but a common one.

I remember the time my wife bought an item that did not prove to be a good purchase. She wanted to return it, but was too embarrassed to do it herself, so she asked me if I would take it back for her. She was very grateful when she learned that I was willing to do that for her.

In reality, Nancy's need was for more than my return of the item. She needed to feel certain that I was not upset with her, that I was even pleased to do this task for her. But even more important, God was not surprised by her request, and He was willing to let this serve as a test that would prove whether or not I would respond to Nancy in a Christlike manner.

I want my wife to know that she never needs to feel bad or guilty for asking me to help her when she feels pressured. I believe that honoring her means protecting her from whatever will be defeating to her and lightening her burden. As Jesus offers us relief, He provides an example that I am admonished by God to follow in behalf of my wife.

MEN ARE OFTEN BLIND TO WIVES' FAMILY NEEDS

Imagine the damage to the spirit of a wife who has spent several years working to put her husband through seminary only to discover that he was taught a set of priorities that would largely exclude her. He has been taught that he can place church members, the community to be won, and often even the church building and its care above her in importance. For some reason, seminary graduates often don't realize they are included in God's injunction through Paul in 1 Timothy 5:8: "But if anyone does not provide for his own, and especially for those of his household, he has denied the faith and is worse than an unbeliever."

That provision includes more than money. It also includes spiritual leadership, emotional care, understanding, comfort, compassion, and friendship. It means that a wife must have a very high priority in her husband's life—and I might add, especially during pregnancy and the months after the birth of a child.

The "using" of wives by husbands is not taking place solely at seminaries. Many wives put their husbands through secular and Christian colleges as a type of investment in the family's future. Yet after all those years of pressure and sacrifice, wives often discover that their feelings and wishes about family plans and goals carry little weight once their husbands graduate and get into the workforce. These husbands are then surprised when their marriages disintegrate several years after they get "real" jobs.

As you can see, a woman determines for herself if a man has Christlike character from a variety of life's experiences. But more than anything, a wife determines her husband's Christlike character by his willingness to let her participate in his life. More often than not, that means that her husband is willing to be held answerable even to his wife as the Holy Spirit alerts her to his character flaws.

Too many husbands, even in our supposedly enlightened generation, reveal the natural tendency to think of themselves as the boss or ruler of the marriage. This attitude is reinforced by the popular notion in Christian circles that a woman's only requirements in marriage are to be a silent, obedient, submissive wife. And that submission, regardless of the conditions, better be with a gracious pleasantness, or she is not a good Christian woman. Implicit in this attitude is that wives are to be flawless—while husbands excuse their behavior by various rationalizations, none of which will hold up when they appear before the great Judge of the universe. God is not deceived by spiritual rationalizations of inexcusable behavior in the home by self-styled Christian leaders.

We read in Proverbs 11:29: "He who troubles his own house will inherit the wind." That's exactly what is happening in Christian marriages all over the world where men are unwilling to let God use their wives to bring about accountability for Christlike character. No woman will permit herself to be continuously set up for spiritual, emotional, and physical defeat and do nothing about it. The staggering climb in the divorce rate among Christians is proof of that. Divorce is not the answer—Christlike behavior by men is, and it will win back alienated and disaffected wives.

You may be saying, "I'm willing to listen, but my wife keeps saying I am not listening. What can I do?" The next chapter provides the answer.

11

THE FINE ART OF LISTENING

No matter which way you look at it, marriage is a commitment—a long-term commitment. In some ways, it is like the commitment required when one invests money in today's mutual fund market. You don't get involved in mutual funds unless you are willing to stick with them over the long haul to get the long-range benefits. The chances for success in the short range are less likely, since there are so many volatile ups and downs over the short term.

Marriage, like the mutual fund market, needs to be regarded with the long-range mentality. Since marriage, like the short-term market, can have so many ups and downs, it is difficult to measure success by today's market value alone. If you recognize the absolute necessity for investing in marriage for the long term, and are committed to persevering through the ups and downs, then, like mutual funds, it will pay off with enjoyable dividends.

HOW PARTNERSHIPS WORK

Mutual funds have investment managers. During the period they manage your investment, many decisions are made—which companies to stay with, which companies are performing better, and how much should be switched over to those companies to gain the most benefits. Once you've made your choice about which mutual funds you are going to invest with, you stick with them and subject yourself to the managers' advice and suggestions. You communicate and work together for the benefit of both parties.

Now think of the long-term commitment you made to your wife. Doesn't the potential for improvement in your investment (your marriage relationship) make it worth working together? Doesn't it make sense to submit yourself to more than one (your own) frame of reference for success? Isn't it wise to use good management techniques, no matter if the business is about money or marriage?

Yet astonishingly few men consider marriage an investment that could use the same sound judgment they apply to business. They don't think about give-and-take communication in marriage—in which they anticipate listening to their wives—because they don't realize it's a part of what will enhance the value of their long-term investment.

To help you understand the importance of approaching marriage with a more carefully thought-through investment strategy, consider another analogy. You have developed a promising new product and believe it represents an unusual business opportunity. So you are looking for a partner with money to help you launch it. You hope to find an investor who will believe in you, your product, and your ability to earn significant profits over time.

Let's say you find such an investor. Before he agreed to the partnership signing on the dotted line, wouldn't you expect him to fully investigate everything about your product? Wouldn't he question your assumptions related to your cost factors, the projected size of the market, and your marketing plans? You would expect the investor to get into all kinds of minute detail, trying to make sure there were no surprises because of something you forgot to consider. And if after investing in your company as a co-owner, the investor saw you doing things that endangered his investment, wouldn't you expect him to exercise the right to challenge your assumptions, your conclusions, and even your operating method and budget?

LIKE BUSINESS, LIKE MARRIAGE

Let's transfer that scenario to your marriage. Let's say you are considering a partnership, investing in the most beautiful, capable, fun woman you've ever met. You're convinced she could be God's gift to you, and you're looking at thirty to sixty years or so of potential enjoyment because of your investment. Wouldn't it seem wise to ask a lot of questions of your potential partner, validating compatibility, discovering her strengths and weaknesses, examining what she projects for the future, so that you can see if those projections will be mutually enjoyable?

Would it not make sense for you to imagine your wife also as a coinvestor in the marriage? With that in mind, does it not make sense that she would want to get to know you better by asking you questions, by examining you with regard to your attitudes, your behavior in a restaurant, at church, in all your associations? After all, her "fortunes" are going to be tied up in how successfully you conduct yourself.

Carrying that analogy a little further, would it not be reasonable, having made the partnership commitment (of marriage) *as co-owner,* that your wife might want to have some say-so in how the "business" is being managed? If she saw things happening that caused her to have questions, if she saw you mismanaging the relationship, shouldn't she have the right *as co-owner* to ask some pointed questions? And no matter how embarrassing the questions might be, wouldn't she be well within her rights *as co-owner* to expect answers?

As co-owner, wouldn't her opinions and solutions merit as much consideration as yours? It's quite possible that your co-owner (wife) may have some good ideas for maximizing your mutual investment. Following the analogy, even though you as the producer-of-the-ideas person may have better ideas about production, she as the financial person may have better ideas about what multiplies money. Representing two different categories these two people in a business environment are different persons and should value and draw upon each other's special capacities.

Although a husband might say his wife represents his most valuable investment, too often he treats her like that's not true. Certainly, her investment counsel is unwanted. She is expected to be totally supportive of her husband's vision for the future and undergird his risk taking as pastor, community leader, businessman, or whatever without the freedom to comment, discuss, question, or sometimes even know what his plans are—let alone be a significant part of them.

I've watched self-assured men, pillars in the Christian community, get nervous and flustered at the thought of letting their wives ask questions and make suggestions about ways they as men can improve in Christian leadership. They muzzle their wives with accusations of not being biblically submissive if they exercise their role of commenting, discussing, or questioning the attitudes and actions of their husbands.

I've lost thousands of dollars by making financial decisions that Nancy disagreed with. Those were losses for her, too, but that didn't matter to me. I was unwilling to listen to her. Some of the money I lost when we were first married was her money, for she earned it herself. But that didn't make any difference to me, either. Yet I can think of only one time when her idea lost us any money. Those memories cause me great heartache now.

King Solomon didn't feel endangered by questions. In all of his majesty he didn't think he was above being questioned by a woman. He welcomed all of the queen of Sheba's questions. We read in 1 Kings 10:1–3:

Now when the queen of Sheba heard of the fame of Solomon concerning the name of the LORD, *she came to test him with hard questions.* . . . And when she came to Solomon, she spoke with him about all that was in her heart. So Solomon answered all her questions; there was nothing so difficult for the king that he could not explain it to her (italics mine).

"But," you say, "I'm no Solomon. God didn't give me the gift of wisdom. My wife can really grill me, and that destroys my self-confidence." The question is not whether you can stand up under the grilling, but whether you see God at work. Is your failure to understand your wife's needs for reassurance or clarification being exposed? Do you know how to meet her needs as Christ would, or do you get rattled?

LISTENING AND RETAINING

We men can't seem to retain husband-wife information. We convey the idea that we are totally without the capacity to carry on a beneficial relationship conversation. We can't remember what they wanted us to pick up for them at the grocery store or what we were supposed to tell the teacher when we dropped off the kids at school! That's another reason wives say, "You just don't listen!"

And yet it's amazing how many details most men will accumulate about sports. We listen to sportscasts by the hour, remembering the answers to thousands of trivia questions—like which player overran second base and was thrown out in a championship series—and we know which team won the 1937 World Series and in how many games. But ask a man what his wife's favorite perfume is, and he probably goes blank. He is unlikely to know what her favorite color is, even though he has seen her in it countless times.

Maybe the following will sound familiar. I come home, and as a passing comment, I ask, "How was your day?"

"It was rotten," Nancy replies.

I respond with my courtesy question: "Oh? Why's that?"

She complains, "The kids were whiny, and I couldn't get the laundry or dishes done because I was giving them so much attention. On top of everything else the dog was digging in the flower bed."

Although I'm hearing all this, my concentration is either on relaxing or doing a project. So I'm thinking, *Do I really need to know about this stuff?* But I don't want to get in trouble for not being a good husband, so I, because I'm so noble, patiently wait for her to finish.

On other occasions, in situations like this, Nancy probably would accuse me, saying, "You're not listening to me." And I would react with, "I am, too!" Then I'm likely to prove it by repeating what she just said. Yes, I was hearing what she said, but I was listening only with my physical ears. I was not listening with my heart. Remember, I said my concentration was elsewhere—my heart was really on relaxing or getting busy on a particular project. I was not emotionally involved in what she had experienced during the day. I was not listening with my heart.

Wives have a God-designed sense about whether we are listening or not in order to *help* us (there's that word again) learn how to relate to them from our hearts. But not just to listen to our wives—they are the training ground for learning to listen from our hearts so we can also listen to God from our hearts.

So what is listening with my heart and getting emotionally involved? That happens when as my wife is telling me about her day, I identify with her. I start to think, *You know, that must really be exasperating, to have the kids whining and hanging on you and tugging at you.* And I start imagining kids hanging on to me: *Daddy, Daddy, Daddy. . . .* Then I imagine the dog in the flower bed, and my wife thinking, *Oh, great! Just what I need. Ken is really going to be mad when he finds out about this.*

At this stage in my recapitulation of her feelings and reactions, I'm really feeling for her, thinking, *No wonder she's down.* I can't help empathizing with her, and I'm attentively communicating my understanding by my comments, my attitude, my looks, and my body language. That will minister to any woman's spirit.

Based on the guys I've worked with over the years, I can imagine some men being ready to throw up by now. All that touchy-feely stuff is too much. A lot of men are quite content with this attitude: "Just give me the facts, ma'am." If that's you, I can guarantee that your wife has said, "You don't listen to me." And you've been exasperated because, like me, you know you could have repeated word for word everything she said. But when wives say that we are not listening to them, they mean, "You don't respond to me from your heart with understanding or empathy. You are not feeling with me."

Despite the so-called gender revolution in which men and women are supposed to have been freed from things being categorized as "male" or "female," most men have a terrible time identifying with their wives' feelings. Men have been taught for generations that emotions are feminine and that women who are emotionally expressive are more of a pain than anything else. This thinking has allowed men to avoid developing their own emotional understanding, thus leaving them unable to identify with and respond to the emotions of almost anyone, especially their wives.

Have we forgotten that our Lord and Master, Jesus Christ, felt deep emotions and was able to share in the emotions of others? Remember the scene as Jesus approached Bethany, having received word that Lazarus had died? First, Martha ran to meet Jesus, and He responded with great warmth and emotion even as she chided Him, "If You had been here, my brother would not have died" (John 11:21). He continued to respond empathetically, "Your brother will rise again" (John 11:23).

So then Martha ran to tell Mary that Jesus had come, and Mary rushed out to meet Him. She also chided Him, "Lord, if You had been here, my brother would not have died." John reported, "When Jesus saw her weeping . . . He groaned in the spirit and was troubled" (John 11:33). Because He cared, Jesus then asked where they laid the body, and they invited Him to see where it was. At that point we read the poignant words, "Jesus wept" (John 11:35). The apostle John revealed that Jesus experienced another wave of deep emotion as He came to the tomb: "Again groaning in Himself" (John 11:38).

Yes, Jesus had lost a dear friend, and He was grieving over that. But it is clear in the exchange between Him and Martha and Mary that He also felt their grief. He was able to communicate at a level that ministered deeply to their spirits.

So if our goal is to be Christlike, then we have to uncover our feelings, uncork the bottle, as it were, so that the emotions God gave us as part of our original equipment can be revived. Only when we do that will we begin to communicate at the heart level with our wives.

RECOGNIZING OUR EMOTIONS

I mentioned earlier in the book that one of my most challenging tasks is helping a man see the need to award high value to emotions. It's extremely difficult for him to recognize the important role emotions play in spiritual leadership.

Most men are not able to interact with their wives on an emotional level. A man will never recognize his wife's emotions and validate them if he does not recognize his own emotions and validate them. Before a man can understand, value, and honor his wife's emotions, he must understand, value, and honor his own emotions. Otherwise he will never communicate with his wife, heart to heart. I'm absolutely convinced he will not be able to communicate with God on a heart-to-heart level, either.

The following is typical of what I hear from men whose wives have given up on the relationship and decided to leave. (This separation results from the fact that the husband is emotionally dysfunctional.)

A husband comes into my office and reports that his wife is leaving him. I ask him, "Why is she leaving you?"

He tells me (as almost all do), "I don't know."

When I ask him, "Why do you *think* she is leaving you?" he responds (as most do), "I asked her why, and she just says, 'I'm not going to tell you again.' And she wouldn't tell me!"

I inquire, "Do you realize she has tried to tell you?"

"When?" he questions.

So I continue, "Have you ever heard her say things like, 'Why do I try to talk with you? You always end up ramming my words down my throat'? Or have you ever heard her say, 'Oh, what difference does it make anyway? You don't care'? Or maybe, 'Why do I bother to get in an argument with you? You always end up being right'?"

Surprised, he answers, "As a matter of fact, I've heard her say all of those things."

I inform him, "She's been trying to tell you what's wrong, but you don't know how to listen to her heart. You just focus on her words."

Wives are always trying to communicate, so from the first days of marriage they start discovering whether or not we know how to listen from our hearts to their hearts.

INDICATORS OF UNSOLVED COMMUNICATION PROBLEMS

The end of a marriage, whether on amicable terms or in anger, is always due to unresolved problems. Poking around in the ruins of a marriage will reveal problems here, some there, more in other areas. I'll discuss some indicators of unsolved communication problems (which are actually an inability to listen as Christ would).

1. The Same Arguments Resurface

Consider the wife who hates to ride in the car with her husband. Despite years and years of expressing her fears, his driving habits still make her arrive at their destination with a knot in her stomach. Yet he rationalizes her fears away, concluding, "She's just high strung. There's nothing wrong with my driving!"

Or what about a wife's not-so-secret attitudes toward certain friends? When her husband is with them, his personality changes. She never can discuss it with him because he gets defensive and denies that his attitude toward her changes and that he gets arrogantly "macho" joining them in putting down women.

Maybe your wife brings up the event that happened at your wedding, the old girlfriend you went to see after getting engaged, a financial investment you made without letting her know, commitments you made in her behalf without checking with her first, the way you never let her know what you do with money, an affair you had, and on and on.

From where I sit, all her constant reminders are meant to help us recognize that we have not yet dealt with the real problems. If we had dealt with them, they would be resolved and not brought up as proof (from God) that we need much more understanding before our leadership is Christlike, since Christ knew (and knows) how to bring healing to relationship problems.

2. Faults or Character Flaws Are Brought Up Repeatedly

In the Christian community, when wives continuously bring up their husbands' faults, they are typically viewed as nagging, unforgiving women. They are wrongly believed to be women who enjoy demeaning their husbands.

But I've found that this is not a legitimate conclusion. Wives who constantly bring up their husbands' faults, privately or publicly, are on a crusade. They have never felt their husbands' approval. In one way or another the wives feel constantly put down, criticized, scolded, or treated like inferior beings. So they are trying to say, "You think you are so perfect, mister, always criticizing me. Well, you're not, and here's my proof (with the list of his past and current faults)."

Even if they were critical of authority before they were married, they need to be healed of their wounded spirits. They need to be shown their worth. They need to hear words of praise and kindness. They need to understand how valuable they are. And they surely must be valuable—God sent His Son to die for them!

If a wife did not have a critical tongue before she met her husband, then he is the one responsible for making her feel devalued. As a result, she is trying to balance the scales by proving that he is not so perfect. So she recites her list of his flaws.

Usually, the husband who has a critical wife doesn't know how to minister to her. He joins the ranks of those who condemn her. She senses the negative perception of her and increases her defensiveness, intensifying her efforts to point out his imperfections.

Before things will change, the attitudes illustrated in this relationship are going to require some serious reevaluation. It will require a complete renewal of a man's listening techniques, learning to translate his wife's negative comments into positive insights. And as he develops the capacity to reinterpret what the attitudes represent in the way of positive insights, he will need to follow up his new translation by expressing his new understanding to his wife in the form of character quality praises.

That was a mouthful! Let me give examples.

When this husband's wife is reciting her list of his faults, he must believe that God is not caught off guard, that He is not unaware of what she is saying and therefore unable to use her in her husband's life. With this in mind, a husband must have two objectives:

   a) Give credibility to your wife's complaints. Discover what God wants to teach you.

- If she says you're a liar, is it because you don't recognize how you are negatively affecting her spirit, and so you evaluate and express her sentiments from your perspective? She hears your expressions as denial on your part, that you are saying that the things she is talking about never happened. And God wants you to realize the truth about how you do not understand her as Christ would!

- If she says you're not a Christian, is it because God wants to show you through her that there is hypocrisy in your life? You're not very convincing to her (much less God) when you condemn her for her shortcomings, since she knows you better than anyone else. She is not convinced you've got it together enough to point a finger at anyone. And God wants you to "seek first the kingdom of God and His righteousness" because He *knows* you're not! You let Satan fool you into being distracted from your need to be Christlike while you busily point the finger of blame away from yourself.

b) *As you hear negative comments, learn how to identify the positive quality those comments can also represent. Develop the capacity to reinterpret negatives into positives.*

- Your wife's recital of a long list of your faults also demonstrates a positive quality. She has a good memory for details. Of course, you don't say to her while she is reciting your faults, "Boy, do you have a good memory!" Anybody could see that *those words* could be interpreted as sarcastic (at least I would hope they could).

  You could say, after she is finished, "I know that God wants me to become more Christlike. He wants me to change every detail of my life that is not like that of His Son. But He knows how unlikely it is that I will see and remember all those areas in my life that need changing. So He has placed in my life someone who has an excellent memory. I want to learn how to be more appreciative of that fact. I want to learn more about the character God wants to build in my life through your help. I want to value you as He does."

- You can use this same procedure with all the negative labels you've used:

  Nagging = motivational reminders.

  Nit-picking = high standards.

  Pointing out hypocrisy = concern for righteousness.

These are only a few examples. But you must believe you are not being Christlike when you are condemning (John

8:2–11). You must be sincere about learning to see God at work in your life and change from accusing your wife to valuing what God is teaching you through her.

3. They Cannot Agree on Priorities, Including Those Related to Work

How would you respond if I asked you, "What are your wife's five top priorities?" That is foreign thinking to most men. It's no wonder men wouldn't have listened well for the answer; they wouldn't have thought to ask the question.

If husbands have not thought to ask their wives about their priorities, what are the chances that any conversation about priorities has ever been held? That husbands would have let their wives know what their own priorities are?

Only when a man sits down with someone (I hope, his wife) and seriously discusses his priorities does he recognize a need for more purposeful priorities. Not having given serious thought to priorities earlier, he may not know that he has unrecognized, deeper priorities that are underlying much of what he does.

Priorities that are not recognized are likely to cause misunderstandings and lead to breakdowns in marriage relationships. Let's say, for example, that a husband is working long hours to endear himself to the boss and gain a promotion. But his wife thinks he is working late because his company demands so much overtime. And he seems to be willing to do that since she never hears him complain. So she resents both him and the company.

Or a wife recognizes their financial resources are not enough to get the living room couches she would love to have, so she gets a job. In his confusion, the husband thinks she is working because she is bored at home or wants to purchase luxuries he cannot supply. He concludes, "She thinks I'm inadequate."

This failure to genuinely seek to discover each other's priorities, and then to establish unified priorities for the family, affects the husband-wife relationship and also relationships in the community, at church, and on the job.

4. They Don't Agree on How to Manage the Children

Perhaps you have heard a husband or wife reject responsibility by saying of their unruly children, "Don't look at me. They're your kids." That statement is an indicator of disharmony over how to discipline children. Children quickly recognize when Dad and Mom do not agree on the same standards in the home, when they do not agree on priorities in the family, when they do not agree on what is appropriate discipline—and when discipline needs to be applied. They also recognize the opportunity to pit the parents against each other, leaving them to their own ways. And the more they experience the tension between their parents, the more undisciplined or unruly the children become.

This problem points to a lack of communication, for the couple should have discussed these things long before children came along. If, however, a husband recognizes the problem of disharmony and approaches it with responsible, Christlike attitudes (not with blame and accusations), the reduction of tensions will make it possible to establish proper priorities at all levels in the home, including discipline of children.

But this again is going to require leadership committed to intense listening for understanding, since each parent has specific reasons for reflecting on parenthood as he or she does.

5. Persistent, Offensive Personal Habits

A Christlike husband who seeks to truly understand his wife and minister to her spirit will become keenly conscious of personal habits that irritate his wife. She will have the liberty to share her feelings with him.

If, however, a husband is not willing to tune in to how his habits affect his wife, he will not make any real efforts to change them. Initially, she might tell him what is bothering her, but when she sees no efforts to change, she concludes he is not interested in how that bothers her: "He's not going to change." She may try to emotionally separate herself from the irritation. But it can still be the cause of a wife's silence or angry outbursts when she is emotionally uptight.

We all joke about how differently we squeeze the toothpaste tube or where men toss their socks and underwear. More serious, though, are habits at the table when guests are present or after mealtimes when wives need help with children. As long as men consider themselves the boss, the king in the castle, it's easy to think, *It's not my problem that she gets so irritated and frustrated over such little things,* and as a result refuse to seriously consider changing.

Once God convicts a man about Christlikeness, and he begins to care about how he is affecting his wife, it's amazing how much more attention he will pay to the need for building oneness of spirit. He and his wife will develop similar priorities—to achieve Christlikeness.

6. The Sexual Relationship Is Not Satisfying

Okay, we all know that when sex is not good or mutually satisfactory, there is trouble in the marriage. Or do we? What if the husband thinks it's great, but his wife (for whatever reason) isn't being honest? She is unable or unwilling to express her true opinion. We'll deal more specifically with the sexual relationship in a later chapter. But at this juncture there may be a need to point out that true sexual satisfaction is the result of total communication.

Romance is not merely bringing home a dozen roses and handing them over to the wife upon arrival at home, though that can be a small part of what encourages a wife's response to her husband. Romance includes being cheerful when walking through the entrance of your home, noticing the children and occupying them while the wife is getting dinner, and helping with the dishes. Consider these added attractions:

• Stopping off at the store and buying her a card for no particular reason

- Setting out a couple of chairs in the backyard and getting a couple of cups of coffee ready so you can sit down and relax together
- Hearing a piece of music on the radio and standing up to invite your "best girl" to have a dance with you
- Using deodorant
- Taking care of bad breath
- Holding her hand whenever you get a chance (and making sure you get many chances)
- Occasionally preparing dinner for her.

The mood is set by thoughtful and caring attitudes and actions every day.

Will you have to put out more effort and become attuned to this kind of thinking to improve communication with your wife?

HARMONY COMES IN MANY FORMS

I was doing respectably well in my sign company, but I felt that I should be doing better. Something was wrong, but I couldn't quite seem to put my finger on it. I voiced my puzzlement one day to Nancy.

"I know exactly what it is!" she offered. How could she be so certain, so fast? Because I was just learning to value her input, her speedy reply almost made me feel threatened—like I must really be dumb to struggle with this for so long and she can instantly come up with the solution. She continued, "There's just one thing you need to do to increase your business. It will gain you more respect as a businessman and more respect from your customers. It will probably even allow you to command higher prices for your work because you will be seen as a classy outfit."

Man! I'm thinking. *What is this one thing—go back to college for six years?* (Just a little bit of smart-aleck cynicism there.) Curious but cautious, I asked, "What?"

Although I didn't recognize it then, I can now in my mind see her thinking over ways to say what she wanted to tell me. She knew it was going to be something uncomfortable for me to hear—it would be outside my comfort zone. She responded to my question, "You know how you wear a T-shirt and jeans to work . . ."

I interrupted, "Yeah. Because I get paint all over and I don't care if they get dirty."

She asked, "Can I finish my answer?"

I nodded, "Yeah. Go ahead."

I wasn't able to enjoy her enthusiasm yet. She started again, "If you were to wear slacks and a dressy sports shirt . . ."

I interrupted again, "Do you know what that will cost? And what will I do when I catch a run with my thumb and go to wipe it on my pants? Paint spots on slacks will look worse than on jeans."

Raising her eyebrow because I interrupted again, she suggested, "You can buy slacks at the Goodwill store for pennies and you can hang a rag out of your pocket for wiping runs on. I'm telling you, it will make a world of difference if you will do this. Can't you just try it? Go to the Goodwill store and see how much it will cost. It can't hurt, can it?"

I reluctantly agreed to try it. The more I thought about it, the more it did make sense. But what would my Levi's think? Would they feel abandoned? Other equally reasonable, defensive thoughts went through my mind.

We went to the Goodwill store. I found a nice pair of slacks for $1.35, a good-looking dressy sports shirt for $.35, and even a button-down-the-front sweater for $.50. If my math is not too far off, it was a total investment of $2.20 for this experiment.

She was right. Existing customers made comments like, "Boy, do you look professional." When I went into offices to meet potential clients and give bids, their secretaries treated me more respectfully. The people I quoted prices to didn't try to get me to reduce prices like I was some kind of cheap labor. When I went to buy materials, the clerks treated me more respectfully, saying stuff like, "May I help you, sir?" and, "Yes, sir," and "No, sir." Clients paid their bills more promptly.

I'm so glad I listened to Nancy (and may I take advantage of this opportunity to say again, "Thanks, hon!").

Early on, I didn't have a clue that there are bonuses for this kind of commitment. The bonus for you of challenging yourself to become an authority on understanding the messages, spoken and unspoken, your wife is trying to convey will be a relationship that is greater than anything you can even imagine. Because no matter what your fondest dreams are about a marriage, they are nothing compared to what God has in mind for you when your ways please God—and being Christlike pleases God!

A CALL TO PEACEMAKING

In the famous passage we call the beatitudes, Jesus said, "Blessed are the peacemakers, for they shall be called sons of God" (Matt. 5:9). That's what I wanted to be, a peacemaker, when I set out to become Christlike in my relationship with Nancy. I knew that to achieve that goal, I would have to study the expressions of my wife, to know her disposition almost as well as I knew myself.

Being a peacemaker also provides living examples for the Christian community. And heaven knows that there is a need in the Christian community for men who are willing to lay down their lives for their wives as Christ did for the church. We will devote all of chapter 14 to more of the benefits derived from being Christlike husbands. In the meantime, chapter 12 will provide insights about the freedom we gain by becoming transparent.

12

GETTING OUR HEARTS TOGETHER

What would happen if you gave your wife the freedom to express exactly how she feels about you and what you are doing? Would you feel threatened? Would you be afraid she might intimidate you?

I've suggested a number of times that men's unwillingness to give their wives the freedom to say exactly how they feel is at the heart of relationship disagreements. I consider it a major reason why wives develop emotional and physical ailments in marriage—and often a key reason they walk out one day, much to the surprise of their husbands. They are finished with living as hypocrites because of the muzzles their husbands have placed on them.

Initially, I was taken aback to discover that some men are threatened by the amount of freedom I give my wife. They reacted strongly when I suggested to their friends, to members of their congregation, the value of giving their wives the freedom to help them recognize where they, the husbands, needed to improve.

Why should husbands have such negative attitudes toward the women with whom they became one in marriage? Here's what men say:

"You can't give a woman that kind of freedom!"

"Some women will abuse such freedom!"

"She'll just make life miserable for me!"

These responses are symptoms of a common malady among men, the desire to be boss, authority, leader, positions such men claim for themselves as their birthright. Yet being born male doesn't give anyone that role, and it certainly is not biblical. Spiritual leadership roles must be earned, or they mean nothing. People may fear a self-styled leader because of his power, but they may not respect him as leader.

I am *not* suggesting that a wife *demand* the right to express concerns to her husband, even though some men could benefit from that. Instead, I believe it is biblical for the husband to ask his wife to help him see himself through her eyes, to help him think something through from a different perspective. By now you are aware of how easily men overlook their imperfections while pointing out another's imperfections, so that a second opinion is most desirable.

Christians in Rome were afflicted by the myopia so common among men I meet. Paul wrote to them, "Therefore you are inexcusable, O man, whoever you are who judge, for in whatever you judge another you condemn yourself; for you who judge practice the same things" (Rom. 2:1). The Christians in Rome apparently loved pointing out the frailties and foibles of others while tolerating sin in their own lives (maybe that's why Paul didn't mention anyone in Rome who stood by him when he was imprisoned). We as men have perfected that kind of hypocrisy, criticizing someone else for something we are doing—though often we do it unknowingly.

I grant you, letting your wife put the binoculars on you and isolate genuine weaknesses, even sin, is not like taking a pleasant trip to the zoo. The prospect may cause even more jitters than the annual review on the job. The danger of a supervisor out to get you is too real to laugh off the possibility. And if you have never let your wife suggest your frailties to you, you may get a real drenching the first time. If, however, your response is like that of Christ or the martyr Stephen, there will be a dramatic reduction in the number of critical comments over time. Your wife will also likely become open to your suggesting some things to her that you have not dared tackle because of the possibility of fireworks. It's amazing what a difference personal transparency makes in a relationship!

Now maybe, just maybe, the reality will be a lot less painful than you imagine. If you've got a piece of paper and a pencil handy, list the areas of your life that your wife might tackle the first time you invite her to suggest improvements in your attitude and behavior. When you've put down the five top areas she could conceivably tackle, put yourself in her place, trying to imagine how she might think. Wouldn't your wife be so taken aback at your audacity in suggesting she indicate areas in your life needing improvement, at the extraordinary change in your attitude, that she would tread softly in case what seems only too good to be true might vanish like a mirage in the desert?

A VESTED INTEREST

Just put yourself in your wife's shoes. Doesn't she have a vested interest in the success and reputation of you as her husband? Is she not building a life around you? After all, she has invested some heavy-duty emotional energy in making the partnership work for as many years as you have been married. Aside from you, she has the most to gain or lose if you make it or end up a failure. Even if she is successful as an executive in a national company, her relationship with you is the most important thing in her life.

So if you have not made it part of your marriage relationship to listen to your wife in as many situations as possible, you are setting yourself up for real difficulty in the long term. A wife will go to incredible lengths to keep a marriage alive, but there does come a breaking point if a husband does not undertake corrective measures.

A WOMAN'S UNIQUE ABILITY TO THINK AHEAD

I have discovered that women have a fantastic capacity to think ahead in marriage and home-related situations. Women have this unique ability to imagine what might happen in a given situation—and then come to conclusions about what to do to take care of potential problems. So the husband who does not regularly talk things over with his wife—and let her freely talk things over with him—will find that she draws conclusions without his reflections. Because her thinking may be based on inadequate information, for which he could have compensated, her decisions may seem ill-advised to the husband.

At that point the husband may find himself reacting negatively as he is being asked to act upon her request without the benefit of their having interacted. Neither would he know how important the issue is to his wife. So he reacts coolly or with disgust, and she responds in anger at being demeaned. But he shouldn't blame her. He should point the finger of blame at himself as a husband who has not drawn his wife into his confidence enough to generate trust and active interaction.

THE REASON BEHIND THE REQUEST

Getting at the reason behind a request can be a real detective game if you have not been actively developing the capacity to discover what is in the mind of your wife. Even educated guesses will not prove to the wife that the husband has a commitment to understand her.

Let's start with a scenario all men can relate to. Let's say Bill Jones has been living on 712 Ocean Street for so long that the mailman would recognize him if they met in the hardware store. He would say, "Hi, Bill, how's it going?" But then one day Bill gets a letter addressed to Joe Smith, 712 Ocean Street. Bill meets him the next day and says, "Hey, you delivered this letter to us by mistake." The mailman looks at the address and says, "No, I didn't."

Bill is too committed to his position to give up that easily. "But I'm not Joe Smith, and you know I'm not Joe Smith. Why did you deliver the letter to my house?" he says.

The mailman is unmoved. "Isn't this address 712 Ocean Street? If it is, I delivered this letter to the right address," he says.

We'll leave that argument, for it could go on for hours. The issue is that they will not find the right solution to the problem because they are arguing over the wrong problem. If the sender were to change the name—or the address—the problem would be solved.

Now if Bill's wife came out the door while they were having the argument, she would say, "Hey, Joe Smith lives four houses down. It's the house with the green shutters."

Why could she solve the problem? She has superior knowledge of her neighborhood that lets her solve the real problem rather than argue over the wrong problem.

Now let's get with a real case in my discipling ministry. Harry had been trying to convince me that his wife, Millie, was trying to bankrupt him with her spending habits (a not-so-uncommon, though mistaken, male fear). I had been trying to help him see how critical, condemning, and harmful that thinking is to a marriage.

One day while Harry and I were talking, Millie called my office and asked for Harry. Although I couldn't track the conversation, I could see that Harry became upset very quickly. He closed the conversation by saying curtly, "I'll call you back and let you know.

"Okay, here's a perfect example of what I've been trying to tell you," he said as he turned to me. "She *is* trying to bankrupt me. That was Millie, and she wanted to know if she could go down and buy a new set of wrought iron patio furniture. I don't understand how she can even ask the question. She knows we don't have the money for it. You said I should learn to listen to her, so what am I supposed to do now? Do I tell her yes or no?"

Harry, I realized, had misunderstood the phrase, "Listen to her." He thought it meant, "Do as she says." So I said to him, "Listen to her means, 'Stop placing little or no value on her words.' Concentrate on what she is saying. Learn to hear what her feelings are saying—not only what her mouth is saying. There are more solutions available to you in this situation than just a yes or no answer."

He said almost defiantly, "Well, you'll have to show me."

Harry was so emotionally caught up in his prejudice toward his wife that he was not free to think of a creative solution to her request. So I explained that if he could know what his wife were thinking, he would be able to avoid misunderstandings that can cause fights. Focusing on understanding her would give him the freedom to discover solutions.

"I think I know what is going through Millie's mind," I said. "I think I know what makes her feel she needs to buy that furniture. You want to hear what I think is in her mind?"

Sounding skeptical, he said, "Yeah." In that one word and his body language, I felt as if he were also saying, "You think you know her better than I do!" So I said, "We've been meeting with the couples in this workshop at your house since Monday, right? And we will be meeting the rest of this week, including Friday, from one o'clock to six o'clock, won't we?"

"Uh-huh," he agreed.

"So I think Millie," I continued, "as an excellent hostess is thinking ahead. After the meeting Friday, we're going to have a potluck dinner. The weather has been beautiful, so she thinks, *Wouldn't it be nice if our guests could have a nice place outside to enjoy their dinner?*"

He was listening now, and when I was finished, he asked, "You really think that's what she is thinking?"

Feeling confident, I said, "I sure do."

He took a deep breath, held it for a second, then exhaled noisily. Then he said impatiently, "Okay, so what now? Am I supposed to buy it or not?"

He still was not quite with me. He needed to think it through even further. So I asked him, "If I've correctly figured out what Millie is thinking, then how long will she need that furniture?"

"I suppose just one day," he answered, though I sensed he was also saying, "Okay, I'll play your little game."

"Okay," I said, "since it is not practical to buy patio furniture for just one day, are there other ways to work this out?"

"What? Rent it?" he challenged.

I was not about to suggest the solution directly, so I asked, "Do you know of anyone who has patio furniture that's not being used?"

His eyes lit up as he joined in the search for a suitable solution.

"Yeah," he said slowly, and I could see his mental wheels turning as he visualized a solution that would make everyone happy. "I've got a good friend who owns a motel, and he has all kinds of patio furniture. Shall I call Millie and tell her?"

Now Harry was involved. But he needed to discover more about solving problems. I wanted him to look farther down the road, so I asked, "If you call her right now, what will be her first thought?" He looked puzzled, so I asked, "Won't she want to know if it is available for her use? Let's first get your plan together so you will have a legitimate solution to present to her. Can you call your friend to see if your suggestion is feasible?"

Harry picked up the phone and called his friend. He discovered that his friend was in the middle of moving. He had a beautiful set of wrought iron patio furniture that Harry could use. In fact, his friend asked if Harry could keep the furniture at his house until he had completed this move—and then return it to his new home. I could see Harry getting more and more excited during the conversation. When he hung up, he was so excited that he couldn't dial Millie fast enough.

The old "wanna fight" attitude permeated his voice when she answered. He had made the plans on the basis of my suggestion of what Millie was thinking, so he was not sure she would respond positively to his solution. But when he told her what he had arranged, she was ecstatic. And I could hear his voice changing while he talked with her, gradually becoming calm and friendly. When he hung up the phone, he said, "I can't believe this. Just fifteen minutes ago I was boiling mad at my wife, and here I am completely over it and even feeling good toward her."

He paused for a moment and said, "What I can't get over is how you knew what Millie was thinking!"

"I learned that to discover how women might think, I had to learn how my wife thinks. You can do the same thing," I said to him.

Harry is doing the same thing now. He has learned what it means to listen and then lay down his life for his wife. In the process he has learned to discover what is in the mind of a woman.

Recently, I heard that someone who knew how bad Harry and Millie's marriage had been had said to them, "It's one thing to see an individual man or woman who has peace, but it's really something to see a couple who have genuine peace in their marriage, especially since we know how close you two were to a divorce in the past."

The friend added, "Even though my wife and I have been considered a happy Christian couple by others, we see that we need and want what you have."

Isn't that what Christ meant when He said, "Let your light so shine before men, that they may see your good works and glorify your Father in heaven" (Matt. 5:16)?

The solution to the problem between Harry and Millie came through understanding. And understanding comes only through an investment of time and the willingness to determine what is causing the lack of understanding. That means a husband has to have such a strong desire for understanding that his wife begins to trust him enough to share her heart with him. She has to feel it is safe to open her heart to him. She sees that he wants to learn to care about her as much as he cares about himself, fulfilling the apostle Paul's challenge in Ephesians 5:33: "Nevertheless let each one of you in particular so love his own wife as himself."

You see, it usually isn't the apparent problem that's the real problem; it's now knowing how to solve the problem that wears men out—and brings on the fights between husband and wife.

THE REASON FOR ALL THOSE QUESTIONS

Most women I know ask a lot of questions. And in so doing, they irritate the daylight out of their husbands.

Do I see your head nodding in agreement? If so, how do you react to your wife's questions? Maybe you react like a friend in our discipleship group when his wife called during one of my visits to his office. When he answered the phone, I quickly realized his wife was on the line by how the conversation went.

He answered, "No, I'm not alone."

She apparently asked, "Who's with you?" for he said, "It's Ken." Her next question appeared to be, "What are you doing?" for his answer was, "Just talking." His next answer indicated she had asked, "What are you talking about?" for he said, "Nothing in particular."

When he hung up, he exploded, "Boy, that's one thing that really makes me mad. She drives me crazy with her questions."

Since he had opened the door, I asked, "Would you like to know why she asks so many questions?"

"I sure would," he responded enthusiastically.

I recognized I needed to prepare him for what I was about to tell him, so I shared with him that there is something almost every woman does naturally, while very few men do it at all. Yet because women think men think like women, they are puzzled when they learn that many men do not do this. It's something women do quite naturally and it happens while they are asking questions.

Let me illustrate it rather than say what it is. Let's say a husband is getting ready to go somewhere and his wife notices what he is doing. She asks, "Are you going somewhere?"

Just those words send up a red flag in his mind. He is irritated because he thinks his wife is checking up on him. He thinks he is a big boy now and does not need to report in. You see, he forgets that he needs to consider his wife's feelings, that she will feel more comfortable knowing where her husband is going. His reaction, however, makes her feel guilty for asking, since his attitude conveys, "Of course, I'm going some-where, dummy. Is that okay with you, Mommy?"

He may not say those exact words, but he is letting her know that he is bothered by her question. And even though he has already shown her his resentment, she hesitatingly asks, "Where are you going?"

With increased resentment, he replies, "To K-Mart!"

At this point most wives would stop asking questions, since they are so keenly aware of the husband's resentment. But to make a point, let's press forward in the illustration. We'll imagine this is a very brave wife who keeps asking questions.

"What are you going to K-Mart for?" she asks guardedly.

"To buy some tires," he snaps back.

With hesitation in her voice and some inner fear, she asks, "What are you going to buy tires for?"

"For the TRUCK!" he is at the shouting stage now.

Braving both physical and emotional danger, she says with hesitation in her voice, "What kind of tires are you going to buy?"

"For crying out loud—whitewalls. Will you get off my back?" he yells.

Just what is there within a woman to cause her to keep asking questions, even though she will be terribly hurt? Because of her husband's frequently expressed resentment, she knows she will feel that she is doing something wrong by asking. She will feel guilty for *his* poor reaction. It goes back to why questions are so much a part of being a woman.

When I use this illustration in a workshop, I know that practically every woman gets an image in her mind of the K-Mart store she is familiar with. You see, most women visual-ize things concerning relationships, but most men don't.

A MATTER OF VISUALIZATION

Here's what is happening. A wife who is pledged to her husband needs to feel she is a part of his life. So her questions are a way for her to enter into his life. She can, *in her mind,* go with him to K-Mart. Let's go through our scenario again with the responses a typical woman will have during that exchange.

WIFE: "Are you going somewhere?"

HUSBAND: "Yes, to K-Mart." (At this point the wife gets a vivid picture of K-Mart in her mind. She has mentally joined him on his shopping expedition.)

WIFE: "Why are *we* going to K-Mart?"

HUSBAND: "To buy some tires." (In her mind she is seeing the tire department.)

WIFE: "What are *we* buying tires for?" (Mentally, she is in front of a rack of tires.)

HUSBAND: "For the truck." (Now she has a picture of his dark green truck in her mind.)

WIFE: "What kind of tires are *we* buying for the truck?"

HUSBAND: "Whitewalls." (*Oh, isn't the truck pretty with its new whitewalls,* she might be thinking as she stands admiring this picture in her mind, almost as if it is reality.)

Now this may seem corny, childish, or hard to relate to for many men, but it actually happens. And it happens often in the life of your wife. If you are not willing to let your wife into your life in this way, you will cause her to feel personally rejected. She will feel hurt and guilty at the same time. Why guilty? Because so many women have been told that a *good* wife doesn't question her husband. She just trusts him. That position, of course, implies that her questions indicate she does not trust him, which is not the case at all.

For the wife, especially a newly married one, questions express a desire, a need, a craving, to be identified with her husband, to sense that she and her husband are one. He has accepted her into his total confidence, which makes her feel she is valuable to him. Then she feels complete.

Remember that passage in which Jesus said He would not call us servants, but friends? Here's the relationship Christ has with us: "No longer do I call you servants, for a servant does not know what his master is doing; but I have called you friends, for all things that I heard from My Father I have made known to you" (John 15:15). Jesus is saying that He would include us in His life and build a special relationship with us. And that is the relationship Christ expects us to have with our wives, even though it is contrary to the instincts of many men.

Remember when we examined what attracted the queen of Sheba to King Solomon? It was his willingness to answer her questions, and that caused her to worship God (1 Kings 10:1–9). Wouldn't you like to see your responses to your wife's questions enhance her worship of God?

A CASE OF WRONG EXPECTATIONS

Yet the process of questioning and visualizing can cause a real problem. A woman tends to think, *I'm a human being, and my husband is a human being. Now since I (a woman) visualize things, all human beings (even men) must visualize things as well.* Men, of course, think all women use the same logical thought process they employ. And couples can live together for decades with these faulty assumptions causing disagreements, fights, and even divorce.

That's why as time goes on, a wife is hurt when her husband does not, through conversation, show that he is interested in her. He doesn't let her ask him conversational questions, nor does he ask her conversational questions. She feels that if he were to ask detailed conversational questions, it would prove to her that he is interested in the details of her everyday life. It's hard for many men to relate to the idea that if they ask their wives questions, the wives believe that their husbands really care for them.

The husband in this next illustration (an illustration I used with my friend who was bothered about his wife's questions) experienced a major breakthrough in his marriage because he learned the value of questions.

When my phone rang that day, it was a call from a wife at the end of her emotional rope. She was distressed by yet another negative experience.

"I need some help. I don't know if I can go on like this," she said. "We just had a big fight, and Dan said to me, 'I don't love you.'"

I suggested I come over so we could talk about it. Half an hour later we were in the middle of getting all the facts together. This woman had said to her husband, "I've got to go to the doctor today." He had responded with his usual indifference: "So go." She felt like she had been slapped in the face, and as she left, his words were echoing in her ears.

When she returned from the doctor's office, she walked up to him in the garage where he was polishing his motorcycle. Hoping he would show he cared by asking a question like, "What did the doctor say?" she stood there for a few moments watching him. No words of caring came from his lips.

This wife's damaged feelings were wounded again by her husband's indifference. Hurt and angry, she went into the house. Then she remembered what they had learned in one of our discipleship groups, that she had a responsibility to be his helpmeet, to remind him to look at his ways and remember the commitment he had made to God to change. So she decided to go back out and give him another opportunity to respond with Christlike, genuine, husbandly interest. It would mean so much to her spiritually, emotionally, and even physically.

When she returned to the garage, she stood by him for a moment. He did not respond to her presence. So trying to ignore her hurt and sound cheerful, she said in a light, musical tone, "I'm home." His response was, "Maybe you think I'm blind?"

You see, he was irritated by all the bothersome interruptions. They were interfering with his task of getting his motorcycle polished.

She lost control after his cavalier response, saying angrily, "I don't think you love me. I don't think you've ever loved me." The lid was off the bottle she had kept corked so long, and accusation after accusation flowed out.

AN HONEST ADMISSION

Although he was irritated, his next response was the result of genuinely thinking through his feelings: "I think you're right. I don't think I do love you." She didn't know that he was honestly facing himself for the first time. She only heard his words, and of course she was devastated.

That's when she called me. After hearing her story in their home, I said to her, "I know that what I'm about to say could sound very cruel to you, but this is something I've been waiting two years to hear him say. You see, he didn't know that he didn't love you. But now that he can see that he doesn't love you, he can also see that he doesn't know how to make you feel loved. That's the first step toward solving the problem—recognizing that there is, in fact, a problem. If a man insists that he does love his wife, even though he makes her *feel* unloved, then it is not likely that he will think that he has a problem."

The husband's next statement was fantastic: "So what do I do now?" He didn't know that even that question was encouraging to her. So I said to him, "Do you realize that just asking that question is encouraging to your wife? It shows that you do care to learn."

Surprised, he said, "You're kidding. Just asking a question shows her that I care?"

He clearly didn't yet know how to experience the feelings of others, not even those of his wife. He hadn't been deliberately trying to hurt his wife—no one had ever taught him how to feel for others. He didn't know how to enter into the lives of others by inquiring and listening. Since then, it has been so rewarding to watch as the Lord has been building in him the ability to understand. He has been learning how to love his wife, how to welcome her questions, and how to picture in his mind things that will make him able to live with his wife in an understanding way.

Remember the husband in my office who was so upset about his wife's asking so many questions? I used the above illustrations to help him understand why women ask so many questions. And remembering the K-Mart example, he asked, "Do most women really visualize like that?" I assured him they do.

When I use the K-Mart illustration at workshops, husbands usually turn to their wives and ask the same question. Wives, in turn, ask their husbands, "You mean you men don't visualize like that?"

Visualizing is one of the reasons, incidentally, that many women get so frightened by the driving habits of their husbands. They can visualize the results of recklessness. It's also why they are so alarmed when their small children are out of sight at a picnic or camp out.

Look at this picture with a double image in it. Some people see one image; some another. Some don't see either one, despite studying the picture intensively. But when someone is able to point out the other image, they say, "Of course, there it is. It's as plain as the nose on my face. Isn't it nutty that I couldn't see it earlier?"

What if you saw an older woman, and I saw a younger woman? And what if I told you that you were wrong when you tried to show me the image of the older woman? Wouldn't you think I was unfair and narrow-minded? You might even think I was unwilling to learn how you looked at things.

That's exactly what goes on between a husband and a wife. He shows the same resistance to what his wife is seeing and fails to see other important issues that his wife sees. He thus resists any attempt at changing how he as a man looks at himself.

Now if we as men take the time to listen and "see" the other subject in our lives, we can use this new understanding to avoid problems. Because we will much more quickly see the reason for most problems, we will be able to solve them. This new understanding will become a powerful tool for building relationships, as well as a powerful tool for seeing into the hearts of others (more on that in chapter 14).

A MATTER OF SEEING INTO THE HEART

A husband and a wife were sitting in my living room to discuss something that had been a long-term irritation to them. When I encouraged the wife to give her side of the story, she said, "He is always disrespectful and mean to my mother. For example, we went over to visit my folks last Sunday after church, and the first thing he did was give her a bunch of bad mouth."

Turning to him, I said, "Do you have anything to say?"

"What a liar she is!" he barked. "I don't know how she can sit there and lie like that."

After he finished telling his version of the story, I said to him, "You're both talking about the same situation, but from two different viewpoints."

Here's why he felt she was lying: "When we went over to her folks' house, the first thing I did not do was bad-mouth her mother. When we walked through the door, the first thing I did was to say, 'Hi,' to her dad. Her dad was sitting on the couch watching the football game, so I went over and sat down to watch the game with him. He and I also talked a little about different things while we were watching.

"But later when her mother hollered that dinner was ready, we didn't jump up and run over to the dinner table. So she started whining about how she had spent all morning getting dinner ready and how we did not appreciate it and on and on. Finally, her dad got tired of the nagging and went over and punched the TV off. Only then did I say, 'We should have stayed home. Then we could have had some peace and quiet. At least we would have been able to see the game without all this hassle.' So the first thing I did not do was give her mother a bunch of bad mouth. And I don't *always* act disrespectful and mean to her."

Each one was providing a "picture" of the situation. What was his wife looking at in the picture of his life? What did she see that he was not seeing? She was seeing offensive attitudes—that's all she wanted to explain.

That was not what he was seeing. He was seeing mechanics, that she was not giving the story in chronological sequence. And because he didn't agree with the way she expressed what she was seeing, he insisted she was wrong. He felt an explanation could be right only if she told it as he saw it.

Imagine the hours of arguing that must have gone on between them before we met, just because he was arguing over her use of words. However, he could have learned some lessons from this situation. For example, he definitely needed to learn how to die to himself (give up what he wants for himself, and prefer others first).

ATTITUDES MOST IMPORTANT

You see, if you want to discover the mind of a woman, you need to recognize that when she is talking to you about what you are doing or saying, she usually wants you to see the *attitudes* you are showing. The life situation is merely a vehicle to help her point out the attitudes troubling her. That's why the exact order of events in the story is not that important to her. And since God's concern is about attitudes, she is reflecting His concern to you.

Men, however, usually do not watch for attitudes but emphasize the *mechanics* of the situation. It's as though we are saying, "If you're going to repeat something, it is only truthful if it is repeated like a movie that has been rewound and then played over again." If a wife rearranges events, then in the eyes of too many husbands the description ceases to be accurate.

Looking at the mechanics only is a limited perspective. It prevents seeing and understanding an awful lot of what is going on in life. There can be many morals to a lot of stories. There are many truths that can be seen in one section of Scripture.

When women talk about husband-wife relationships, they usually emphasize attitudes and emotions. When we as men hear our wives repeating events, we want (as we put it) just the simple facts. But that's telling our wives what they should or should not *see* when they look at what is happening in the marriage. It's insisting that they see things only from our perspective. Need I remind you that God says a husband's responsibility is to understand his wife—not vice versa?

Let's consider the difference between what women see and men see in the chart "Perspectives of Women and Men."

Attitudes and emotions are key elements in being human. They make life more valuable. Like salt and pepper on food, they make love taste better. You will miss a lot of beauty in life if you insist on looking only at the facts. The person who refuses to open up to emotions and is not willing to tackle attitudes will become a cold, hard person.

The apostle Paul addressed this issue when he wrote to the Galatians: "But the fruit of the Spirit is love, joy, peace, longsuffering, kindness, goodness, faithfulness, gentleness, self-control" (Gal. 5:22–23). All of these qualities reflect emotion or attitude.

Wise is the man who has ears that are listening intently for anything that will help him improve. When my wife repeats a situation or an event to me, I conceivably would expect her to see it only from my perspective. But insisting on listening only to what I wanted to hear would condemn me to a narrow slice of life. Insisting that she see my side doesn't make me more understanding—it makes her more understanding, which increases the relationship problems.

Perspectives of Women and Men

Women See	Men See
A deep violet soft velvet gown with delicate lace trim.	A dress! (How much does it cost?)
A precious, cuddly, soft, warm little baby that's hungry or wet.	A kid! (Can't somebody keep that kid quiet?)
A man who makes her nervous when he drives behind her, but will keep her and her children safe from crime.	A cop! (Who's he after?)
A sweet elderly grandma having a hard time crossing the street.	An old lady! (She's slowing me down.)
A romantic dinner at home, dimly lit with candles, followed by sitting beside the fireplace, listening to soft music, and talking.	Mush! (I can't see what I'm eating, and I'm missing my TV program.)
An enjoyable time window-shopping together.	A waste of time! (We're not going to buy anything.)

Sure, go ahead and insist that your wife understand you. But it would be more Christlike if you said to yourself, "I'm going to demand that I settle for nothing less than completely understanding my wife, even if it seems one-sided. I'm going to insist that she help me see my poor attitudes and emotional weaknesses." That selflessness on your part will not remain one-sided. Your wife will be drawn to you with deep, deep love for you. And after all, isn't deep, deep love what you want from your wife?

CONVEYING CONVICTIONS

Sometimes when a husband is expressing his convictions, he will end up in a big fight with his wife. Then he will feel that she is fighting his convictions. That is usually not the case— she may only resent the attitude with which he presents his convictions. Consider the case of Steve and his wife, Irene.

Steve insisted that his family go to church *every* Sunday. One Wednesday his mother-in-law became ill and needed someone to help her out. So his wife, Irene, volunteered to pitch in and care for her mother. By Saturday night, Irene was exhausted. So she hinted around, saying, "Tomorrow morning sure is going to come around early."

Steve caught the nuance and said unsympathetically, "You're still going to church tomorrow."

What did Irene hear?

"You heathen, trying to neglect God again, huh? It's a good thing you've got me to keep you straightened out."

As a result Irene responded, "I don't have to be in church *every* Sunday to be a good Christian, you know."

Steve didn't realize that his attitude had been condemning. He felt that his convictions about church attendance were being attacked. So he replied in a commanding tone of voice, "Well, you're going to church tomorrow, so you might as well get used to the idea."

"But I'm totally exhausted," Irene complained, exasperated by Steve's inflexibility.

Not listening to what his wife was really saying, not catching the emotion in her words, Steve barked, "That's your tough luck. You have other relatives who could have helped your mom, but you had to be the little do-gooder," with his continuing tirade building accusations upon accusations.

Was Irene arguing against Steve's convictions about church attendance? No, she was reacting to his condemning, demeaning attitude. Because Steve had to be the boss, the commander in chief in his home, he had effectively lost his position of spiritual leader by his browbeating attitude.

Suppose Steve had decided to re-evaluate whether or not he was portraying Christ. He could have asked questions like, "What bad attitude is the Lord trying to show me through this situation? Am I being impersonal and putting church attendance above the need for compassion? Do I make my wife feel that my rules are more important than my need to love her and care for her needs? Is this an attitude that shows up in other areas of my life, at work, in my volunteer activity at church as well?"

Shouldn't a daughter care for her mother—and shouldn't her husband be glad she has a compassionate heart? After all, he might be diagnosed with cancer some day, have a stroke, or become bedridden because of an accident. Wouldn't he want her to demonstrate the same caring attitude at that time? Because we as men think short term so much of the time, we don't recognize the long-term implications of our attitudes and behavior—often until it is too late.

And why couldn't Steve also demonstrate care when his wife became involved with her mother? Couldn't he have assumed some of the duties around the home to take a load off her? He could have even gone over to his mother-in-law's home and provided relief for his wife. Isn't that what Jesus would have done? And think how such a servant's heart would draw others to Jesus—and how grateful his wife would have been. Because she would not have been exhausted, there would have been no question about her attending church.

Christlikeness in our attitudes toward our wives and children solves many problems before they occur. Just as in medicine we know that prevention is better than the cure, so prevention through Christlike attitudes produces loving emotions and Christlike responses. That's what our wives are trying to help us see—if we will only listen for attitudes and emotions rather than only for the facts.

Jesus reinforced the serious impact of attitudes expressed in words when He said,

Either make the tree good and its fruit good, or else make the tree bad and its fruit bad; for a tree is known by its fruit.

Brood of vipers! How can you, being evil, speak good things?
For out of the abundance of the heart the mouth speaks. A
good man out of the good treasure of his heart brings forth
good things, and an evil man out of the evil treasure brings
forth evil things. But I say to you that for every idle word
men may speak, they will give account of it in the day of judgment. For by your words you will be justified, and by your
words you will be condemned (Matt. 12:33–37).

In addition, Jesus gave us the be-attitudes in His Sermon
on the Mount (Matt. 5:3–12). For too long many Christian men
have relegated those attitudes to a future kingdom, while
Jesus was speaking to men living in the now. A careful self-
examination while reading the be-attitudes will make us much
more receptive when our wives remind us of attitudes and
words that are demeaning and hurtful.

There's no time when a Christlike attitude is more necessary than when we think of the marriage bed, the times of intimacy with our wives that are an expression of our oneness. I
discovered, to my shame, that selfishness is more in style
than unselfishness when it involves us as men and sex. But
that's another chapter.

13

"I'M JUST WEIRD"

Are you married to one of those women who doesn't seem to have a sex drive? Do you wish that just once she would take the initiative?

As part of my effort to become Christlike in my attitudes and behavior toward my wife, I stumbled across my need to discover what my wife's *true* sexual desires were. I believed I had married a normal woman, though I was puzzled by her apparent lack of interest about an experience that really interested me. So I started talking to her about our contrasting desires, trying to determine her true feelings.

There were so many questions that it was sometimes embarrassing to us to be so open with each other. Sometimes her answers seemed so unique that I would respond, "You're kidding! Do all women feel that way?" She would reply, "I don't know if all women feel that way or not. All I know is that's the way I feel!" Since I travel cross-country in my ministry, I offered, "I'll find out. I'll ask other women as I travel." Alarmed, she pleaded, "No, no! Don't do that! Then everybody will find out how weird I am. It's just me that's so weird!"

I assured her that I could ask questions without anyone knowing who I was talking about. Although she never really agreed to my asking questions, she seemed a little more relaxed about it.

As I traveled around the country, questions about sexual incompatibility frequently came up. That gave me the chance to start conducting my survey so I could discover the true, heartfelt perspectives of women about sexuality.

The most common questions clearly pointed out how husbands are much more sexually motivated than wives. I'd inform the wife, "You know you're not alone when it comes to being unmotivated sexually. Some women have practically no sex drive." And women everywhere would tip their heads slightly to the left and squint their eyes as if to say, "How did you know that?" As they were doing that, they'd say in astonishment, "Yeah, that's me! But I just assumed that I was weird."

The first time I broached this subject with a husband and wife and validated the similarity I went home and told Nancy that another woman felt and thought just like she did. Nancy said, "Okay, so there are two of us weirdos. That doesn't prove anything."

As time went on and I talked to thousands of women, I discovered that all the women I talked to thought the same way. And they all thought they were weird because they couldn't measure up to the sexual expectations in their marriages.

Another thing I discovered is that most women are trying desperately to live up to others' sexual expectations. These come from all kinds of sources; other women, rumors from men, movies, TV, magazines. And women are so concerned about being seen as a failure that they never tell each other, or their husbands, the truth about what they really feel. If they don't talk about it, then no one will find out how weird they are.

I believe a man should purpose in his heart to understand his wife, discovering her true perspective about sexual intimacy in their relationship. He should learn to understand the contrast between the thinking of men and women concerning sex. And a key to that discovery is recognizing that most men think that women think about sex as mechanically as they do—and most women think men think about it at an emotional level, as they do.

AN ATTITUDE AND DESIRE CHECK

Few of us men recognize the degree to which selfish attitudes determine our sexual activity and how this can hinder a loving relationship. This truth really came home to me late one night back in 1972. I was getting ready for bed. Nancy was already asleep, and I was thinking about waking her up to satisfy myself. Something strange happened. Deep within, my conscience prompted me, "But she's asleep." (I believe it was the Spirit of God at work.)

From what I now know was my flesh came the reply, "So?"

An argument ensued: "If she's sleeping and you wake her up, isn't that selfish?"

That's the first time those thoughts had occurred to me. But then my flesh spoke up again, "Do I care?" Adding, "That's her job—to be there for me!"

Next my conscience probed deep into the motives of my heart with a soul-searching question: "Okay, Mr. Christlike Christian, whose needs are you really seeking to meet right now?"

That question made me wonder, "With regard to intimacy, what are Nancy's needs?" I realized that I didn't have the faintest idea about her genuine, heartfelt needs. Another question that occurred to me was, "So what is right? What is acceptable? What is not acceptable?"

I quickly realized that most of us men base our understanding about intimacy on our own thinking. That being the case, I reasoned, how accurate is my thinking compared to God's thinking? What am I going to do now, since I don't know how to control my sexual nature? I was confused because I had never asked myself these types of soul-searching questions before.

Then a really powerful question struck me: "How much, or how little, am I controlled by my lower, sensual nature, my carnal nature?" And I reached the conclusion that even though I was a Christian, in this instance I fit the description in Romans 7:14: "But I am carnal, sold under sin."

As I examined Scripture I rediscovered that I was to be self-controlled, yet I wasn't. Something else about the lack of self-control occurred to me, and it really disgusted me. I was overwhelmed with the thought that the basic difference between me and a dog walking down the street was the structure. The sexual instincts and urges were frighteningly similar.

I felt animalistic, and the longer I thought about it, the more I resented the control that sensuality had over my life. I really felt it controlled me, and thinking it had so much influence over me bothered me. I'm not trying to say that a sex drive is wrong; the lack of self-control demonstrated by my selfish sensual focus was wrong.

A lot of women, I discovered, feel disgusted by being sexually intimate with their husbands because they sense that selfishness in them. Women have told me, "While I'm having sex with my husband, I feel so used. I feel so dirty. After he's finished and falls asleep, I have to get up and go to the bathroom and throw up—because *I know* he doesn't love me. We were not involved in an act of love; it was an act of lust." And their husbands are blind to how their wives are affected.

Some women have tried to tell their husbands how they feel. Every time I've expressed the following exchange, people have asked, "Do you have a tape recorder at our house?"

> WIFE: "You don't love me."
> HUSBAND: "Yes, I do."
> WIFE: "No, you don't. You just love my body."
> HUSBAND: "What! Are you trying to tell me that you and
> your body are two different things?"
> WIFE: "Yes, they are."
> HUSBAND: *Oh, great, Now I have to live with a woman
> who's gone insane.*

A husband caught in this exchange usually doesn't understand what his wife is saying—nor does he try to find out what she means. Yet from her perspective, since he emphatically demonstrates interest in her body, and she knows he does not demonstrate a genuine interest in her heart—or understand her emotions—she is convinced he does not love *her,* just her body.

Developing the understanding that establishes the proper priority for the sexual aspects of marriage is absolutely vital.

GETTING IN FOCUS

All wives have three key areas of need. Husbands are required by God to understand those needs and responsibly care for their wives in those areas. First, there is a wife's spiritual need (the need to care for her spirit), and that requires a high level of spiritual maturity on the husband's part. He gains that maturity only by living in keeping with God's will.

Second, a wife has emotional needs, and they can be met only if a husband has an understanding of emotions and illustrates emotional stability.

Third, a wife has physical needs, and caring for his wife physically will require a husband's moral strength. That comes only when he begins to understand and to accept that his wife is much more than a sexual being.

Usually, there is a much greater natural sensitivity among wives to the things that can build or destroy a relationship. And as we've been discussing, an area of great dissatisfaction is the sexual relationship. A wife may feel that she is required to be subject to a husband's advances, even though he disregards her spiritual, emotional, and physical condition. Although deeply offended and emotionally wounded, she may respond to him sexually out of a sense of what has been labeled Christian duty.

Trying to discover Nancy's true desires introduced me to another concept. What are the effects of sensuality on spirituality? So I examined passages like Galatians 5:17: "For the flesh lusts against the Spirit, and the Spirit against the flesh; and these are contrary to one another, so that you do not do the things that you wish." I looked at 1 Peter 2:11: "Beloved, I beg you as sojourners and pilgrims, abstain from fleshly lusts which war against the soul." I examined Galatians 6:7–8: "Do not be deceived, God is not mocked; for whatever a man sows, that he will also reap. For he who sows to his flesh will of the flesh reap corruption, but he who sows to the Spirit will of the Spirit reap everlasting life."

The passage that really hit me right between the eyes was Romans 8:5–6, where Paul jolts the reader by saying, "For those who live according to the flesh set their minds on the things of the flesh, but those who live according to the Spirit, the things of the Spirit. For to be carnally minded is death, but to be spiritually minded is life and peace."

I began to recognize that there is a distinct correlation between sensuality and spirituality. They cannot be equally operative at the same time. Either the flesh is in control, or the Spirit is in control.

So I determined that I wanted to understand how much my life was influenced by sensuality, no matter what the cost to make some changes. I decided offensive acts had to go. But part of my problem was, I didn't know what offensive acts were. In time, however, I discovered that *simply the attitude* of wanting to give up offensive acts had a healing effect on our relationship.

I decided I would let God's Word be the judge between what is God's design for the marital relationship and what is man's design. I knew that was safe because 2 Timothy 3:16–17 states, "All Scripture is given by inspiration of God, and is profitable for doctrine, for reproof, for correction, for instruction in righteousness, that the man of God may be complete, thoroughly equipped for every good work."

I recognized that it is quite natural for men to be attracted to, and accept, the sexual standards of the non-Christian world. That is true, especially if the standards were accepted and set up by people considered to be professionals: psychologists, pastors, and others recognized as experts regarding human nature. Yet I also discovered that many of those professionals do not consider that, from God's perspective, these human standards are highly offensive and destructive to the spirit of a woman.

A HIGHER STANDARD NEEDED

I realized that a much higher standard than that of Kinsey and other sexologists had to be established about what is best in a marital relationship—and what is loving. The Scriptures reinforce that we cannot be trusted to come to godly conclusions if we operate on natural human insight. The writer of the book of Proverbs reminds us, "There is a way that seems right to a man, but its end is the way of death" (14:12).

Scripture illustrates how human it is to struggle with sensuality. It provides accounts that show how even the great men of God have struggled against the power of their lower, sexual nature. Samson, for example, had a problem. When his parents said, "Aren't there any women in Israel who please you?" he said, "I want that woman. Get that woman for me." He was sexually motivated and was willing to disobey God by marrying someone who was not a Hebrew.

David had the same problem, as we all know. Solomon also had a problem with it. And even Paul confessed to it (compare Rom. 7:8 with 1 Thess. 4:4–5). Because of personal struggles, Job declared, "I made a covenant with my eyes not to look lustfully at a girl" (Job 31:1 NIV).

Jesus pointed out that a man's struggle involves much more than yielding or not yielding to physical activities, but that the struggle begins in the heart. He said in Matthew 5:28 that adultery can be committed in the heart, even though it isn't acted on physically. He revealed that immorality starts in the heart, the spirit; it is not only a physical function.

I reached the conclusion that as a practical means of establishing godly standards, a man could ask God to reveal to him, especially through his wife, any aspects of his sexual nature that were out of control, thus causing damage to the marriage. A man can purpose that the greatest influence in his life will be the Holy Spirit. In the power of the Spirit a man can develop a mutually beneficial love, as opposed to selfish love. In the process, he will also discover that there is a need to understand the elements of affection without ulterior motives.

It's not unusual for a wife to react negatively when I encourage a husband to hold or hug her as a means of letting her know that he wants to care for her. That's because she has been so sexually offended by her husband that she doesn't want him to hug her. She is accustomed to hugs meaning, "I am moving in for sex." That is why a man will probably need to learn what affection without intentions means to his wife.

Also, a man may think that doing things around the house mechanically should impress his wife. He cannot imagine that expressing an emotion such as joyfulness while doing his tasks lets a wife know that he is motivated by the high value he puts on her happiness. So she is not impressed by his mechanical performance.

Mechanical performances in a relationship do not awaken romantic desires within a wife. So, having completed a task, when a wife expresses the feeling that her husband doesn't love her, he is astonished. He reasons, "How can she say that I don't love her? I do all these things. I haven't left her. I'm still here, am I not?"

I've said to men, "That's a faulty form of evaluation. If 'being there' is a legitimate means of determining love, then her car must really love her, too, because it's always there."

Men who operate from a frame of reference that measures love by things done also try to figure out how to generate a greater sexual appetite in their wives to selfishly satisfy themselves. Yet rarely will those men try to increase their emotional capacity as a means of helping them identify with their wives and their emotional needs.

Even when a husband is being offensive, a wife may look for ways to become more sexually stimulated for him because she knows that is what he wants. Because she is making that kind of effort, can't you imagine she also wishes her husband was challenging himself with: "How can I become more spiritually stimulated for my wife?"

Having a strong spiritual focus will benefit all areas of a man's life, bringing balance to his spiritual, emotional, and physical character. This balance is absolutely necessary as a way to prevent a man from being preoccupied with sex. A strong spiritual focus might even permit a man to miss an opportunity for sex with his wife without feeling cheated. Abstinence for a period of time is not contrary to godliness, but it can be a meaningful aid to self-control and spiritual maturity.

WOMEN DO NOT HAVE A SEX DRIVE

Up to this point, I have been laying the groundwork for an uncommon frame of reference. You remember when I mentioned how women would tilt their heads to the left and, with eyes squinting quizzically at me, wonder how I knew what they really felt—deep down in the secret places in their hearts? The following statement really freed those women to be honest: "Especially *compared to men,* women don't have a sex drive."

You see, the primary trigger for the human sex drive is testosterone, and women have almost no testosterone. Let me give you an idea of why that is a basic fact to know and how this knowledge will help men and women understand each other better. Because of the technical equations involved, I want to try to simplify them. To do that, I want to substitute the technical numbers with recognizable objects. Let me try by comparing the amount of testosterone in the blood to the number of pellets of shot in shotgun shells. (Let's say each shell holds one hundred pellets.)

Everybody knows how preoccupied and spellbound men can be about anything pertaining to sex! Let's say that the high level of attention and dedication to sex in men is stimulated by testosterone in quantities of 37 to 100 percent of *one* pellet of shot in one hundred shotgun shells. Now keep this in mind—I'm talking about one pellet or less in one hundred shotgun shells (or 10,000 pellets), and that ratio of testosterone in the blood is what gets men so fired up about sex.

Then there's women. Using the same comparison, let's say women's testosterone level is 0 to 10 percent of one pellet of shot in one hundred shotgun shells. Do you realize what I'm saying? We're talking about one-tenth of one pellet (on the high side) in one hundred shotgun shells.

What does that say to you?

Just in case I didn't make my point, let me make one more attempt using chips in chocolate chip cookies. Let's say men have a level of testosterone that is a little over one-third of a chip to one whole chocolate chip per one hundred cookies. Women, on the other hand, have none to one-tenth of one chocolate chip per one hundred cookies. With that ratio in mind, you might wonder why they would even be called chocolate chip cookies, wouldn't you?

That's why I say, "Compared to men, women don't have a sex *drive.*" Hearing that, many women have said to me, "I cannot tell you how much pressure you have lifted off me. I always thought something was wrong with me. I thought maybe I was frigid, or something else was terribly wrong."

I add, "No, you're okay. It's normal for women to be without a strong sex drive."

Let me further explain what I mean when I use the term *sex drive* in discussing the differences in attitudes between men and women. I'm not talking about women not experiencing pleasure—nor am I saying women do not have a capacity for desire. I am focusing on what motivates a person sexually. This difference also explains why men attempting to become spiritual leaders must not let their sex drive control them. They must learn to control their sexual appetites.

On occasion, women have said to me, "I'm sorry to disagree with you, but I do have a strong sex drive." I answer those women by saying, "In the past, when women have told me that, I have made the following suggestion. There are many women who never hear their husbands say, 'I love you.' There are husbands who never use romantic words or expressions that tell their wives they are desirable. There are never any indications that their husbands are interested in them at all as persons. There are men who are never affectionate, who never gently touch their wives. There are no hugs, no holding, no kisses—*except during sex.*

"As these women were shown the difference between the sex act and acts of affection—recognizing they can separate the two—they realized it was the attention, the acceptance, and the kindness that they wanted after all. It was not the sex! These women have concluded, 'In that case, I guess I don't have a sex drive. I have a craving-for-loving-attention drive.'"

A husband may think it is the actual penetration that his wife likes and is motivated by, but it is not. This mistaken idea may have been generated because of his wife's responsiveness during the time of sexual involvement, since it was the only time she got her husband's full attention.

THE DIFFERENCE IS REAL

When we look at the difference between desire and drive, we need to go to Genesis 3:16, which says, "Your desire shall be for your husband." Some say the word *desire* here refers to sexual desire, yet all the commentaries I've read say it does not. Some commentaries say to make the word *desire* refer to sexuality is a gross perversion. The word *desire* in Genesis 3:16 actually assigns to a woman "a craving for value and acceptance as a wife-woman." That's a part of God's design—instilling in a woman a craving that makes her determined to make her marriage work, even in the face of overwhelming odds.

I'd like to further illustrate the differences between men and women by the following scenario. Imagine you found a young woman and a young man who have been living isolated from modern society. Neither has ever met the other before. Both are inexperienced adolescents. Consider what would happen if you placed them alone in a room together, and as they were facing each other, all of a sudden the young man were to have all of his clothes stripped away. The young woman would be embarrassed, ashamed, humiliated—and desperately trying to get out of there. That would be the typical response of an inexperienced young woman.

On the other hand, if the young woman suddenly had her clothes removed, the young man might be embarrassed, but he would also be instantly aroused. That's testosterone kicking in. That's the nature of drive.

Let me approach it from another angle. How many times have you heard of husbands punishing their wives by denying them sex? But you've probably heard of a lot of wives punishing their husbands by denying them sex.

THE DIFFERENCE IN PRECONCEIVED NOTIONS

We were talking in one of our classes about relationships. A woman mentioned that when she met different men, she would fantasize about them. I stopped her and said, "Hold it right there. We need to discuss this. I know what these guys are thinking when you say you fantasize about men." And she answered, "Oh?"

I said, "Let me see how close I can come to describing what you mean when you say you fantasize about men. You think, *Gee, he's got a nice voice. He seems very pleasant. I wonder if he'd be a good father and a good conversationalist. If he were married and out with his wife, would he pay attention to her and make her feel special? I wonder if he would be pleasant to be with all the time?*"

"Of course that's what I mean. What else?" she answered.

"I had to stop and clarify this because when you use that word, you don't understand what men think women mean," I explained. "You see, fantasizing means something altogether different to men. It means the thoughts of the mind are exploring sexual activity: frequency, variations of involvement, location."

Her face showed disgust as she reacted, "Yuck! No! Good grief, that's horrible!"

The men all unhesitatingly reassured her (even in the face of her contempt), "Yep, that's exactly what we thought she meant, and that's exactly what it means to us."

INCREASE DESIRE?

Men think that if they can increase their wives' pleasure by various means, they will also increase their drive, imagining they will be the happy beneficiaries of all that increased sexual appetite. But without the needed spiritual care (which illustrates love), that's not what women are thinking about. That focus in a man will actually decrease a wife's desires and pleasure, causing her to become more distant and to reject opportunities that might present themselves.

Some wives take a stand, refusing to be used, so their husbands try to coerce them into being more cooperative by assaulting them with misused Bible verses. They use the passage in 1 Corinthians 7, saying, "Wait a minute. You can't deny me because it says here that your body belongs to me, so I'm telling you to stop resisting me."

That's an improper use of the apostle Paul's instruction. In the first place, those people in Corinth were deeply involved in immorality. They had been involved in temple prostitution as an act of worship. So they had a corrupt lifestyle. Paul in effect was saying, "Let me give you God's perspective about husband-wife relationships."

Back in Corinth of that day, a husband might say, "Since we've become Christians, I don't feel right about this temple-prostitution-as-worship stuff."

His wife might say, "Well, you don't have to go if you don't want to, but I think I'll just keep on."

Her husband probably insisted, "Well, I'd rather you didn't."

As new Christians wondering what to do, they questioned Paul. Paul gave them God's perspective. In this passage Paul was not trying to assign dominion of one person over another. He was trying to get them to change their focus, to begin seeing each other as very valuable and, as a result, change their habits out of consideration for each other. They were to start demonstrating the Christian principle of laying aside one's own life ambitions for what is best for the relationship.

However, back to the misuse of this passage. When I'm working with a couple and I hear that the husband has been using this passage to lay down the law, saying, "Your body does not belong to you anymore. It belongs to me, so you've got to satisfy my needs," I say, "If that's how you want to interpret that passage, then read on. The apostle Paul also said that *your* body belongs to *her,* that she has control over your body. That being the case, and your wife using this passage as you used it, she could say, 'Okay, fine, I won't deny you. But your body belongs to me as well, and I say you cannot use it.'" In chess I believe the result of that exchange would be called checkmate!

That Corinthian passage was never meant to be used in that sense. You have to recognize that it was given in the light of both spouses having been involved in temple immorality, and they were struggling with a lack of self-control. That's why the apostle recommended that they say to each other, "Let's take some time for prayer and fasting so we can get our sensual appetites defeated."

So why did God make men with such a strong sex drive? Well, that's simple—balance. Because men are work oriented, if women had the same sex drive as men, no work would get done. On the other hand, if men had the same sex drive as women, there wouldn't be any children born. So the problem is not the sex drive, but that we keep it in control instead of its controlling us.

That's why a woman needs a husband who is a spiritual leader, who is Christlike in his behavior toward her, and who will live with her in an understanding way, even sexually.

I could never see Christ forcing Himself on anyone. That being the case, would a Christlike husband ever have sex with a wife who was not interested because she sensed that her husband's primary interest in her was sexual?

To gain a better understanding of the sexual dynamics between us, I purposed that I would not approach my wife until she expressed an interest. And, boy, was I in for a long wait! We did volumes of talking. I gained tons of information, and my wife learned that I did care about her more than her body. At the same time I learned what the difference is. If I did, you can, too. God bless your efforts and commitment!

By now you may wonder if all this self-control, self-denial, and focus on understanding the mind of a woman will really pay off. It does, and well beyond your relationship with your wife, as the next chapter will reveal.

14

IMPACT ON OTHER RELATIONSHIPS

"**O**kay," you say, "I agree that if I listen more carefully to my wife, thoughtfully minister to her spirit, and care for what is going on in her life, our relationship will be improved. But does that really make a difference in other relationships? Will I be more effective as a pastor, get a promotion sooner, sell more products as a salesman, or be more effective as a teacher if I apply the principles in this book?"

You are asking whether being Christlike pays off, aren't you? Of course, the first payoff comes in a wonderfully improved relationship with our Father in heaven. But does Christlike behavior have application in the real world you and I live in beyond our homes and our churches?

Intuitively, you and I know that we do not live only in relationship with our wives, that what home is like radiates out into every other area of our lives. And it's a well-known fact that if men or women leave home angry, they are much more likely to have accidents than if they left home feeling at peace with themselves and their families. Yet we may never have stopped to consider how much being Christlike really affects some of the other areas of life—and what a motivator that can be to become more open to receiving input from our wives about where we are not Christlike.

IMPROVED IN-LAW RELATIONSHIP

Why does the term *mother-in-law* arouse such a negative emotional response that comedians can capitalize on it year after year to get them laughs? Is it that a wonderful mother suddenly becomes a relationship wrecker when a son or daughter gets married? I discovered that this is not true. The problem was not with my mother-in-law but with me.

You see, my mother-in-law had watched me treat her daughter in an offensive way on many occasions. And on many occasions she had let me know exactly what she thought of my behavior. Like other men, I always reacted negatively to her expressions of concern.

My reasoning went, "I am the boss in this home, and you are going to find out that I can make my wife do what I want her to do—especially in front of you. You will see that I am the authority in this home, and that what I do is right because I'm doing it."

When the Holy Spirit got through to me on how offensive I was in the way I treated my wife, I also recognized that my attitude to my mother-in-law was inappropriate. So I went to my wife's parents and asked their forgiveness. They were willing to forgive, but with reservations. They were not at all sure my new attitude would last.

We would visit them on vacation and at other times, and they would say, "Ol' Ken, he'll never change." They were saying that I was basically the same person, even though I was trying to change my attitudes. Ten years later my mother-in-law said to Nancy, "Ken has really changed." Boy, did that feel good! That's the kind of blessing my efforts to become Christlike brought.

Unfortunately, the average man doesn't know much about this kind of blessing, for he has little with which to compare his attitude. Growing up he has no model illustrating the benefits of Christlikeness, no observable experience against which to match his.

You see, if you have a one-hundred-dollar bill in your hand and suddenly it is gone, you know the difference. But if you've never had a one-hundred-dollar bill in your hand, you really don't know what you are missing. So if you have never been sensitive to others, your relationship with your in-laws has never been great, and you don't know the blessing an improved relationship with them can bring.

IN THE OFFICE

"Sure," you say, "getting along with my in-laws is important, but I struggle on the job. Does Christlike sensitivity on the job have a positive effect?"

My associate Eldon was discipling the manager of a plant manufacturing industrial material when that issue came up. I'll let Eldon tell the story:

"This manager said to me, 'I cannot be Christlike and carry on my business.' You see, he was the person in charge of hiring and firing and did not see how what I was teaching him applied in his job.

"I said to him, 'Keep working on it with your wife.' So he said, 'But I cannot be two people, one at home and another at the office, because my wife works in the same office with me. So if I am practicing these things, I am practicing them on the job site. Others will see how I treat my wife.' The important thing was that he was committed to caring for his wife's spirit.

"This man was going to have to let go an employee in another city because he was not productive. So he decided to apply the principles he had begun to apply to life with his wife. He drove to the city to meet with the employee. Instead of going in and saying, 'Listen, we've talked about your productivity, and you are not producing. So I'm going to have to let you go,' he sat down with the man and set about ministering to the man's spirit. He talked to the employee about the condition of his spirit, asking questions like, 'How are you feeling? What is happening in your life?'

"The employee was taken aback, for he had never experienced this kind of caring attitude from a boss. So he shared about the really tough times in his family and how they were affecting his productivity. After my friend left, the man's productivity rose significantly, and he became a fine performer on the job.

"My friend came back just aglow over how his visit had gone. He said, 'I went down to fire the guy and came back with a more devoted employee than I had ever thought possible.'"

Maybe you've heard of bottom-up management. Or maybe you call it the upside-down corporate structure. If you want to truly implement that approach to management, consider beginning to care for the spirits of those who work for you.

I have a friend who as president of a company decided to make his associates' emotional health and personal growth his priority. When he had to call an associate in because of a breakdown of relations with another associate, or because of failure to treat others fairly, he would say, "I am more interested in your growth as a person than I am in your contribution to this company." And he would take the time to help the associate work through the problem relationship.

Employees could not believe their ears, but over time the president's actions showed he meant what he said. In every case the "problem" associate improved in attitude and behavior. Associates often admitted to a relationship breakdown and asked him for help, even before he called it to their attention.

In executive group meetings he would say, "I want you to hold me accountable just as I am holding you accountable. If you see me doing something that you believe is hurting others or the company, come to my office and tell me."

The resultant improvement in team spirit increased the staff's performance so significantly that the company made an impact despite a less-than-thriving financial environment.

Ministering to your associates' spirits results in a tremendously improved atmosphere at any level in companies, including corporate giants. When associates know you care for them as people, not only as staff or employees, their positive response will surprise you.

IN PROFESSIONAL LIFE

"Fine," you say, "maybe it works in corporate life, but I must relate to others in high-pressure professional environments. And I am so busy, I don't have the time to sit down and discover how to minister to the spirits of people I work with."

Have I got news for you! An article in the November 23–30, 1994, *Journal of the American Medical Association* reveals that researchers at Vanderbilt University School of Medicine discovered that the main difference between obstetricians who were sued for malpractice and those who were not was not the quality of medical care. Physicians who were not sued were considered "concerned, accessible and willing to communicate." Those who were sued were viewed as "hurried, uninterested and unwilling to listen and answer questions." This group of obstetricians also kept patients waiting longer, spent less time with them, and spent less time "connecting with patients." The conclusion of the researchers was that many doctors are sued because of their poor interpersonal skills, not their lack of medical skills.

I'm thinking of a doctor who came to me for discipling in his relationship with his wife. Two years after he first came to me, he reported, "My nurses are coming to me and saying, 'You have really changed.' And they are coming to me with questions about relationships because they have seen such a change in me. I am now enjoying a relationship with my staff that I never dreamed possible."

As a doctor, this man is under great stress. He has to make decisions that mean life or death for his patients. Yet as a result of his Christlike attitude, his associates have become much more proficient, they are willing to work at things together, and they help implement ways to save money.

This doctor reported that everything has really changed, even the way he talks to the young woman at the checkout counter in the grocery store. He can tell when she has had a bad day, and if her response is poor, he can change her reactions with a couple of encouraging comments.

I have worked with lawyers employed by large corporations. Just that sentence probably evokes the image of a hard-driving, ruthless corporate lawyer. And if you have ever tried to get through to one of those lawyers, you know how protective the executive secretaries are—it's like breaking through a brick wall to get past them. Yet it's amazing what can happen when their lawyer boss starts demonstrating new attitudes.

For example, when I call the office of the lawyer I am working with, I can get through to him instantly. As soon as I identify myself to his secretaries, they say, "Oh, yes," and put me through. Their boss has mentioned me to them, and they are delighted to have me spend time with him because they are seeing such positive changes.

If you are a professional or a business executive, ask yourself what kind of spirit you are creating when you go into a restaurant. "Oh," you say, "when I get to the restaurant, I don't have time to minister to anyone's spirit except my client's." Yet if you develop sensitivity to your wife's spirit, you will be amazed how quickly you will sense it when a waiter or waitress is having difficulty. When you minister to the server's spirit, you can be sure the service will improve immediately!

I remember eating at a restaurant where the waitress was really curt with me. I said to her, "You know, knowing me, I would not put it past me to have done something that might have offended you. Could you help me by telling me what it is?"

She said, "Huh? Oh. What? Huh? Oh, the guy that was at this table before you was really a jerk. I'm sorry I came across that way. You shouldn't have to pay for what he did." Everything was fine from then on.

You see, if I accept responsibility for having the capacity to offend people, I have taken the first step in improving relationships. And if I can do it with my wife, everybody else is a cinch.

IN EDUCATION

If you think being Christlike in an office is tough, try reflecting a caring spirit in today's environment in the classroom. Yet it is possible to be so radically Christlike that you can break through to even the toughest kids.

I was working with a teacher in 1978 who was learning to minister to the spirits of his wife and several daughters. He was a great big guy who could easily come across as intimidating. For that reason the principal had shifted all the incorrigibles in the school into his class. So he asked me to accompany him to school to help him learn how to be a better teacher.

The first thing he did was show me a list, saying, "This is a list of things I am going to tell my class that they cannot do."

I said, "Do you want to know what I would do?"

"Yes," he replied.

"Well, the first thing I would do is wad it up and throw it away," I said. "These kids are unruly. They'd love to have a list of things to violate. You give them a list like that, and they are going to have a field day."

"So what do I do?" he asked.

"If I were you," I responded, "I would get up in front of the class the first day in school, and after getting their attention, I'd say, 'God wants me to be a better teacher (remember, he's in a public school), a better husband, and a better father. I would be willing to enter into an agreement with you something like this: you help me learn how to be a better teacher, and I will teach you how to be better students.'"

We devised tests so that they could test him. Each quarter they would grade him on his character and then let him know how they had graded him.

I went to his class the first day. The first person to walk into the room was a petite teen. In her hands she had a huge history text, and she threw it down with a loud bang. She kicked it, and it slid all the way to his wall. She sat down and proceeded to go to sleep. The whole class was like that.

"Who's the guy, Teach?" one of the kids asked.

"Oh, he's my counselor," the teacher said.

"Oh, your shrink, eh?" replied the kid.

I saw the teacher talk with this kid for a while. Then he finally got the class's attention and started his presentation: "I want God to help me be a better husband, father, and teacher. . . ."

The girl who appeared to be sleeping half lifted her head. Then she raised her head and looked at him in utter disbelief. From then on, he had her attention. He worked on his deal with them.

At the end of the school year the kids in his class passed on their own merits for the first time, not because they were getting too big for their seats. Because he was so successful, and the administrators could not figure out why, the principal had him come in the next year and teach the other teachers what he did that made the class so successful. So he got to teach them about caring for the kids' spirits, having the kids help them become better teachers.

I have given you just a few examples of the far-reaching impact of becoming Christlike in our attitudes and behavior. Our Lord honors those who honor Him by living in harmony with His Holy Spirit's promptings, who are humble enough to let others become His prompters for Christlikeness. The honor may not come in terms of worldly recognition, but it comes in improved relationships and the domino effect of that improvement.

I think of the father of three sons whose wife was planning to leave him in eight years, four years after the youngest was out of high school. She had it all figured out. She would go to nurses' training during the last four years because the son would be in college, and she would not have to be at home for him. Then she would be financially independent and could divorce her husband.

The husband and father was not aware of her plan, but he knew the relationship was in trouble. He came to me for discipling in becoming a Christlike husband and father. Within two years his wife had decided she was not going to leave him, and she would maybe stick around because she was enjoying what was happening to him and the family.

When the oldest son decided to get married, he came to his dad and said, "I knew you before. I know you now. I want what you have for my marriage." The other sons have already said the same thing. That is awfully enjoyable!

We cannot, however, forget that we have an enemy who is determined to prevent us from becoming Christlike. So he is going to tempt us in various ways. But we also know that God lets us experience tests to deepen our faith and commitment. That's what we'll tackle in the last chapter.

THE ACID TEST OF COMMITMENT TO CHRISTLIKENESS

The greatest stumbling block to a Christian's achieving Christlikeness is the flesh's creativity—it instantly develops all kinds of arguments, excuses, and reasons to resist dying. The flesh does not have to be taught how to protect itself; manufacturing excuses to prove it is not the problem is a natural reflex. The flesh is amazingly skillful at developing rabbit trails that let us avoid the real issues or justifying our behavior when someone attempts to point out its sinfulness.

Even though someone might claim they have made a commitment to Christlikeness, their flesh easily proves its superiority over that commitment with irresponsible statements like these: "Hey, nobody's perfect"; "I'm only human; too much is expected from me"; "That's your interpretation"; "Yeah, but . . ."; "How about her? She's not got her act together, either"; "When is someone going to straighten out her?"; "I'm not the only one around here who makes mistakes, you know."

Christlikeness requires Christlike attitudes, a behavior no one is naturally familiar with unless they have begun to live the Christ life. Because we need to develop this new attitude and behavior, we will need to be on the hot seat of exposure every day, especially if we give our wives and associates the freedom to feed back to us when they see the flesh in control. In addition, we can be assured that Satan and his accomplices are going to target us, just like he targeted Christ and every apostle in the early church. And if we know our Bible, we recognize that God is willing to let us be tested so we can see whether we mean business with Him.

Freedom is a human demand. The typical guy I talk to thinks that being free means not having to pass any tests or be accountable to anyone for anything. He thinks he is free when no one is telling him what to do, especially his wife. It's against the very nature of a man to submit to women, to have his fleshly nature challenged or exposed, to have his spiritual encumbrances highlighted. That's why the Bible says that the way is narrow and hard to find, and few stay on it.

This tendency is also evident as we minister to people who attend our seminars. We feel especially privileged to assist those who get involved with our intensive discipleship program and bless us as we watch them develop Christlikeness. Many more say they are enthusiastic about the concepts we present, but they find all kinds of reasons for not signing up for the follow-up. Then others sign up but drop out once they realize that the acid test of Christlikeness is commitment that perseveres despite the extraordinarily humbling process of being held accountable by God—through their wives. And they miss out on the truly overwhelming blessings of Christlikeness in new and exciting relationships with their wives and children.

LIFE IS FULL OF TESTS

If you think about it, life is full of tests that hold us accountable. If you want to drive a car, you are tested. If you own a vehicle, most states require emissions tests every year or two. If you want to advance in business, you might be required to go back to school for an advanced degree with all the testing accompanying that.

We should not be surprised, then, that God has also designed tests for us. That's how God helps us discover our strengths (what walking in His ways has accomplished in us) and our weaknesses (how we still have areas of our lives that are not yet submitted and Christlike). The Scriptures reveal that God constantly tested those whom He used the most.

We may look at Israel's forty years in the wilderness as punishment for disobedience. Yet God gives us another perspective in Deuteronomy 8:2: "And you shall remember that the LORD your God led you all the way these forty years in the wilderness, to humble you and test you, to know what was in your heart, whether you would keep His commandments or not." Wow, what we have perceived as punishment was a test revealing the condition of their hearts to them.

We all remember the story of Satan appearing before God and getting permission to test Job's loyalty. We remember, too, that Jesus Himself was tested. We read in Luke 4:1–2: "Then Jesus, being filled with the Holy Spirit, returned from the Jordan and was led by the Spirit into the wilderness, being tempted for forty days by the devil." So who permitted that testing of the human embodiment of the Son of God? Wasn't it God Himself? Jesus was living according to His Father's will as He was led by the Holy Spirit into the wilderness. His total submission to the Father's will was evident in Gethsemane when He prayed, "Nevertheless not My will, but Yours, be done" (Luke 22:42).

The proof of Jesus' commitment is the durability of His work—it remains tried and true. I must draw my confidence from His ways, knowing they will stand the test described in 1 Corinthians 3:13–15:

The work of each [one] will become (plainly, openly) known—shown for what it is; for the day (of Christ) will disclose and declare it, because it will be revealed with fire, and the fire will *test* and *critically appraise* the character and worth of the work each person has done. If the work which any person has built on this Foundation—any product of his efforts whatever—survives (this test), he will get his reward. But if any person's work is burned up [under the test], he will suffer the loss (of it all, losing his reward), though he himself will be saved, but only as [one who has passed] through fire (AMPLIFIED, italics mine).

The practical, joyful results of persevering while being tested are highlighted by James, who wrote, "Blessed, happy, to be envied is the man who is patient under *trial* and stands up under temptation, for when he has stood the *test* and been approved, he will receive [the victor's] crown of life which God has promised to those who love Him" (1:12 AMPLIFIED, italics mine).

TESTING HAS PRACTICAL PURPOSES

As much as we might find testings distasteful, they are beneficial. Testing is a way of determining our abilities while at the same time revealing where we need improvement. Using the imagery of the military, Jeremiah wrote,

If you have run with the footmen, and they have wearied you,
Then how can you contend with horses?
And if in the land of peace,
In which you trusted, they wearied you,
Then how will you do in the floodplain of the Jordan?
   (Jer. 12:5).

We're talking "be prepared" here.
Jesus used an image from the financial world when He spoke about testing: "Therefore if you have not been faithful

in the unrighteous mammon, who will commit to your trust the true riches?" (Luke 16:11). We're talking "know the difference" here.

For all of us who want to be respected as spiritual leaders, notice who the apostle Paul says must qualify us: "Be diligent to present yourself approved to God, a worker who does not need to be ashamed, rightly dividing the word of truth" (2 Tim. 2:15).

PREQUALIFIED IN THE HOME

There is an immense need for workers in the field of crumbling marriages. But those workers need to be tested first for Christlikeness in their own lives before they can be qualified for service in restoring marriages. The home is the place where that testing must occur, where a man can learn how to effectively function as a leader. The home is the training ground where effective ideas and methods are developed for a man's own use within his family. It is there a man learns how to discover and confirm God's ways for his life.

If we go through the trials of learning how to lay down our lives for our wives and experience success, then we become the husbands and leaders God wants us to be. As we become victorious soldiers, we also become qualified to lead others through battles. We must see leadership as being a servant to others instead of an opportunity to be served by others.

Learning the Christlike response to the pressure of laying down our lives for our wives—and expecting nothing in return—will prepare us for the pressures of having no expectations from others as we serve them. We will then develop the attitude recommended by the apostle Paul: "And whatever you do, do it heartily, as to the Lord and not to men, knowing that from the Lord you will receive the reward of the inheritance; for you serve the Lord Christ" (Col. 3:23–24).

When the apostle Paul wrote that, a servant was a possession. He could be bought or sold. He had no rights. Here's how I see this passage: Jesus is the Lord, and I am the servant. So I make the following transfer: I am the servant, and everyone else represents Jesus (especially my wife). As a servant, I am willing to make the preferences of others more important than my own. Now I can be happy and excited about doing what is best for others (especially my wife), even if I never get to work on my preferences, because it is just as if I'm doing it for Jesus.

As I set out to serve others, I can avoid confusion over what to do—and determine whether or not the service will bring glory to God—with the following question: Will what I am about to do cause me to violate God's Word or cause me to do anything that is not Christlike? (To determine this, I'd better be more and more familiar with the Word of God.) If it does neither of those, then I am free to serve without reservation, being careful not to sacrifice my wife and family by dismissing their place of priority in my life, making them pay the price of my preferential treatment of others. (This would be an example of the question above: Will I be violating God's Word? The answer is, "Yes, I would be." [See Eph. 5:25; 1 Cor. 7:32–33.])

We discover that setting aside our own desires and wishes is very difficult when we determine to become a servant to others. That is to be expected. Although extremely difficult, wouldn't it be wonderful if we could come to the point of not feeling cheated, insecure, or threatened when others are not seeking to meet our needs, and we can keep right on serving them?

TESTING FOR A SERVANT ATTITUDE

How about getting practical about this testing stuff! Let's say you are going to paint your house. You have visualized it as white with yellow trim. Your wife would like it to be yellow with white trim. Keeping in mind the principle of doing it as unto Jesus, who are you going to let choose the color?

You are thinking about going on a vacation. You have been wanting to go to Disneyland. Your wife has been dreaming of a trip to her mother and father's home in another state because they are getting older, and she wants to enjoy them as much as she can before they die. Since you are doing it as unto the Savior you love, where do you go? Wouldn't you fulfill your wife's dream and bring her joy (for Him)?

Now suppose you gave up your preference in each of the above cases. What would be your feelings as you did so? *The real test* is this: Is there *sincere joy* in your heart because you realize you have the privilege of being a servant?

This would be a good time for me to make a point. It would be wrong of me to allow anyone to conclude that since I am presenting all these godly principles and attitudes, I consistently illustrate them in my life. I do not. But I also need to make the point that every time I do not respond to life with Christlike attitudes and actions, I am wrong!

As a Christian, I have an obligation to God to always respond in a Christlike way. But because I know what my commitment to Christlikeness is, and I have learned to accept as a simple fact that I am always going to fall short of the glory of God (which is why I am grateful that I have a Savior), I can live with the knowledge that when I am not Christlike, I am wrong!

The possibility of gaining real joy in situations where I have the opportunity to die to self increases if I concentrate on this idea: I do not have to have my own way. In most cases it won't make a noticeable difference if I do or do not get my own way.

While looking at the concept of dying to self, consider how much a dead man worries about getting his way. A dead man does not exist anymore. A man who does not exist has no need to please himself, does he? This does not mean the death of personality, but the death of the egotistic self—death of the flesh's rule.

Asking a man to give up his wants worries some people. They think I am advocating that a man should give a woman her own way in everything. Yet notice that I am asking a man to give up only personal preferences or personal opinions, not godly convictions. And I am not commanding it—only asking a man to consider it, since the focus is laying down his life to become Christlike.

Wasn't that the attitude of Christ? In prayer, He said to the Father, "Nevertheless, not as I will, but as You will" (Matt. 26:39). He told His followers: "My food is to do the will of Him who sent Me, and to finish His work" (John 4:34). In other words, He was saying, "Not what I want, but what You want, God."

The apostle Paul was on his final journey, returning to Jerusalem with a gift of money for the church. A prophet told him that going to Jerusalem would be dangerous, so his loving friends pleaded with him not to go; they urged him to be concerned about his well-being. But the apostle Paul was willing to be troubled and to die for the privilege of presenting Christ. When his friends saw that they could not persuade him to put his safety first, they agreed, "Okay, then, the will of the Lord be done" (Acts 21:10–14).

Each Scripture passage cited touches on our willingness to set aside the flesh's preferences and strive to acquire biblical attitudes in its place.

Yet when I present this attitude, I get many expressions of concern typified by this question: Won't a wife who is consistently shown preferential treatment develop a very selfish perspective? I say that will not happen. Paul in Ephesians 5:25–27 emphasized that if a man will learn how to lay down his life for his wife (as Christ laid down His life for the church), then as Christ in laying down His life for the church presented the church holy, so a husband in laying down his life for his wife will present his wife holy (which is not selfish!). That is not my promise—it is God's promise.

The principle of giving up my preferences may be hard to accept, but regardless of what my wife is like, I am commanded to become an example of Christ to her. Rather than tell her to be like Jesus, I need to show her how to be like Jesus. Showing Christlikeness is catching and quickly infects those in the Christlike person's home with similar attitudes.

A scriptural principle is involved in this it-will-catch-on philosophy. To receive the blessings of caring for others and being a role model, we must give an example of Christlikeness. The promise of Jesus Himself in Luke 6:38 is, "Give, and it will be given to you: good measure, pressed down, shaken together, and running over will be put into your bosom. For with the same measure that you use, it will be measured back to you." Similarly, Jesus affirmed in Matthew 6:33: "Seek first the kingdom of God and His righteousness, and all these things shall be added to you." These passages are not referring only to physical giving and receiving. Rather, Jesus gives us a principle primarily related to spiritual considerations.

For example, if I concern myself with becoming spiritually mature, I will understand more about spirituality. That knowledge will give me a burden for others to have that blessing. It will allow me to minister in an understanding way to the spirits of others. Knowing I have done that will bless me, and those whom God has blessed through me will return my blessings in thanks. They will also be able to bless others with spiritual understanding—and that in turn will multiply my being blessed. That's an even better return than the best multiple-level marketing program.

If you, for example, decide to prove God, you will be delighted to discover that your wife cannot resist showering you with preferential treatment in response to your Christlike unselfishness. If you are like most men, you may think that preferential treatment means you will be rewarded with more sexual intimacy. Boy, talk about a single-track mind, as I indicated in a previous chapter. But we are talking about the motivation for unselfish giving, not about finding ways to receive more of anything in particular.

THE TEST OF KEEPING YOUR WIFE ENCOURAGED

If you are like me, you find it much easier to encourage others. People at church or on the job, friends, or anyone else is easier to encourage than a wife. Yet that became your primary assignment from the Lord when you agreed to get married.

I've already indicated that the home, the relationship with your wife, is the key testing ground God uses to reveal how much the flesh is still in control. Those tests may come hot and heavy at times, so let me remind you of a promise that has validity even when being tested in the home. The apostle Paul wrote,

> For no temptation—no trial regarded as enticing to sin [no matter how it comes or where it leads]—has overtaken you and laid hold on you that is not common to man—that is, no temptation or trial has come to you that is beyond human resistance and that is not adjusted and adapted and belonging to human experience, and such as the man can bear. But God is faithful [to His Word and to His compassionate nature], and He [can be trusted] *not to let you be tempted and tried and assayed beyond your ability and strength of resistance and power to endure,* but with the temptation He will [always] also provide the way out—the means of escape to a landing place— that you may be capable and strong and powerful patiently to bear up under it (1 Cor. 10:13 AMPLIFIED, italics mine).

With this verse in mind, think of coming home after a hard day at the office, having experienced a lot of pressure. You don't feel you can handle any more when you walk in the door. Your wife has also had a very difficult day and needs to unload her burdens on you. Can you pass the test of letting her unburden on you in light of the preceding promise? Can you convey to her that she can come to you at *any time* with *any problem,* and you will minister to her as Christ would?

You will fail the test if you let her know that she doesn't have the freedom to give her burdens to you. You can let her know how upset you are with her for even considering giving you more pressure, by excusing yourself with the explanation, "After all, I'm only human." But don't forget that we discussed that this excuse indicates that the flesh is in full self-protection mode.

The other option Christ gives us is whether we will, in the light of God's promises, evidence Christlikeness in our responses when we arrive home. We know, of course, that Christ went through a great deal more suffering than we ever do, proving Himself a worthy leader and thereby setting an example for us to follow. He has been through it all for us, for we read, "We do not have a High Priest who cannot sympathize with our weaknesses, but was *in all points tempted as we are, yet without sin*" (Heb. 4:15, italics mine).

If your wife feels she cannot come to you as her husband because you make her feel that you cannot handle the extra pressure, you will be denying her one of the main outlets for emotional and physical overload God has provided for her. Yes, she can come to God as well, but if you as her husband do not permit her to use the outlet God has specifically assigned to—and provided for—her, she will develop a spirit of desperation. That will grow into resentment, which begins to have emotional and physical consequences.

You may respond, "Oh, yeah! Well, what happens when I get overloaded?" Don't you remember? God said He would not let you get overloaded. Is He faithful, or isn't He? I sometimes wonder if God doesn't let my load get heavy as a way of forcing me to turn to Him in prayer. Prayer and understanding are the ways I can get rid of my desperation.

But you might say, "How come she gets to get overloaded, and I don't?" That's a fair enough question. I'd like to make two points:

1. I'm not saying one has the privilege of getting overloaded and the other doesn't. I'm only talking about who gets to turn to whom for relief. Refer to the Scriptures already used. Both men and women can turn to God in times of need, but when it comes to marriage, wives are supposed to turn to their husbands as they would to Christ. The results are that we prove to be Christlike or we fail to illustrate Christ. This will help us recognize whether we can rejoice in how we have yielded to God or how and where there is more work for us to do.

2. Notice again how protective and defensive the flesh is. It does not say, "Okay, how would Christ approach this situation? How can I become more godly through this experience?"

What a privilege to represent Christ to my wife! Representing Christ requires that I accept the responsibility of protecting and caring for her. God has given us as husbands a serious charge, and more marriages need an unchanging, genuine, until-death-do-us-part commitment by the husband to provide encouragement, protection, and caring.

AN UNBIBLICAL COP-OUT

We as men should never feel that we have the freedom to excuse our wrong behavior by saying, "My offensiveness may be wrong, *but* (there's another flesh-protecting word) God is using it to teach my wife how to deal with her resulting wrong attitudes." Nor do we have the freedom to say, "God is teaching my wife patience and trust, since she thinks she is supposed to do the work of the Holy Spirit in my life. She's not willing to wait for Him to speak to me or wait for Him to show me any of my un-Christlike characteristics. No, no! She thinks she's gotta do it for Him."

Certainly, wives have an opportunity to develop a more meaningful relationship with God in these situations. But no one should ever lead anyone to believe that God plans to be tolerant of a husband's sins just to teach his wife to have a proper response. She is supposed to learn proper responses from his example.

It is unbiblical to imply that the length of time a wife will have to put up with her husband's cruelties depends on how long she takes to straighten herself out, change her "naughty" ways, and respond properly to him—that her husband is God's rod of reproof to her. And it is unscriptural to teach that a husband has no control over his un-Christlike ways, that he is just an innocent pawn in the hands of God, or that he is being held back from a more meaningful relationship with God because of his wife's immaturity. This approach is destructive to a couple's relationship, negates the husband's accountability to God for his sin, and only hinders him from becoming Christlike.

We can never blame our wives for our failures. We can never rightfully neglect our responsibilities as husbands—to be a Christlike example. Our obligation to represent Christ to our wives is too intensely important to even consider trying to escape it.

By now you may have identified with some of the conditions presented herein. Maybe your marriage is in pretty good shape but you see some warning signs and want to apply some preventative medicine. Then again, maybe you have become aware of some serious needs in your marriage, some deep hurts, some grave wounds to be healed. You may understand now why your wife seems to have withdrawn from the marriage. Maybe you see, too, why she seems to have lost her zest for life or is dead in her response to you.

If this is the case, try to remember that there have probably been times in your life when others hurt you deeply. Can you remember how you totally withdrew from them or how you were very cautious toward them, being very careful about letting them get close to you again? You did not want to give them another opportunity to hurt you. You may have avoided all contact with them because you could not stand them. Just seeing or hearing of them revived the bitterness you felt toward them.

If you can remember feelings like that, let that memory help you understand how your wife may now be feeling. She may have said that she has forgiven you. But remember that there is a difference between being willing to forgive and feeling free to let someone who has been destroying her back into her innermost self. A wife who has emotionally, and maybe even physically, taken herself out of your life because of severe hurts will be fearful that you will again trample on those tender feelings that she has hidden deep within herself. She is protecting herself. She has been trying to become immune to your insensitive ways. Sometimes it takes years before a wife will totally trust her husband again.

DON'T GIVE UP TOO SOON

You have probably seen a movie or television program where the main character has to cross a desert. The whole story is about his struggles as he makes that attempt. He runs out of food first. Then his horse or truck dies. He gets baked by the sun until his lips are cracked and swollen with sores. Then he runs out of water. He still tries to go on, but it's too much for him. He decides to give up and die.

Then the camera backs away and gives you a panoramic view, and you see the whole area around him. And there, just over the next sand dune, is civilization with shade, cool water, and food.

"Don't give up!" you want to scream at him. As a spectator, you can see that he is about to make the discovery that will save his life. But he does quit, and you feel so disappointed and desperate for him.

I see too many men in that situation, giving up too soon. A man may struggle for a month or two, or even a year or two, and then decide it is time for his wife to recognize the enormous progress (in his own eyes) that he has made. He may decide that it is time for his wife to stop hurting and see him as a different person *now*. But the fact that he is ready to quit shows that he is not really a different person yet. Yes, he may be learning how to be a different person, but he is not changed enough yet. Only a wife can say when (or if) her husband has successfully made her feel safe and loved.

OUR GOAL AS HUSBANDS

Our goal as husbands is to be in it for the long haul, to be committed to understanding our wives and learning to meet their needs. We ought to stick with becoming Christlike, no matter how long it takes our wives to recognize it, no matter how many sacrifices we have to make.

I certainly have had times when I felt that I had put out enough effort to prove that I cared. I thought that it was about time I got more honor or relaxation or credit than I had been getting. I started feeling sorry for myself, but I was wrong when I started thinking that way. My problem was that I started looking at how much I had improved, at where I had been, and at how far I had come. Instead, I should have been looking at Christ and His example to see how far I still had to go.

As time goes on, you may begin to feel sorry for yourself. I can empathize with that. Yet we must not permit ourselves the luxury of continued self-pity. We can receive the benefits that come from a sincere commitment only if we learn to keep on giving of ourselves to our wives with no expectations or time limits. Our goal in dying to self should be to become more like Jesus, no matter what it takes.

Getting discouraged is not unusual. And since we can be faced with it often, we should let 2 Corinthians 4:8–12 be our encouragement. Here is how I have paraphrased it for my personal benefit:

> We have many problems everywhere we turn, yet we do not think we are without help. We are puzzled, but we do not think there are no answers; treated mean, but we do not think that no one cares; ashamed in front of others for Christ's sake, but our reputation is not ruined in God's eyes. Our suffering allows us to show Christ's response to those who mistreat us. If we did not suffer, we would not have the chance to show others what Christ's response would be. Your persecution of us, even unto death, gives us the chance to show you that even though there is death, we have life through Christ, and you can have life, too. We have God's Spirit, which allows us to visualize what God intends to do. David said in Psalm 116:10 [paraphrased]: "I can say this because I believe it." So we, too, can say, "I wouldn't be telling you this if I did not believe it myself."

God is completely committed to us. Let us learn what that really means and deepen our commitment to Him!

TESTIMONIES ABOUT COMMITMENT

In conclusion, let me share some testimonies from other men. They prove the positive results of a commitment to persevere for whatever time it takes.

A staff supervisor in a Christian organization declared, "My work involves rebuilding broken lives and relationships.

Not only did I attend a great number of seminars for successful living, but I also taught adult education classes on family living. I had been in full-time Christian service for more than ten years and thought I had all the answers.

"Then some things looming on the horizon made me realize that what I was parroting to others had not helped me realize my own needs. My wife was attending a Life Partners 'Discovery Seminar' while fully intending to divorce me.

"Suddenly, reality came crashing in all around me. Literally overnight, I came to realize that I had been consistently abusing personal relationships. I had also totally failed in my marriage. I was more concerned about what others might think of me than about what my wife might think of me.

"At that point I realized that I needed to become a 'real' person and a loving husband. I also needed to become concerned about inward growth and openness before God. The three years since then have been the most challenging and rewarding (as well as the hardest) as I have been learning how to become the Christlike person God wants me to be. I'm learning to trust God and follow His ways in everyday circumstances. I'm finding that God's ways work, even in seemingly impossible situations.

"Because of God's grace, I have seen my marriage turn from a disaster and near divorce into a warm, loving relationship. I am enjoying a marriage relationship that I never even dreamed possible."

A headmaster of a school shared his experience: "My wife and I attended a 'Discovery Seminar' of Life Partners. My initial reaction to the biblical principles presented was deep resentment. I resented the focus on me. I have always been quick to see my wife's un-Christlike attitudes, but have resisted being honest about my own un-Christlike attitudes. In fact, I could make any of my sins look as though they were her fault.

"During that seminar God stripped me of my defense mechanisms and caused me to see my wife as a helper rather than an accuser. I know now that God gave her to me to help me to become more like Christ. Because she knows and understands me so well, she is better equipped than anyone else could be to help me see my need to become more sensitive to the leading of the Holy Spirit. God made her that way (Gen. 3:16). Getting to know and understand her (1 Peter 3:7) is the most exciting thing that ever happened to me.

"God's ways do work! There is now a two-way communication in our marriage that never before seemed possible. The practical advice we received at that seminar has made this the most wonderful years of our marriage (we have been married fourteen years). Our children are also becoming increasingly more sensitive to the Holy Spirit."

A carpenter said, "I have seen the validity of God speaking to a husband through his wife on many occasions. Two of the most memorable times involved the shaping of my career.

"The first occurred when my wife felt God speaking to her about having me take over the responsibility of handling the monthly finances, a burden which up to that time I had allowed her to carry. I had always felt that God would indicate the time for her to quit her job by increasing my salary or providing a job that would equal our combined incomes. She felt that if we were obedient to God's priorities, He would be faithful. So in a step of faith she tendered her resignation. Even though my job as a carpenter paid well, our financial responsibilities were greatly in excess of my monthly earnings. Two days later I was offered a job totaling our combined incomes. My starting day was on her last day at work.

"This job of remodeling restaurants met our financial needs, but after a time it wore greatly on the family's needs, since there was an increasing amount of out-of-town and overtime work required. My wife, voicing her own need as well as the children's needs for more of my time, suggested that I might possibly seek a career change. I, however, insisted that this was the job God intended me to have, since He had provided it.

"As the year went by, things got worse. I finally agreed that if a job offer came with the same salary and a company car (as we had sold our second car), I would accept it as being God's will.

"We began praying. Shortly thereafter I received a job offer that initially looked less attractive, but did meet the prerequisites I had stated, so I accepted it. As I discussed the position with my new employer, I stated my priorities of not working nights or weekends, since I felt the necessity to spend those times with my family. He agreed to these conditions and has never imposed on me. He even agreed to have family get-togethers when extra job time was needed for conferences.

"This position has not only helped me meet the needs of my wife and family, but it has also become very lucrative, since my boss has generously provided a profit-sharing program.

"Through these and many other instances I have learned to appreciate the special insights God gives to a wife. I am anxious now to seek out her thoughts and insights on the decisions we have to make. I am able to deeply appreciate this additional source of input God has provided, especially since I had previously ignored her for so long."

A sales representative discussed what happened to him: "Our marriage had reached the point where my wife insisted that we get outside help. This surprised me, for I did not know we were having any serious problems. Through a chain of events, the Lord led us to join with several other couples to attend the Life Partners ministry. I had many fears about the method and emphasis of the ministry, but decided to give it a chance.

"Over the last two years the Lord has done a remarkable work in the life of our entire family. I have learned about myself and my attitudes by listening to my wife share her feelings. This has been very difficult, even more difficult than I imagined. God has, however, given me a dear gift in my family, and He continues to give me encouragement as He brings us all closer to each other and to Himself."

A pastor stated, "In seeking help for a couple with seemingly insurmountable marital problems, I first encountered the principles leading to spiritual oneness in families. This couple, very special friends of my wife and myself, allowed us the privilege of being present at several of their counseling sessions with Ken. As the principles were shared, God began to convict me of deficiencies in my own relationship with my wife and daughter. He showed me my responsibility to 'love my wife even as Christ loves the church and GAVE Himself for it.' This Christlike giving began for me when I finally committed myself to fulfilling several projects dealing with my attitudes toward my wife. These challenges truly accomplished their designed purpose of revealing my insensitivity!

"After three years of application, there is still much for me to learn, and I must confess to occasional lapses into the old attitudes. However, the joy I experience in working toward spiritual oneness with my wife—as evidenced by her freedom to share her deepest thoughts, desires, and hurts with me— has made every painful step away from self-centeredness worthwhile. An added bonus has been to see these lessons strengthen and deepen my relationship with our nine-year-old daughter. And remarkably enough, as I have become more sensitive to my wife's and daughter's spirits, the instances of fruitful ministry with my congregation have increased.

"I am grateful to God for the opportunity to learn and apply these life-changing principles. I am also thankful for His continued supply of wisdom and strength to my wife to withstand my periods of rebellion, and for her willingness to do it. It is not an easy way of life, but the results are tremendous— and eternal!"

WHY WAIT?

Is your wife still living with you? Why wait until your character forces her to leave before you decide to learn how to live with her in an understanding way? Too many men wait until their wives have left them before they realize something must be done. This is not necessary. So why not start learning now? Let your wife read this book, highlighting those parts she feels illustrate problem attitudes in your marriage. And then give her the freedom to share her heart with you so that the two of you more and more can become one.

If you decide to proceed, I know what is ahead of you. I pray God's blessings upon you, for Satan will try to prevent you from becoming a living testimony of Christlikeness. That is the last thing Satan wants, a light in his darkness. But that is exactly what God wants. God is light, and the more you are like Christ, the more light you will be—and that light cannot be hidden in darkness. Light is attractive to people who are looking for something. You may be their proof that it is possible to be a conveyor of God's light.

May your marriage be the proof that God's answers applied in the lives of Christians will eliminate divorces, for God's answers bring solutions, eliminating the need for divorce as a solution.

> For the eyes of the LORD run to and fro throughout the whole earth, to show Himself strong on behalf of those whose heart is loyal to Him (2 Chr. 16:9).

Along with the prophet Samuel, you could say, "Here I am, LORD." And then get ready because you cannot outgive God!

About the Author

Ken Nair has discipled more than five hundred men in how to be Christlike husbands—all of whom have experienced a renewal of their marriages. He is the founder and president of Life Partners, a discipleship ministry. He is also a seminar leader and maintains a private and group counseling program in Phoenix, Arizona, where he lives with his wife, Nancy.